MW00777122

"Goodyear-Brown and Yasenik 1   ss
the field to share their wisdom o.   .y.
Rich case descriptions offer the reader an authentic exploration of how we
experience Polyvagal power with the children we serve in play therapy."

Dee C. Ray, PhD, *Regents Professor and Co-Director of*
Center for Play Therapy at the University of North Texas

"This pioneering and innovative volume skillfully weaves complex constructs
from Polyvagal theory together with practical, embodied, and transformative
play-based therapeutic interventions. It is a must-have masterpiece that will
change child and play therapists' perspectives on healing."

Ana M. Gómez, MC, LPC, *author of*
EMDR Therapy and Adjunct Approaches with
Children: Complex Trauma, Attachment, and Dissociation

Polyvagal Power in the Playroom

Polyvagal Power in the Playroom shows therapists how to treat children using play therapy to address the hierarchy of autonomic states. What do children need, and how do play therapists purposefully use the principles of play to increase the feeling states of safety and regulation? Step inside the playroom and discover how trained play therapists are addressing treatment using Polyvagal theory when working with children and teens.

The book is organized into three parts:

1. *Interruptions* explores developmental derailments brought about by relational betrayals such as domestic violence, child sexual abuse, and attachment ruptures implicated in a myriad of adverse childhood experiences. In these cases, the neuroception of safety scaffolded through "good enough" rhythms of healthy caregiver/child interactions is either compromised through a thousand relational cuts (parental addiction or parental mental illness) or abruptly ended (divorce, death or incarceration of a parent).
2. *Happenings* explores events that involve an external intrusion, such as natural disasters, wars, and pandemics.
3. *Expressions of Risk and Resilience* explores mental health symptom clusters such as depression, anxiety, dissociation, and explosive behavior through the lens of dorsal vagal or sympathetic nervous system states, as well as specific play therapy methods for healing the nervous system.

The therapeutic powers of play are illustrated through case examples and in practical, play-based interventions woven throughout the book.

Child and play therapists will come away from *Polyvagal Power in the Playroom* with the tools they need to help children and their caregivers achieve deeper levels of safety and connection.

Paris Goodyear-Brown, LCSW, RPT-S, is the creator of TraumaPlay™, the Executive Director of the TraumaPlay Institute, the Clinical Director of Nurture House, and author of twelve books including *Play Therapy with Traumatized Children*, *Trauma and Play Therapy*, and *Parents as Partners in Child Therapy: A Guide for Clinicians*.

Lorri A. Yasenik, PhD, RPT-S, CPT-S, is the Director of Rocky Mountain Play Therapy Institute in Calgary, Alberta, Canada, and the co-author of *Play Therapy Dimensions Model: A Decision-Making Guide for Integrative Play Therapists*.

Polyvagal Power in the Playroom

A Guide for Play Therapists

Edited by
Paris Goodyear-Brown and
Lorri A. Yasenik

Routledge
Taylor & Francis Group

NEW YORK AND LONDON

Designed cover image: Warchi © Getty Images

First published 2024
by Routledge
605 Third Avenue, New York, NY 10158

and by Routledge
4 Park Square, Milton Park, Abingdon, Oxon, OX14 4RN

Routledge is an imprint of the Taylor & Francis Group, an informa business

Library of Congress Cataloging-in-Publication Data
Names: Goodyear-Brown, Paris, editor. | Yasenik, Lorri, editor.
Title: Polyvagal power in the playroom : a guide for play therapists / edited by Paris Goodyear-Brown and Lorri A. Yasenik.
Description: New York, NY : Routledge, 2024.
Identifiers: LCCN 2023041896 (print) | LCCN 2023041897 (ebook) |
   ISBN 9781032393728 (hbk) | ISBN 9781032393667 (pbk) |
   ISBN 9781003352976 (ebk)
Subjects: LCSH: Play therapy. | Play therapy—Methodology. | Autonomic nervous system. | Affective neuroscience. | Social interaction in children.
Classification: LCC RJ505.P6 P655 2024 (print) | LCC RJ505.P6 (ebook) |
   DDC 615.8/5153—dc23/eng/20231221
LC record available at https://lccn.loc.gov/2023041896
LC ebook record available at https://lccn.loc.gov/2023041897

ISBN: 978-1-032-39372-8 (hbk)
ISBN: 978-1-032-39366-7 (pbk)
ISBN: 978-1-003-35297-6 (ebk)

DOI: 10.4324/9781003352976

Typeset in Goudy
by Apex CoVantage, LLC

We would like to dedicate this book to all the children who have informed our practices and who entrusted us to find a way to connect and "be with" them through the difficult and joyous times. Understanding the rhythms and unspoken energy between people is art and science combined.

We are grateful for the significant contribution made by Dr. Stephen Porges, who has made neuroscience more accessible for clinicians while validating the importance of social connection and play as a neural exercise.

Contents

    Shifting States Towards Safety
    CARMEN RICHARDSON

17 Animal Assisted Play Therapy™ as a Polyvagal Process   219
    MARY ROTTIER AND REBECCA DICKINSON

18 Digital Play Therapy™   232

    Harnessing the Felt Sense of Safety in the Digital Space
    JESSICA STONE AND RACHEL ALTVATER

    Index   245

Foreword: Play Therapy Through the Lens of the Polyvagal Theory

As the originator of the Polyvagal theory, I am pleased to write the foreword for *Polyvagal Power in the Playroom*. In this edited volume, Paris Goodyear-Brown and Lorri Yasenik have brought together experts in the emerging field of play therapy to create a comprehensive volume documenting how the principles of Polyvagal theory can be integrated into play therapy. The book provides a platform to observe, through the therapists' own voices, how the lens of the Polyvagal theory has transformed how they conduct their therapy and especially how they deal with traumatized children who present profound state regulation difficulties and hypersensitivities. As I read the chapters, I was impressed with the passion, compassion, and persistence of these brilliant and intuitive play therapists as they expand the impact of the theory through their work.

It is not a surprise to me that play therapists are interested in Polyvagal theory. In many of my talks, I emphasize that play is a "neural exercise" that enables the co-regulation of the physiological state to promote neurophysiological states that support mental and physical health. Put more succinctly, when play is appropriately structured and implemented, play is therapy. Play, similar to other "movement" therapies such as dance, yoga, and even martial arts, involves a dyadic interaction requiring reciprocity that (in Polyvagal terms) supports co-regulation. This volume confirms this view, illustrates how the core principles of Polyvagal theory fit well with the practices of play therapy, and convincingly documents that play provides a natural platform for Polyvagal-informed therapy. Polyvagal theory provides a neuroscience language to explain what play therapists have observed and intuitively understood. This language, including concepts such as autonomic state, co-regulation, and neuroception, is frequently used in this volume to provide a neurobiological explanation for the behavioral and psychological phenomena observed during play therapy.

We often think of play as an amusement or a diversion from the "real" work in our lives. When we observe children playing, we might judge the time engaged in play as a distraction from opportunities to learn. This view, denigrating play and revering classroom learning opportunities, is consistent with our cultural view of education. Educational systems attempt to maximize opportunities for classroom instruction and to minimize opportunities for social interactions available during recess and other interactive forums requiring co-regulation such as team sports, music, and theater. From an educator's perspective, play is the antithesis of learning; play steals the precious time that could be dedicated to learning. Similarly, within work environments, management often frowns when workers play and enjoy social interactions.

This perspective is based on assumptions derived from learning theories that were outlined by behaviorists about 100 years ago. What if this perspective, prevalent in our society, is outdated? Is misinformed? What if play, rather than displacing learning experiences, actually provides a neural exercise that would facilitate learning and enhance both mental and physical health?

Is our conceptualization of play inadequate? Are our views of play restricted interpretations dependent on a limited understanding of learning embedded in our educational institutions, parenting styles, expectations of socialization, and mental health treatment models? Can we take a different perspective and emphasize that play provides opportunities to exercise features of our nervous system that would foster learning, social behavior, and mental health? If play were perceived from this perspective, then play, as a neural exercise, might foster state regulation, enabling individuals to transition efficiently from active to calm states. Consistent with this perspective, the ability to move rapidly into a calm state would facilitate efficient learning and optimize spontaneous and reciprocal social behavior. The importance of play is dismissed in the cognitive-centric world of education. Within theoretical models of learning, little importance is placed on how bodily feelings, as an intervening variable, influence the ability to learn. Although we may want to sit and attend, at times our body may want to run, fight, or hide. Calmly sitting enables us to attend and to efficiently learn. However, when our body wants to run, fight, and hide, we are in a physiological state that supports defense. During these physiological states, neural feedback from our body to the higher brain structures will interfere with cognition and learning. Missing from the cognitive-centric perspective is the role that play may have in strengthening these neural circuits that can rapidly down-regulate defense systems to foster learning and sociality by enabling us to sit calmly and attend.

The roots of play and play-related therapies are linked to the evolution of a neural mechanism that enables mammals to shift between mobilized fight/ flight and calm, socially engaging states. From an evolutionary perspective, mammals had to rapidly detect whether a conspecific was safe or dangerous. If the interaction was dangerous, they needed to be in a physiological state that would produce sufficient energy to defend (fight) or facilitate an instantaneous escape (flight). If the interaction had cues of safety, then the physical distance could be reduced, and physical contact might ensue to foster parenting and development of trusting relationships.

To mate or to be in close contact with a conspecific, defense reactions have to be inhibited before cues of aggression or fear are expressed. An immediate decision has to be made to distinguish potential mate from potent threat. This process was so important to survival of both the individual and the species that the neural mechanisms were subjugated to brain processes outside the realm of conscious awareness.

Within the context of the Polyvagal theory, the instantaneous process of evaluating risk outside the realm of awareness is called *neuroception*. This concept is used in several of the chapters. Neuroception is the neural process through which our body reacts to features in the environment and shifts physiological states to deal with potential risk. Neuroception is not perception, because the process does not require awareness. If the cues trigger a neuroception of safety, our physiological state calms immediately, then we can easily socially engage or attend. If the cues trigger a neuroception of danger, our body prepares for movement. If the cues trigger life threat, then we lose social contact and immobilize. Although we are not aware of the stimuli that trigger our sense of danger or safety, we can become aware of our bodily responses via interoception triggered by neuroception. Thus, the cues from our body influence our personal comfort, which will vary as contexts and interactions with people change. Play therapy by providing opportunities to harness the power of neuroception of safety to down regulate feelings of threat functions as a neural exercise promoting resilience and enhanced biobehavior regulation.

Play and Co-regulation: Insights from Polyvagal Theory

Principles of establishing relationships are similar to play and include the following:

- Reciprocity
- Movement and inhibition of movement
- Face-to-face interactions and/or prosodic vocalizations to dampen potential defensive reactions to movements, proximity, and touch

In Polyvagal terms, reciprocity is observed as co-regulation. In play we see this as turn taking, and in good relationships, we see it as listening to and witnessing the other and when appropriate engaging with words and behaviors. In fact, we can map the behaviors of dyads and evaluate contingent behaviors and appropriate role reversals as markers of co-regulation. It is this capacity to co-regulate that can reframe sociality as a neuromodulator with the capacity to calm another's nervous system (see Porges, 2021, 2022; Rajabalee et al., 2022).

From the perspective of the Polyvagal theory, play can be seen functionally as a neural exercise in which cues of safety and danger are alternately expressed and explored (Porges, 2021, 2022). The ability to safely transition through "dangerous" states of disconnection—breaks in flowing emotional containment—is crucial to the development and internalization of a child's robust sense of self (Hughes, 2004; Schore, 1994). During play risks are taken, dangers are survived, and connections are repaired through co-regulation. As an example, we can think of the simple game, peek-a-boo, that a mother may play with her infant. By hiding her face and removing the cues of safety normally generated by the social engagement system (prosodic voice, facial expressions), the mother is creating a state of uncertainty in the infant. This state of uncertainty is followed by the mother startling the infant by showing her face and saying, "Peek-a-boo!" The sequence of the peek-a-boo game is ended when the mother uses a prosodic voice with warm facial expressions to calm the startled infant (e.g., Kolacz et al., 2022).

Deconstructing the behavioral sequence involved in "peek-a-boo," we see the neural exercise embedded in this play behavior. "Peek-a-boo" may be a model for how aspects of play therapy may work. First, the initial hiding of the mother's face elicits a state of uncertainty and vigilance. This state is associated with a depression of the infant's social engagement system, including a withdrawal of the myelinated vagal pathways to the heart. This puts the infant in a vulnerable state in which a "startle" stimulus could easily recruit sympathetic activity to support mobilization (i.e., fight/flight behaviors). The mother provides the startle stimulus by showing her face and stating "boo" in a relatively loud and monotonic voice. The acoustic features of the mother's vocalizations support the unpredictable presentation of the mother's face, since the vocalizations of "boo" have acoustic features that are associated with danger and lack the prosodic features that would be calming. The cues of this sequence trigger a detection of danger, which recruits increased sympathetic activation. The next step in the sequence of this game provides the opportunity for a neural exercise that will promote resilience and enhance the infant's ability to calm.

After the infant is motorically and autonomically activated by the "boo," the mother calms the infant with her social engagement system using a prosodic voice with warm facial expressions, which trigger a neuroception (detection) of safety. The infant calms as the social engagement system comes back online and the myelinated vagal pathways down-regulate the sympathetic activity. When effectively implemented, "peek-a-boo" provides opportunities for the infant to "neurally navigate" through a sequence of states (i.e., from calm, to vigilant, to startled, and back to calm). Repeating this game provides opportunities for the social engagement system to efficiently down-regulate sympathetic activation via social interactions. The child will need this "neural" skill to adapt throughout every aspect of life.

Kittens playing provide a relevant example. Visualize kittens in bouts of rough-and-tumble play. They are using their claws and teeth, but they rarely injure each other. In fact, if you have a kitten, you may be surprised that they know when to retract their claws and relax their jaws once they make a gentle bite. However, an extremely important feature often goes unnoticed. The kittens maintain face-to-face interactions during most of the play. If a bite hurts, there is an immediate face-to-face interaction of their social engagement systems, and they cue each other that there was no intention to injure. But kittens, like children, vary in their ability to be aware of each other in a play scenario. If awareness of the other is poor, then injury may occur. In primate social groups, the juveniles who enthusiastically engage but, due to a lack of awareness of others, may injure peers are ostracized and marginalized from social groups.

We can observe similar situations on the playground. For example, when playing basketball, players are often shoved and fall. If the social engagement system is employed following this event, aggressive behaviors will be dampened. For example, aggression is defused if the person who did the shoving makes eye contact with the person on the floor, helps the other person off the floor, and asks whether the person is okay. However, a fight might be triggered if the person who did the shoving just walks away.

By deconstructing the play of other social mammals, whether we are observing kittens, dogs, or children on the playground, we see a common feature of behaviors that simulate features of fight/flight that are actively inhibited by social engagement behaviors (e.g., facial expressions, head gestures, prosodic vocalizations). We can see that play transitions into aggressive behaviors if the social engagement systems are not employed to down-regulate any potential neuroception of danger.

The process of play is about active inhibition of the neural circuit that promotes fight/flight behaviors. Play functions as a neural exercise that improves the efficiency of the neural circuit that can instantaneously down-regulate fight-flight behaviors. If we translate this into the classroom or clinic, we can identify children with difficulties in down-regulating the neural circuits that promote fight/flight behaviors. These children have difficulties in sitting, in attending, in listening, and in socializing. If we watch these children on the playground, we might see deficits in their ability to play with others. They may not accurately anticipate the behaviors of others and, instead of a reciprocal interaction that inhibits fight/flight behaviors, they may functionally be physically bouncing off their peers with dire consequences in their abilities to develop trusting relationships.

The Polyvagal theory explores why this might be the case. In the process of risk detection, external cues are not the only source of information. Afferent feedback from the viscera provides a major mediator of the accessibility of prosocial circuits associated with social engagement behaviors. Polyvagal theory predicts that states of mobilization compromise the ability to detect positive social cues. Functionally, visceral states distort or color our perception of other people. Thus, the features of a person engaging another may result in a range of outcomes, depending on the physiological state of the target individual. If the person being engaged is in a state in which the social engagement system is easily accessible, a reciprocal prosocial interaction is likely to occur with the calming benefits of co-regulation. However, if the individual is in a state of mobilization, the same engaging response might be responded to with asocial features of withdrawal or aggression.

A Polyvagal-informed definition of play, similar to other forms of co-regulation, requires reciprocal and synchronous interactions between mammals while using the social engagement system as a regulator of mobilization behavior (e.g., fight/flight). This definition of "play" may differ from the use of the term to describe interactions between an individual and a toy or computer. Play with a toy or computer lacks face-to-face interaction and will not exercise the social engagement system as a regulator of the neural circuits that foster fight/flight behaviors. Thus, as mammals, we need to respect our phylogenetic heritage and appreciate the importance of synchronous face-to-face interactions as an opportunity to exercise our social engagement systems. As the neural regulation of our social engagement system improves, we gain resilience in dealing with disruptions in our lives.

Many of the features of play are shared with psychotherapy. A deconstruction of a therapeutic session will find the client (and often the therapist) shifting states from calm to defense and back to calm. Fortunately, we as mammals have a social engagement system that evolved to employ cues from face-to-face interactions to efficiently calm our physiological state and shift our fight/flight behaviors to trusting relationships.

Conclusion

By deconstructing the play of mammals, whether we are observing kittens, dogs, or children on the playground, we see a common dynamic in social behavior—features of fight/flight are continually stimulated *and* actively inhibited by social engagement behaviors (e.g., facial expressions, gestures, prosodic vocalizations). Play is a natural and powerful therapeutic tool. From the polyvagal perspective, play can be conceptualized as an efficient "neural exercise" that uses social engagement to actively inhibit fight/flight behaviors. A sensitive adult can attune herself to a way of communicating that recruits a child's social engagement system and down-regulates defense. As illustrated in this volume, therapists who work actively through playful modes consciously leverage this process. It is crucial that the therapist engenders a feeling of safety for the child via sensitive attunement. The experience of safety increases the frequency of spontaneous reciprocal interactions. It is through these interactions that there is a resetting of the neuroceptive threshold, from a defensive baseline to a robust sense of safety.

As described by the authors, children frequently referred for play therapy are in neurophysiological states that support mobilization, withdrawal, and shutdown. In these states, cognitive processes are greatly compromised, and there is a loss in the awareness of the emotional states of others. Polyvagal theory informs clinical practice that there is a neural circuit that can rapidly down-regulate mobilization behaviors to foster the calm states that optimize social behavior. Although play is frequently characterized by movement and often recruits many of the neural circuits involved in fight/flight behaviors, it may be operationally distinguished from defense, since during play mobilization maintains access to the calming social engagement system, which easily can be recruited to promote calmness. However, the effectiveness and efficiency of the social engagement system to down-regulate fight/flight behaviors require a type of learning through practices involving structured "neural exercise."

Opportunities to gain competence via neural exercise usually start early in a child's development through play. However, trauma may disrupt the child's ability to feel safe and to exhibit spontaneous social engagement behaviors. Given this situation, similar to the clinical examples provided in this volume, clinicians need to provide the child with unambiguous biological signals of safety through intonation of voice, facial expressions, and gestures. Moreover, once these signals effectively trigger a spontaneous engagement by the child, the intuitive therapist must be ready to respond with reciprocity. Reciprocal exchange of cues of safety, between therapist and child, function as playful neural exercise of the social engagement system, the mechanism that shifts mobilization from defense to play and trust. The chapters describe individualized therapeutic strategies in which signals of safety foster co-regulation between therapist and client, enabling the client to experience the capacity to down-regulate threat reactions and shift autonomic state from being locked in a state of defense to enable spontaneous social engagement with others. From a Polyvagal perspective, this is the central objective of therapy.

Stephen W. Porges, PhD
Distinguished University Scientist
Founding Director, Traumatic Stress Research Consortium
Kinsey Institute,
Indiana University Bloomington
Professor of Psychiatry
University of North Carolina at Chapel Hill

References

Hughes, D. (2004). An attachment-based treatment of maltreated children and young people. *Attachment and Human Development*, 6(3), 263–278.

Kolacz, J., daSilva, E. B., Lewis, G. D., Bertenthal, B. I., & Porges, S. W. (2022). Associations between acoustic features of maternal speech and infants' emotion regulation following a social stressor. *Infancy*, 27(1), 135–158. https://doi.org/10.1111/infa.12440

Porges, S. W. (2021). Polyvagal theory: A biobehavioral journey to sociality. *Comprehensive Psychoneuroendocrinology*, 7, 100069. https://doi.org/10.1016/j.cpnec.2021.100069

Porges, S. W. (2022). Polyvagal theory: A science of safety. *Frontiers in Integrative Neuroscience*, 16, 27. https://doi.org/10.3389/fnint.2022.871227

Rajabalee, N., Kozlowska, K., Lee, S. Y., Savage, B., Hawkes, C., Siciliano, D., Porges, S. W., Pick, S., & Torbey, S. (2022). Neuromodulation using computer-altered music to treat a ten-year-old child unresponsive to standard interventions for functional neurological disorder. *Harvard Review of Psychiatry*, 10–1097.

Schore, A. N. (1994). *Affect regulation and the origin of the self.* Lawrence Erlbaum.

About the Editors

Paris Goodyear-Brown, LCSW, RPT-S, and EMDRIA-approved consultant, is the creator of TraumaPlay™, a flexibly sequential play therapy model for treating trauma and attachment disturbances in family systems. She is the Executive Director of the TraumaPlay Institute, the Clinical Director of Nurture House, and an adjunct instructor of Psychiatric Mental Health at Vanderbilt University. Paris has an international reputation as a dynamic and compassionate speaker, a master clinician, and a prolific author. She is a thought leader in the fields of child trauma and play therapy, has received the APT award for Play Therapy Promotion and Education, gave a Ted Talk on trauma and play therapy, and served as the Executive Director of the Lipscomb Play Therapy and Expressive Arts Center. She is on the board of TNAPT and is the author of multiple chapters and articles as well as 12 books, including *Play Therapy with Traumatized Children*, *Trauma and Play Therapy*, *Parents as Partners in Child Therapy: A Clinician's Guide* and *Big Behaviors in Small Containers*, and finds great joy in training clinicians all over the world in helping children heal.

Lorri A. Yasenik PhD, RPT-S, CPT-S, is the Director of Rocky Mountain Play Therapy Institute and the Co-Director of the International Centre for Children and Family Law (ICCFL) in Australia/Canada. Lorri is a registered and certified supervisor of child psychotherapy and play therapy, and she delivers approved training programs nationally and internationally in the areas of child and play therapy, play therapy supervision, and child inclusive practice in the family law sectors. Lorri has expertise working with treatment of trauma, separation and divorce, children's adjustment and developmental issues, and a range of other presenting problems for impacting children and youth. Lorri is the co-author of the books *Play Therapy Dimensions Model: A Decision-Making Guide for Integrative Play Therapists* and *Turning Points in Play Therapy and the Immergence of Self: Applications of the Play*

Therapy Dimensions Model. In addition, Lorri has authored and co-authored 12 chapters and peer-reviewed articles in the areas of play therapy supervision, play therapy practice, play therapy case conceptualization, children's voices, and children and family law. Lorri has a fellowship at Deakin University in Australia and currently sits on Deakin University Advisory Board for the Child Play Master's Degree Program.

Contributors

Rachel A. Altvater, PsyD, RPT-S, Creative Psychological Health Services, Frederick, Maryland

Sue C. Bratton, PhD, LPC-S, RPT-S, professor emerita and director emerita, Center for Play Therapy, University of North Texas

Jennifer Buchanan, MBA, MTA, founder, JB Music Therapy in Calgary, Alberta, Canada; award-winning author; recipient of the Norma Sharpe Award

Isabella Cassina, MA, TPS, CAGS, PhD candidate, head of project management at the International Academy for Play Therapy, founding member of the International Consortium of Play Therapy Associations in Switzerland

Janet A. Courtney, PhD, RPT-S, Founder FirstPlay® Therapy, Boynton Beach, Florida

David A. Crenshaw, PhD, ABPP, RPT-S, chief of clinical services, Children's Home of Poughkeepsie; recipient of the Lifetime Achievement Award 2021 from the Association for Play Therapy

Marie J. Dhaese, PhD, RCC, ATR, RPT-S, CPT-S, Centre for Expressive Therapy, Parksville, BC, Canada

Rebecca Dickinson, PhD, LISW, RPT-S, CAAPT-I, Assistant Professor of Social Work, University of Northern Iowa, Certified Animal Assisted Play Therapist™, Instructor

Lisa Dion, LPC, RPT-S, founder of the Synergetic Play Therapy Institute, co-founder of the Synergetic Education Institute and creator of Synergetic Play Therapy in Boulder, Colorado

Bridger D. Falkenstien, MS, NCC, LPC, creative director of Beyond Healing Center & Institute, Springfield, Missouri

Maggie Fearn SFHEA; MA DATP; MA HIPPT, Integrative Child Psychotherapist ECIP; BAPT Play Therapist and Filial Therapist, BAPT & ECIP Clinical Supervisor

Jackie Flynn, EdS, LMHC-S, RPT, clinical director of Counseling in Brevard and founder of EMDR and Play Therapy Integration Support, Cocoa, Florida

Richard L. Gaskill, EdD, adjunct faculty, Wichita State University in Kansas; recipient of the Lifetime Achievement Award 2023 from the Association for Play Therapy

Natalie A. Hadiprodjo, PhD, RPT-S, senior lecturer in Play Therapy at Deakin University, Australia

Linda E. Homeyer, PhD, LPC-S, RPT-S, professor emerita at Texas State University; director emerita, Association for Play Therapy

Sueann Kenney-Noziska, MSW, LCSW, RPT-S, founder and director of Play Therapy Corner in Las Cruces, New Mexico

Marshall Lyles, LMFT-S, LPC-S, RPT-S, owner of The Workshop, Austin, Texas; EMDRIA- approved consultant

Claudio Mochi, MA, RP, RPT-S, founder of the Association for Play Therapy Italy, director of the training program at the International Academy for Play Therapy in Switzerland

Judi A. Parson, PhD, MA Play Therapy, BN, RN, APPTA RPT-S, discipline leader and senior lecturer in play therapy, School of Health and Social Development at Deakin University in Geelong, Australia

Carmen Richardson MSW, RSW, RCAT, REAT, founder and director of Prairie Institute of Expressive Arts Therapy, Calgary, Alberta

Mary Rottier, EdD, CAAPT, RPT-S, clinical director, Pawsitive Counseling Center, Fremont, Michigan; certified Animal Assisted Play Therapist™, instructor, and supervisor

Marilyn R. Sanders, MD, neonatologist, Connecticut Children's Medical Center; professor of pediatrics, University of Connecticut School of Medicine

Karen Stagnitti PhD, BOccThy, GCHE, Professor Emeritus, School of Health and Social Development, Deakin University Australia

Jessica Stone, PhD, RPT-S, Fruita, Colorado; CEO Virtual Sandtray; CPO AscendantVR; affiliate of the East Carolina Neurocognition Science Laboratory

Alyssa M. Swan, PhD, LCPC, RPT, core faculty in the School of Social and Behavioral Sciences at Capella University, Bloomington, Illinois

Lynn L. Wonders, MA, LPC, CPCS, RPT-S, PhD candidate at Saybrook University; owner and director of Wonders Counseling Services, LLC, Ormond Beach, Florida

1

How the Science of Relationships Impacts Our Thinking About Development

Interruptions, Happenings, and Expressions of Risk or Resilience

Marilyn R. Sanders

Overview

Everyone has a story. And for many of us, it is a birth story. Under ideal circumstances, parents and their babies spend the initial minutes, days, and weeks in each other's loving care, choreographing the dance most parents and their healthy babies do. The relational connection between mother and newborn creates dependability, predictability, consistency, and safety for the developing baby and infant that is vital to survival. All too often, however, sometimes even before the relationship begins to flourish, there are interruptions in this connectedness because "things happen," and the responses to these events are expressions of resilience or risk. Mammals cared for and nourished who lack a primary attachment figure die or survive with serious social-emotional disturbance (Fraiberg et al., 2003). We now understand that secure attachments are not "just nice"; they are essential to healthy development.

In this chapter, I will lay the foundation for understanding the science of relationships beginning in pregnancy and continuing through early childhood. However, relationships are imperfect, and there are always disruptions in even the most solid relationships. As Tronick reminded us, it is not the disruption but the repair that determines how dyads move forward in their increasingly complex work. An important component of the "repair" becomes the meaning the parent-baby dyad make of their own connection (Tronick & Cohn, 1989).

DOI: 10.4324/9781003352976-1

The Privileged Relationship of the Pregnant Woman and Her Fetus

At no other time in our lives will our bodies tolerate "foreign" protein without developing antibodies or absolute immunological rejection. Yet, in a healthy pregnancy, the fetus coexists within the maternal uterus in dual physiology (Weinstein, 2016). Indeed, for the healthy fetus and mother, it meets both their evolutionary expectations. The uterine wall and amniotic fluid provide safe containment. The placenta provides nourishment and temperature control. And there is a pregnancy pause in immunologic responsiveness that nurtures and protects the fetus. The placenta also protects the fetus from stress by producing an enzyme, 11 β hydroxysteroid dehydrogenase, that converts the stress hormone cortisol to an inactive form, cortisone, through most of the pregnancy (Sandman et al., 2011). As fetuses begin moving and "quickening" occurs, parents construct mental representations of their fetuses based upon ultrasound images (Ammaniti & Gallese, 2014).

Finding Safety Moving from the Womb to the World: Polyvagal Theory Provides "an Explanation"

The uterus is the econiche for the healthy fetus. At birth, most babies go from the womb to the mother's chest, where they will continue to find temperature control, nourishment, and co-regulation. This is the beginning of the "sacred hour" when the mother, the non-birthing partner, and the baby begin to choreograph another dance: that of an emerging family (Phillips, 2013).

As thought leaders like Jinpa and neuroscientists including Stephen Porges detail, social engagement leading to social connectedness assures young mammals survive and thrive. Polyvagal theory, developed by Stephen Porges, anchors the survival of young mammals in the biological imperative to seek safety (Porges, 2011). This theory, based upon the evolutionary neurobiology of threat detection, describes vertebrate responses to danger as a hierarchy of response beginning in the earliest terrestrial vertebrates. Polyvagal theory details an integrated autonomic, automatic, or unconscious nervous system consisting of two divisions—the parasympathetic nervous system and the sympathetic nervous system. The parasympathetic nervous system consists of the neurons of the 10th cranial or vagus nerve. It is termed the vagus or "wandering" nerve because its branches reach out from the brain to the heart and the most distant body parts. Among the most important functions of the vagus nerve above the diaphragm is control of the electrical activity of the heart. Were it not for the vagus, the heart would beat very quickly, allowing little time for filling the lower chambers. The vagus thus acts as a brake on the heart's intrinsic electrical activity, controlling the heart rate to optimize the heart's work, sending oxygenated blood to the body. When the vagal brake is lifted, the heart rate increases. For example, when we have a meal, the heart rate increases to supply more energy to metabolize the food we ingested. And when the vagal brake is applied, the heart rate slows, allowing us to rest and digest (Porges, 2011).

The sympathetic nervous system responds to stress and releases the hormone(s) epinephrine or adrenaline and cortisol. Under the influence of epinephrine and cortisol, the heart works harder; blood flow is sent to vital organs; the airways open up to allow more oxygen to get into the lungs; and the liver converts stored starch to glucose that is released for energy. Non-vital functions such as digestion slow down. Both the parasympathetic and sympathetic components, working in tandem, are vital to mammalian health and wellbeing.

The limbic system, a primitive part of the midbrain, consists of the amygdala—the central alarm system, the hippocampus—the seat of memory, the thalamus—the receiver of sensory information from the body, and the hypothalamus—the origin of the hypothalamic-pituitary-adrenal axis that eventually produces cortisol. The limbic system is constantly scanning the environment for signs of danger. Vertebrates exhibit behavioral responses based upon their unconscious sense of whether they are safe, in danger, or in a life threat environment, termed *neuroception*. Neuroception, below conscious awareness, derives from sensations of the external and relational environments as well as the interoceptions, or internal sensory responses created by the environment outside the body (Porges, 2014).

For example, if you are walking to your car after dark, you will likely be watching carefully as you leave the building. Your pupils will dilate to allow for a large field of vision. Your muscles may feel tense, and you may have your hand on your keys as you move farther from the building, an experience of lack of relational environment as no one is accompanying you to mitigate your uneasiness. Your interoceptive sensory input is the feeling in your body of tense muscles and perhaps some anxiety. Now, if you see someone approaching in the distance, your tension and anxiety may increase. However, when the person in the distance gets close enough to greet you warmly, and you realize it is an office colleague, your body relaxes; the tension leaves, and you return their warm greeting. In just moments your neuroception has transformed from one of danger to safety based upon clues from the environments both outside and inside your body.

Vertebrates, or animals with a spine, are always unconsciously surveying the environment for signs of danger. Primitive vertebrates such as lizards and reptiles have only one possible response to danger—to blend in or camouflage, hoping that the predator will simply leave. This response is driven by the neurons of the dorsal vagal complex located toward the back of the brainstem. As vertebrates continued to evolve, however, the sympathetic nervous system came on-line. So later vertebrates, such as fish, have the capacity to stay and fight or flee. Colloquially, this is referred to as the "fight or flight" reaction. However, only in mammals is this threat system repurposed to promote social engagement. Thus, mammals use the social engagement system when they feel "in danger." The origin of the social engagement system is located farther forward in the brain stem in the ventral vagal complex. When mammals feel in danger, they use their social engagement system to return to safety. Only when their social engagement system fails them do they become sympathetically activated or, in a life threat situation, immobilize or collapse (Porges & Furman, 2011).

The Work of Infancy Is Establishing Social Engagement and Connectedness with Caregivers

Mammals are vertebrates that nurse their young. From an evolutionary perspective, young mammals expect to go from the mother's womb to the mother's body after birth. Mammals' evolutionary expectations of their caregivers include their social and emotional proximity, their sensitivity and attunement, their contingent responsiveness, and their social engagement and social connectedness. Social connectedness as defined by Porges is the ability to mutually (synchronously and reciprocally) regulate physiological and behavioral states (Porges, 2019).

When the human newborn transitions from the womb to the mother's body and is skin-to-skin on her chest/at her breast, the process of social engagement leading to social connectedness begins. In a well-choreographed and reproducible series of movements, a healthy newborn will move to the mother's breast and latch onto her nipple. The mother's body regulates the newborn's temperature, and her breast provides breast milk at body temperature. Babies who rest with their mothers during the first hour after birth or "sacred hour" have increased physiologic stability, increased breastfeeding rates, and longer duration of breastfeeding. In addition, this vital time after birth promotes optimal brain development, promotes maternal attachment behaviors, and protects against the negative effects of maternal-infant separation (Phillips, 2013).

Moving to *Nurture*science from *Neuro*science to Support Developing Young Infants and Their Families

Neonatologist Nils Bergman proposes a paradigm shift for understanding the trajectory and outcomes of infant development moving to *nurture*science from *neuro*science. Zero separation of mother and infant is key (Bergman, 2019). Bergman stresses the critical importance of the mother's body as the "proactive and purposeful continuation of the normal neurodevelopmental trajectory based on ecologically salient/expected sensory inputs" (Bergman, 2015, p. 143). A *nurture*science perspective emphasizes the first 1,000 minutes of a baby's life as the mother and her newborn in skin-to-skin contact coregulate each other. The focus is on boosting calming parasympathetic activities, and relational health and interdependence are key objectives. By contrast, a *neuro*science perspective emphasizes the first 1,000 days of an infant's life with the focus on calming sympathetic activity and self-regulation with key objectives of independence and self-actualization (Bergman et al., 2019). From the *nurture*science perspective, the self-actualization of the neuroscience perspective is replaced by "mate acquisition, mate retention, and parenting" (Kenrick et al., 2010, p. 293).

Based upon the work of developmental psychologist Myron Hofer, Bergman further comments, "All sensory inputs from the mother are necessary, each has a (sic) unique impact on a specific physiological aspect, collectively over different periods of time" (Bergman, 2019, p. 1093). Upon separating a mother rat from her litter, Hofer discovered a predictable pattern of distress responses beginning with ultrasonic vocalizations. To prevent these ultrasonic vocalizations, baby rats needed a range of sensory inputs provided by the mother rat to prevent the distress cry (Hofer, 1994). Hofer named these inputs "hidden regulators" and commented that "in infants of species with the necessary cognitive capacities, mental representations of caretakers are formed out of the individual units of their experience with the regulatory interactions" (Hofer, 1994, p. 16).

Play as a Neural Exercise

As the securely attached infant and toddler matures, life stresses will increase particularly when s/he/they are asked to leave the safety and security of home and family and to venture out into the world. We can prepare children for these separations using play as a *neural exercise* (Porges, 2015). From the earliest games, such as peek-a-boo, the adult caregiver engaged in play challenges the developing child's autonomic nervous system's regulatory capacity. As the caregiver puts their hands over their eyes, shielding themselves from the child's sight, the child is stressed by the sudden removal of the attachment figure. Initially, they are confused. Where did mommy or daddy go? The confusion may turn to a momentary startle or fear as the caregiver says "peek-a-boo" in a lilting tone and takes away their hands, returning to the child. However, as repetition reinforces the continuing return of the caregiver to the child, the startle soon turns to ventral vagal delight as the child and caregiver are engaged in a reciprocal dance of pleasure.

As children age, the play becomes more complex, and the stress potentially increases. The Center on the Developing Child (n.d.) emphasizes the key role of "serve and return" interactions to build flexibility, resilience, and a sense of agency and lists five explicit steps:

1.   Notice the serve and share the child's focus of attention.
2.   Return the serve by supporting and encouraging.
3.   Give it a name.
4.   Take turns and wait.
5.   Practice endings and beginnings.

When caregivers engage in healthy "serve and return" interactions, the child's internal working model of relationships as a self, worthy of love and care, is reinforced. Costello (2013, p. 85) describes these internal working models as a "kind of guidance system that tells us what to do and what to expect when we are with another person. They are scripts for social interaction."

Priming Children to Seek and Approach Novelty: Supporting Children into School and Community

As children move out of the home into school and community, they will experience separations from their primary caregivers. If they were well-scaffolded in their early experience by caring adults, the disruption or separation may cause temporary distress. Their "guidance system," however, supports the transfer of their trust to other adults in the environment. Children are naturally curious and novelty-seeking. For the curious child, the presence of adults creates an environment of safety and protection that is activated when the adult neurocepts possible danger. The prefrontal cortex is the organizing part of the brain that weighs potential dangers and makes quick assessments of the risk involved. Is the calculus one of safety, relative safety with little risk, moderate risk, or life-threatening danger? We want children to seek new experiences, but we also want them to develop assessments of risk in a graduated manner.

Depending upon their early experiences, both children and their caregiving adults may have alterations of their risk-assessment capacities. Adults who were not themselves well-scaffolded or who had frightening experiences as children may be hypervigilant and become sympathetically activated when children engage in typical childhood neighborhood play. And since children are experts at reading the room around them, they too may become fearful and avoidant. Other adults who are equally poorly scaffolded may be passive and shut down, allowing children to engage in activities that are clearly dangerous to them. These children will also be challenged to make self-protective risk assessments. Both kinds of children have faulty neuroceptions that guide their daily lives. One child may be so risk aversive that typical activities of childhood—playground, sleepovers, summer camp—are out of reach. The other child may plunge headlong into a series of thrill-seeking behaviors that are potentially dangerous (Sanders & Thompson, 2021).

Reaching a balance of safety and curiosity is well described in the Circle of Security parenting program that supports parents to be both a *safe haven* to whom the child can return for protection and comfort as well as a *secure base* who promotes exploration (Powell et al., 2013).

Interruptions of Early Relationships: What Happens When the Baby Is "Whisked Away?"

Throughout most of our evolutionary history, mammalian infants remained with their mothers after birth; however, beginning in the 19th century newborns were increasingly separated from their mothers. Some of these separations resulted from developing technology that permitted survival of infants, such as those born premature, who were previously considered non-viable. Unfortunately, the separation philosophy overflowed into typical term births as well. By the 1960s, separation of mother and her infant became the norm (Bergman, 2019).

In many such separations, the newborn is "whisked away" from their mother and delivered to the hands of unknown caregivers for some time period. These scenarios may include babies who require newborn intensive care services, babies whose mothers are ill, and babies whose mothers plan on adoption. The common thread of these scenarios is that the baby goes from their evolutionary econiche, the maternal womb, to one that does not meet their evolutionary biological expectancies of the emotional and physical proximity of the caregiver, sensitivity and attunement, contingent responsiveness, and social engagement. Just as the baby's biological expectations are violated, so too are the parents' who often describe the pain of separation, disconnection, helplessness, powerlessness, and fear.

For those who go to a modern newborn intensive care unit, the sensory environment of the womb is substituted with loud noises, bright lights, unpleasant to painful touch, and the absence of a scaffolding caregiver who provides the necessary sensory inputs. And for parents, their prior mental constructs of a memorable, private, and intimate time where they begin building their family often dissolves in terror when a healthcare provider may say, "We need to deliver you now."

Happenings Become Interruptions of Social Engagement and Connectedness: When Mothers, Babies, and Families Are Left Alone

I don't think Tommy knows what a smile is.
How would he know?
Pediatric trainee about a hospitalized infant during COVID-19

As this chapter is written, we are finishing the third year of the COVID-19 pandemic. The global response to COVID-19 is highly variable. In the United States, people outside healthcare settings are now largely unmasked. Epidemic levels of influenza and RSV, a virus causing the common cold, are overwhelming children's hospitals (Baumgaertner, 2022). The response to COVID-19 vaccination remains highly politicized. The epidemic was and is an ongoing interruption of social engagement and social connectedness. And this interruption reaches down into our youngest persons, our young children. Indeed, parents who delivered babies during the past three years refer to them as *pandemic babies* (Wong, 2022). From the *nurture*science perspective, the ecology of the mother includes the family unit and her community. During COVID-19, mothers, babies, and families were left alone to protect against COVID-19 transmission. So extended family, often including grandparents, rather than being a source of tangible support, were isolated from new babies and young children. And young children were seen as a potentially "dangerous" source of infection for aging family members. Rather than the expected emotional and physical proximity of caregivers, there is/ was social distance and quarantine. The cues of danger around other people replaced cues of safety accompanying warm social engagement. Preoccupation with losses interfered with attunement. Cues of danger impaired contingent responsiveness and social connectedness. Preliminary studies suggest COVID-19 pandemic-related social distance and quarantine impacted early childhood development. Columbia University showed small delays in gross motor, fine motor, and communication skills compared to babies born before the pandemic (Shuffrey et al., 2022). While it is not clear these will be permanent delays, there is even greater concern these developmental delays are more significant in low-income children, especially children of color.

The impact of social isolation/quarantine and a more sedentary lifestyle potentially leads to delays in immunizations and other health surveillance, more screen time, increased economic and food insecurity, higher obesity rates, and elevated rates of domestic violence and child neglect and abuse. Children and adolescents who are neurodivergent, have learning differences, and attentional challenges are at even higher risk for delays. Again, children of low socioeconomic status and children of color are particularly affected (Irwin et al., 2022).

From Risk to Resilience: Moving from Caravans of Risk to Caravans of Resource Passageways

Stress is ubiquitous, and not all stress is bad. Some stress promotes growth. The Center on the Developing Child describes the hierarchy of stress: 1) Positive stress: brief increases in heart rate and mild temporary elevations of stress hormones; 2) Tolerable stress: serious temporary stresses buffered by supportive relationships, and 3) Toxic stress: prolonged activation of stress responses in the absence of buffering relationships (Center on the Developing Child, n.d.). In addition to pandemics, our youngest children and their families are subject to the toxic effects of climate change, mass migration, wars, poverty, racism, and violence. Many of our most vulnerable children are affected by adverse childhood experiences (ACEs). Felitti et al., 1998, documented the lifelong impact of adverse exposures experienced by adults during their childhood. Many of these adults had multiple exposures, and for those who experienced more than four ACEs, there was a 60% chance they developed a chronic illness of adulthood, including heart disease, diabetes, and high blood pressure. They were also ten times more likely to engage in substance misuse. A unifying characteristic of the ACEs is their interruption of social connectedness either through traumatic losses, bereavements, or separations or impaired caregiving secondary to parental mental illness or substance misuse.

Many children and families are enmeshed in "caravans of risk passage-ways." These are redundant and multiplicative environmental conditions that *detract, undermine, obstruct, or impoverish their (sic) resource reservoirs.* To transform caravans of risk into caravans of resource passageways requires developing individual, family, community, and population resilience. Now considered to be a state rather than a trait, one working definition of resilience is "the ability of people, families, or communities to withstand stressors and to return to their pre-stressor state when that stressor ends" (Hobfoll et al., 2015, p. 3). Not surprisingly, the transformation depends upon building successful relationships. Positive childhood experiences or Counter-ACEs focus upon developing and sustaining social engagement with an adult even when primary caregivers may not be physically or emo-tionally available for scaffolding. Having at least one caregiver with whom you felt safe, at least one good friend, at least one teacher who cared or an adult who could provide support or advice mitigated the impact of ACEs (Narayan et al., 2018; Bethell et al., 2019). Adults who had Counter-ACEs had lower stress and depression, fewer sleep difficulties, an improved locus of control, higher forgiveness/gratitude, higher familial closeness (Crandall et al., 2019). Bad things still happen or may happen, but those persons who report Counter-ACEs are better able to manage the bumps, ride the waves, and engage in practices that build better health and wellbeing.

Conclusion

Family physician and psychiatrist Herbert Adler said the provider-patient relationship requires "the person-to-person attunement that is essential for the development of the newborn" (Adler, 2002, p. 887). Whether in work with children, their families, or other staff, we can use the foundation of Polyvagal theory to meet their evolutionary expectancies of relationships. We use our physical and emotional proximity to keep ourselves and move others toward a ventral vagal state of calm and social engagement. We lev-erage our sensitivity and attunement to deepen and maintain these devel-oping relationships while building the trust that will assist in repair and see us through disruptions. And finally, as the culture of neurobiological safety emerges and becomes iterative, we live in the reciprocal and synchronous co-regulation of physiologic and behavioral states, social connectedness, where humans thrive.

> **Treatment Takeaways**
>
> - Mammals' evolutionary expectations of their caregivers include their social and emotional proximity, their sensitivity and attunement, their contingent responsiveness, and their social engagement and social connectedness. *Social connectedness* defined by Porges is the ability to mutually (synchronously and reciprocally) regulate physiological and behavioral state.
> - Mammals exhibit behavioral responses based upon their unconscious sense (or neuroceptions) of whether they are safe, in danger, or in a life threat environment. All mammalian behaviors are in the service of survival.
> - There are disruptions in even the most solid relationships. It is the repair, not the disruption, that determines how dyads move forward in their increasingly complex work.
> - Stress is ubiquitous, and not all stress is bad. Some stress promotes growth.
> - Resilience is a state, not a trait. Resilience is the ability of persons to withstand stressors and to return to their pre-stressor state when the stressor ends.

References

Adler, H. M. (2002). The sociophysiology of caring in the doctor-patient relationship. *Journal of General Internal Medicine, 17*(11), 883–890.

Ammaniti, M., & Gallese, V. (2014). *The birth of intersubjectivity: Psychodynamics neurobiology and the self.* Norton.

Baumgaertner, E. (2022, November 3). 'This is our March 2020': Children's hospitals are overwhelmed by RSV. *New York Times.* www.nytimes.com/2022/11/01/science/rsv-children-hospitals.html

Bergman, N. (2015). Neuroprotective core measures 1–7: Neuroprotection of skin-to-skin contact. *Newborn and Infant Nursing Reviews, 15*(3), 142–146.

Bergman, N. J. (2019). Historical background to maternal-neonate separation and neonatal care. *Birth Defects Research,* 1–6.

Bergman, N. J., Ludwig, R. J., Westrup, B., & Welch, M. G. (2019). Nurturescience versus neuroscience: A case for rethinking perinatal mother–infant behaviors and relationship. *Birth Defects Research,* 1–18.

Bethell, C. Jones, J., Gombojav, N., Linkenbach, J., & Sege, R. (2019). Positive childhood experiences and adult mental and relational health in a statewide sample: Associations across adverse childhood experiences levels. *JAMA Pediatrics*, *173*(11), 1–10.

Center on the Developing Child. (n.d.). *A guide to toxic stress*. https://developingchild.harvard.edu/guide/a-guide-to-toxic-stress/

Costello, P. C. (2013). *Attachment-based psychotherapy: Helping patients develop adaptive capacities*. American Psychological Association.

Crandall, A., Miller, J. R., Cheung, A., Novilla, L. K., Glade, R., Novilla, M. L. B., Magnusson, B. M., Leavitt, B. L. Barnes, M. D., & Hanson, C. L. (2019). ACEs and counter-ACEs: How positive and negative childhood experiences influence adult health. *Child Abuse & Neglect*, *96*, 104089.

Felitti, V. J., Anda, R. F., Nordenberg, D., Williamson, D. F., Spitz, A. M., Edwards, V., Koss, M. P., & Marks, J. S. (1998). Relationship of childhood abuse and household dysfunction to many of the leading causes of death in adults. *American Journal of Preventative Medicine*, *14*(4), 245–258.

Fraiberg, S., Adelson, E., & Shapiro, V.(2003). Ghosts in the nursery: A psychoanalytic approach to the problems of impaired infant-mother relationships. In J. Raphael-Leff (Ed). *Parent-infant psychodynamics: Wild things, mirrors and ghosts* (pp. 87–117). Routledge.

Hobfoll, S. E., Stevens, N. R., & Zalta, A. K. (2015). Expanding the science of resilience: Conserving resources in the aid of adaptation. *Psychological Inquiry*, *26*(2), 174–180.

Hofer, M. A. (1994). Early relationships as regulators of infant physiology and behavior. *Acta Paediatrica Supplement*, *397*, 9–18.

Irwin, M., Lazarevic, B., Soled, D., & Adesman, A. (2022). The COVID-19 pandemic and its potential enduring impact on children. *Current Opinion in Pediatrics*, *34*, 107–115.

Kenrick, D. T., Griskevicius, V., Neuberg, S. L., & Schaller, M. (2010). Renovating the pyramid of needs: Contemporary extensions built upon ancient foundations. *Perspectives on Psychological Science*, *5*(3), 292–314.

Narayan, A. J., Rivera, L. M., Bernstein, R. E., Harris, W. W., & Lieberman, A. F. (2018). Positive childhood experiences predict less psychopathology and stress in pregnant women with childhood adversity: A pilot study of the benevolent childhood experiences (BCEs) scale. *Child Abuse & Neglect*, *78*, 19–30.

Phillips, R. (2013). The Sacred hour: Uninterrupted skin-to-skin contact immediately after birth. *Newborn and Infant Nursing Reviews*, *13*(2), 67–72.

Porges, S. W. (2011). *The Polyvagal theory: Neurophysiological foundations of emotions, attachment, communication, and self-regulation* (1st ed.). Norton.

Porges, S. W. (2014). *The transformative power of feeling safe* [Paper presentation]. Presented at the Cape Cod Institute, Eastham, Massachusetts.

Porges, S. W. (2015). *Play as a neural exercise: Insights from the Polyvagal theory.* www. legeforeningen.no/contentassets/6df47feea03643c5a878ee7b87a467d2/sissel-oritsland-vedlegg-til-presentasjon-porges-play-as-neural-exercise.pdf

Porges, S. W. (2019, September 20). *Social connectedness as a biological imperative: Implications of Polyvagal theory in the classroom* [Paper presentation]. Presented at the Educational Neuroscience Symposium, Butler University, Indianapolis, Indiana.

Porges, S. W., & Furman, S. A. (2011). The early development of the autonomic nervous system provides a neural platform for social behaviour: A polyvagal perspective. *Infant and Child Development, 20*(1), 106–118.

Powell, B., Cooper, G., Hoffman, K., & Marvin, B. (2013). *The circle of security intervention: Enhancing attachment in early parent-child relationships.* Guilford.

Sanders, M. R., & Thompson, G. S. (2021). *Polyvagal theory and the developing child: Systems of care for strengthening kids, families, and communities.* Norton.

Sandman, C. A., Davis, E. P., Buss, C., & Glynn, L. M. (2011). Prenatal programming of human neurological function. *International Journal of Peptides*, 1–9.

Shuffrey, L. C., Firestein, M. R., Kyle, M. H., Fields, A., Alcantara, C., Amso, D., Austin, J., Bain, J. M., Barbosa, J., Bence, M., Bianco, C., Fernandez, C. R., Goldman, S., Gyamfi-Bannerman, C., Hott, V., Hu, H., Hussain, M., Factor-Litvak, P., Lucchini, M., . . . Dumitriu, D. (2022). Association of birth during the Covid-19 pandemic with neurodevelopmental status at 6 months in infants with and without in-utero exposure to maternal SARS-Cov-2 infection. *JAMA Pediatrics, 176*(6), e215563.

Tronick, E. Z., & Cohn, J. F. (1989). Infant-mother face-to-face interaction: Age and gender differences in coordination and the occurrence of miscoordination. *Child Development, 60*(1), 85–92.

Weinstein, A. (2016). *Prenatal development and parents' lived experiences: How early events shape our psychophysiology and relationships.* Norton.

Wong, A. (2022, June 9). Pandemic babies are behind after years of stress, isolation affected brain development. *USA Today.* www.usatoday.com/in-depth/news/education/2022/06/09/pandemic-babies-now-toddlers-delayed-development-heres-why/9660318002/

2

Listening Inside Our Bodies, Outside Our Bodies, and Between Bodies

Interoception, Exteroception, and
Setting Up a Polyvagal-Informed Playroom

Paris Goodyear-Brown and Lorri Yasenik

Overview

Play therapists are invited to examine the Polyvagal-informed playroom
(PIP) with a focus on exteroception (what our bodies tell us from the outside
in). Consider first the many physical decisions related to the play therapy
room detail such as size, color, light, shape, space, and play therapy materials.
Then, in conjunction with a focus on the physical, examine five main areas
of therapeutic use of self. Safety between two players begins with a heightened awareness of the self of the therapist, as the therapist is a significant
co-regulator of the process. Safety in the physical space and safety between
two people are core to the ventral vagal state of social connectedness.

Setting the Stage

Polyvagal theory posits that we are always listening inside our bodies, outside our bodies, and between bodies without conscious awareness that we
are doing so (Dana, 2018, 2020). All three of these processes are critically
influenced by the felt sense of the space that we occupy while we listen. The
drama that unfolds in our moment-to-moment neuroception of safety, danger,
or life threat is powerfully influenced by the physical environments in which
humans find themselves. I (Paris) double-majored in theater and psychology
in my undergraduate degree program. During my years at Duke University,

DOI: 10.4324/9781003352976-2

I had the privilege of performing in a variety of settings: a black box theater with audience members seated close up, a proscenium thrust theater with lights blinding me to the audience, a beautiful but drafty cathedral with great distance between me and the audience, and theater in the round with audience on all sides. Actors access different parts of the self under the influence of the space in which they are performing: nuanced micro expressions are amplified in power on film, while the use of voice, tone, and body language may all need to be over-exaggerated in a grand theater space. The audience too may use their bodies, voices, and witnessing presence differently based on the space. Parts of a person are invited or disallowed as a result of the practical configuration of the concrete space. Playrooms (both indoor and outdoor) are the physical space in which the drama between therapist and client unfold. A Polyvagal informed playroom (PIP) scaffolds specific decisions related to size, sound, color, light, shape, space, and the chosen toys and tools themselves upon the foundational value of providing the neuroception of safety for the play client. One way to think about the process of play therapy is as a series of relational risks. Once a neuroception of safety has been established in both the physical space and the therapeutic relationship, children can begin taking those risks. Through a polyvagal lens, play itself is seen as a neural exercise (Porges, 2015), and play therapy invites clients to dance at the edges of their windows of tolerance for excitation and distress in blended vagal states.

Interoception, what our bodies tell us from the inside out, and exteroception, what our bodies tell us from the outside in, are intimately connected to a variety of environmental stimuli, including *objects in* and *characteristics of* our physical environments. Nowhere is this truer than in a playroom. When a child enters a playroom that includes prominently displayed play swords and shields, the nonverbal invitation to sword fighting is processed. If the child decides to experiment with the objects in the playroom, activation of the sympathetic nervous systems *within them* (the client and the play therapist respectively) will be mitigated by the social engagement system *between them*. Will limits be set? Will they fight one another? If so, what roles will they each play? Or do they join together to fight a foe . . . and if so, do they decimate the enemy or get captured or killed? And what is the felt sense in each of these scenarios? These sensory impressions often happen outside our conscious awareness and contribute to the felt sense of safety humans experience in space.

While Polyvagal theory informs some qualities of environmental stimuli that are predictive of felt safety—like higher frequency, prosodic sounds vs. lower frequency tones—other sensory markers of felt safety may vary greatly between individual clients. If *safety is the treatment* (Porges, 2011, 2017, 2021), then the physical space must offer multiple points of access to the experience of safety. Parameters of the physical space itself, the bigness or smallness of space, the colors, the light, the sound, the temperature, the smells, the tactile offerings, and the sensory experiences all make up the unique character of a playroom. Individual playrooms are as unique as the play therapist who occupies them. Just as no two play therapists offer the neuroception of safety in exactly the same way, no two play spaces are exactly the same. Basic parameters based on our understanding of sensory needs merit exploration.

Listening Inside Our Bodies

Body-Based Need Meeting: Temperature, Hydration, Nourishment, Toileting Needs

Easy access to a bathroom can increase the felt sense of safety for certain clients. Young children are often potty training. One powerful way to support interoception is to become curious with children about what their bodies are communicating to them. The four-year-old who is bouncing up and down while holding his private parts in one hand while continuing to build a block structure with the other is helped to tune into his interoceptive sense with the question, "What is your body telling you right now?" Early on in treatment, the interpretation of the child's nonverbal cues may need to come from the therapist, "Your body is letting me know that you might need the bathroom. Let's go, quick!" Afterwards, there can be a celebration of the powerful way the client's body communicates its needs (Goodyear-Brown, 2019).

The provision of water or juice and snacks helps create an early neuroception of safety for clients. Big behaviors (Goodyear-Brown, 2022) can be fed by a lack of hydration (Benton & Young, 2015; Booth et al., 2012; Edmonds & Jeffe, 2009; Liska et al., 2019) or unsatiated hunger. The first stop at Nurture House is in the main hallway, where there is easy access to the bathroom, the snack cart, the gumball machine, and the refrigerator. It is standard practice to invite a moment of interception: *Before we choose a room, let's check in with our bodies. What is your body telling you it needs?* While gum chewing can provide both proprioceptive and vestibular input, giving children quicker focused access to their executive function, offering a variety of snacks can harness the gustatory sense. Some children are alerted by the sour sting of some candies, others may feel soothed by the sweetness (and suck) of a lollipop, while still others are viscerally affected by the crunch of a chip or carrot stick. From birth, the caregiving relationship is paired with resources. Mother's milk is paired with her warm, nurturing embrace. Offering these most fundamental need meeting experiences increases the felt sense of safety for the individual client while solidifying relational safety with the play therapist.

The Playroom as a Co-Therapist

Bigness and Smallness in Space

TraumaPlay™, a flexibly sequential play therapy model for treating traumatized children, gives therapeutic primacy to the enhancement of safety and security for each child (Goodyear-Brown, 2009, 2019). To this end, TraumaPlay therapists view the playroom space itself as a co-therapist, an ally in increasing the neuroception of safety experienced by the client. Some children, those who are big in their bodies or hyperkinetic, might come into a large, open playroom and run in circles, filling the space—and this will feel good to them. Other children may need a sense of containment in order to feel safe. Smallness of space (Goodyear-Brown, 2019) can be achieved within larger playrooms by creating definitive quadrants within the larger room (for example, two book cases placed perpendicular to one another to separate a play kitchen area from the sand tray), a pop-up circus tent placed in a small closet, or even an old sheet thrown over two chairs to make a fort. An energetic five-year-old boy may need a qualitatively different physical environment than a fifteen-year-old female client in order to neurocept safety.

The author has had the great privilege of creating a multitude of playrooms, each with its own unique flavors. For instance, we have expanded Nurture House (our home-like treatment center that currently offers ten indoor playrooms and five unique outdoor play environments). Our work spaces have ranged from a variety of school-based settings that included a broom closet, a full-sized classroom, the locker room adjoining the gymnasium, and the landing of an unused stairwell all the way to magnificent old buildings with multiple nooks, crannies, and large spaces. Wherever your space and whatever your space constraints, there are things that can be done to amplify the invitation to the neuroception of safety.

Light

Lighting choices can influence our felt sense of safety. Lighting can influence our affective mood and our cognitive function (Blume et al., 2019; Knez,

1995; Kong et al., 2022). Additionally, the lighting conditions associated with a particular trauma may need to be understood. For example, a child who was sexually abused repeatedly in the semi-darkness of their bedroom may associate a low-lit room with a neuroception of danger. Another child, perhaps a chronically ill child who associates brightly lit rooms with their extended hospital stays and invasive medical procedures, may neurocept danger in a fluorescently lit room. Choosing a playroom that has one or more windows can let in an abundance of natural light, which may contribute to a felt sense of safety for many. However, if there are windows in the room, it may be difficult to make the room entirely dark, and occasionally a child client needs to turn off all the lights, experience the dark, and use a flashlight, a lantern, a candle, or even a strobe light (Goodyear-Brown, 2009). The most versatile playrooms will have options for lighting, including windows, shades/blinds to cover the windows, ceiling light, lamp light, and smaller light sources such as flashlights. LED lights and other decorative light strands offer clients the potential to change color, pattern, and ambience within the playroom, increasing their sense of agency and enhancing their voice through choice.

Sound

Porges has added meaningfully to the idea of sound as influential in offering safety (Porges, 2017, 2021; Porges & Lewis, 2010; Porges et al., 2014). The discovery that tendrils of the ventral vagus attach in the muscles of the jaw and the inner ear has led to a deeper understanding of the use of our voice as influential in establishing a neuroception of safety with and for our clients. Prosody, particularly the motherese that comes almost unconsciously to many parents of young children, and the pitch, tone, and cadence of the play therapist's voice matter. Musical instruments that allow for all sorts of sound and rhythm can help child clients to externally modulate their internal chaos (Goodyear-Brown, 2009), practice attunement with others, or restore lost early rhythms of regulation. Play therapists often place white noise machines in or just outside their playrooms for sound masking purposes. Inviting the client to choose which sound setting feels right for them is one easy way to enhance agency. Noises that hum along at a lower pitch, such as hospital machinery, air conditioning units, construction noise, or the thrum of a vehicle's motor, may hearken back to evolutionary associations with predators and our body's heightened sense of danger when we hear these sounds. Music, from heavy metal to lullabies, can influence our felt sense in an instant and can be used powerfully in playrooms. The Safe and Sound Protocol (Porges et al., 2014) can be offered as a sort of sound diet to clients and/or to their parent(s) to help in the enhancement of their own neuroception of safety.

Temperature

Indoor playrooms should be kept at a mild, mid-range temperature. However, the wise play therapist will have offerings (a blanket, a fan, a space heater, hot and cold beverages) that imply permission for a client to need a colder or warmer temperature to feel safe. Clients can become distracted when they are too hot or too cold. The temperature of outdoor spaces will obviously fluctuate, and clients can benefit from conversations about what they need to regulate effectively in the outdoor space: a thick winter coat, gloves, rain boots, a heated blanket, a cold drink, a shady spot, etc. Encouraging the client to check in with their bodies about the temperature and ask for what they need to feel "just right" can be another powerful tool for establishing a neuroception of safety. The play therapist models checking in with their own body's needs throughout the session. When the therapist and the client are experiencing the same environment differently, the stage is set for powerful learning to occur around individual differences, empathy, and perspective taking.

Touch

Offering a range of sensory materials encourages clients to explore what their bodies need. Is the client sensory seeking, sensory defensive, or a complex presentation of both? Presenting the client not only with a classic white sand for sandtray work, but also with the extra-fine Jurassic sand, the packable kinetic sand, and trays of shells, rice, or beans extend the client's potential expansion of self-knowledge. Art materials such as clay can be offered across a sensory continuum: wet clay that requires some force to mold, PlayDoh, Model Magic, Sculpey, Air Dry Clay, and plasticine each provide a unique sensory experience and will evoke a variety of felt senses across a variety of clients. Within a "Nurture Nook" (Goodyear-Brown, 2021), the play therapist might offer a multitude of pillows: one that is fuzzy and soft, one that is made of rough burlap, one that is shiny or silky, some that are squishy, and some that are more supportive. Slime-making ingredients can offer more or less texture, intensity of color, and viscosity.

Smell

The olfactory bulb is the only part of our central nervous system that is exposed to the elements, so it is the fastest way in for a change of state. One simple way to amplify choice is to offer a set of essential oils and to explore the various scents and determine which is most upregulating or alerting and which is more down-regulating or calming. These can be diffused as needed or made into sachets for use outside of session. Certain smells may be intrusive for sensory defensive clients, so it is worth exploring how the smell of microwaved foods, perfumes, and body lotions might affect different clients and their neuroception of safety, danger, or life threat. Certain smells may be associated with particular nurturers or, conversely, with certain perpetrators. Trauma triggers may need to be assessed around smell.

Invitation to Movement/Rhythm

Proprioception and the vestibular sense are also experienced across a continuum and can influence a sense of felt safety. Sensory-seeking children may need intense touch that reaches deep tissue when receiving an arm massage from mom, giant jumping when playing on the Jumparoo outside, or hard hitting when playing tetherball. For these children, other therapeutic goals may need to be paired with significant kinesthetic involvement for the bulk of each session. Sensory-defensive children may avoid big body play that might involve climbing, swinging, or spinning.

What Does the Therapist Need to Feel Safe?

The neuroception of safety being experienced by the play therapist at any given moment in the therapy process is a powerful partner in the work, while a neuroception of danger (or life threat) can be incredibly dysregulating for both the therapist and the client. To maintain a Safe Boss presence in the room, it is important that the play therapist follow the age-old maxim *Know thyself*. The wise play therapist works to understand their own neuroception around light, sound, smell, bigness or smallness in space, and works to titrate the dose of whatever environmental influences the client needs while remaining grounded and anchored themselves. Titration of the dose of any one of these environmental qualities may need to be tweaked for the therapist to remain fully present. Strobe lights, for example, may be so dysregulating to the therapist that this particular form of lighting may need to be removed from the choice offerings within the playroom. The curation of playroom space, then, is an organic, evolving process that includes the physical constraints of the space, the needs of the client population being served, and the bare minimum regulation needs of the play therapist.

Entering the Stage

The therapist has set the stage and prepared the environment. It is now time to enter the stage. The child client and the therapist previously unknown to each other meet in anticipation. Previously unknown to each other, meet in anticipation. The scene is carefully laid out with all the props, materials, costumes, and stage. It is a dance of knowing and getting to know the other's movements, rhythms, emotions, intentions, energy, and lines. The story is yet to unfold, and each has a critical part to play. Who will lead, and who will follow? Who will fall on the sword, and who will be brought to life again through magical command? Each actor moves to the other's beat, influencing the play in inexplicable ways.

Play therapists and child clients are the primary actors in a series of scenes that encompass the unspoken yet powerful elements of a therapeutic relationship. As Act 1 begins, each actor turns toward the other, scanning for safety and predictability. The character of the actors is unveiled little by little. Not unlike "personality actors" who use their own personalities to bring life to a character, the play therapist and child client find themselves using parts of themselves to engage on the play therapy stage.

Between Actors

The "self" of the play therapist is critical in creating safety in the space and safety in the relationship with a child. A safe and connected space between the two actors sits in the center of the ventral vagal "stage." Creating this space requires a close look at therapist use of self from a multifactorial point of view. The nuanced movements, energy, and tones expressed by the therapist all contribute to an interpersonally felt experience of safety. The Neuroception of Safety Scale (NPSS) (Morton et al., 2022) is one of the first scales informed by Polyvagal theory that begins to explore the factors related to psychological safety in adult clients. The preliminary breakdown of the scale includes 29 items and 3 subscales (compassion, social engagement, and body sensations). Kirby et al., 2017, note that compassion including soothing voice tones, breathing, and eye contact all help to co-regulate the autonomic nervous system with another person. Children who have received a regular dose of compassion during early childhood will have a greater ability to self-soothe and therefore self-regulate in later years, whereas those without such experiences will lack this ability. Therapeutic use of self in play therapy increases the possibility of enhancing a child's self-soothing capacities through a process of co-regulation between therapist and child (Grant et al., 2020).

Play therapists are invited to reflect on psychological, emotional, relational, and physical safety in play therapy using the *Degree of Immersion: Therapist Use of Self Scale* (Yasenik & Gardner, 2012, 2018, 2020). Safety between two players can only begin with a heightened awareness of the self of the therapist, as the therapist is the guide and co-regulator of the process. The scale not only considers the therapist's use of self and degree of immersion in the process, but it also asks the therapist to identify the *child's responses* to the therapist's degree of immersion. If the therapist's use of self is over- or under-played, the therapist is informed how to shift in a given session or for the next session based on the responses of the child. Safety between the two players is a reflexive process. The following provides a deeper look at the therapist use of self on the play therapy stage. Five main areas for reflection and self-rating are reviewed: 1) Verbal Use of Self; 2) Emotional Use of Self; 3) Physical Use of Self; 4) Self System, and 5) Cultural Use of Self.

Verbal Use of Self

Verbal use of self relates to four ways a play therapist may verbally engage with a child client and is divided into four subscales: 1) Here-and-now discussion about the child's life or the child outside of the play activity; 2) Reflecting and tracking statements (tracking what the client is doing or what the play objects are doing and reflecting statements or guesses about what the therapist thinks the client or play objects are experiencing; 3) Restating content (paraphrasing what the child said during the play without adding meaning or interpretation; and 4) Interpretations (utilizing play material to assist a child to develop new understanding and meaning by bringing a link between play and the child's lived life to greater conscious awareness). The pressure to "talk" or use one's voice in the process can sometimes be high, as play therapists may be influenced by parents, third parties, and/or a theoretical model of play therapy. How verbal are *you*, and how responsive is the child? Are you creating a safe and engaging space, or are you imposing and closing in on the child's need for distance or personal and psychological space? Are you aware of your tone, cadence, timbre, rhythm of voice? How does your verbal "use of self" support or interrupt safety?

Emotional Use of Self

Emotional use of self is divided in two subscales: 1) Emotionality (the degree of emotional intensity that you assigned to either reflective statements or by inserting an emotion or emotional meaning to a character or characters in the play metaphor. If you were in a role, consider the intensity of use of emotions including tone, prosody, duration, volume, and facial expressions.) and 2) Emotional self (to what degree were you personally emotionally involved during the session)? This may include your awareness of feeling a particular intense emotion or noticing yourself shut down or becoming numb or temporarily losing track of following the client. You may become aware of a personal experience or be triggered to a personal memory. The emotional "use of self" scales ask the play therapist to self-evaluate and identify personal feeling states that may arise during the play process and to identify child responses. How did the emotionality or emotional self of the therapist impact the child or the play process? Did you notice an over- or under-expression in the use of self? Did your emotional "use of self" deepen the play or shut the play down? Did it create or stop a sense of safety and connectedness? Did you feel safe? Did the child feel safe?

Physical Use of Self

The physical "use of self" subscale requires the play therapist to identify the degree of physical involvement during a given session. Physical self includes physical movement in play activities such as physical proximity or touch, level of physical energy, physical involvement, and physical interaction. Was there a sense of physical joining? Did you feel engaged or withdrawn from the physicality of the play? What happened between you and the child? Was there encouragement from the child for you to physically join with them? Did you encourage the child to join with you? Were you able to keep the environment and actions between you and the child safe and energetically rhythmic and co-regulatory?

Self-System

The self-system subscale (embodiment) asks the therapist to rate the self-system related to body energy and awareness of the self in relation to "other" (the child). The scales assist the therapist to connect to internal states of "self" related to interoceptive awareness. It is the ability to identify, access, understand, and respond appropriately to the patterns of internal signals. When prompted, therapists may notice a sense of disembodiment whereby they are mostly operating in a cognitive, disconnected embodied space during a session. Conversely, the therapist may become aware of being lost in embodiment as internal signals increase and flooding occurs. Maltreated children who have poorly organized sensory systems are prone to sensory misperceptions, resulting in inadequate body awareness and integration of self, body, and environment (Barfield et al., 2012). During the Embodiment (E) stage of the E-P-R developmental paradigm, the child's embodied experiences are essential for establishing a 'body-self' and are critical in forming security and trust (Jennings, 2005, 2014). The embodiment scale capturing the interaction between therapist self-system and that of the child is an important Polyvagal theory consideration for the co-regulation process.

Cultural Use of Self

The cultural "use of self" subscale leads play therapists to rate themselves on their acknowledgement of their own cultural orientation and cultural sharing in combination with the child's cultural referencing during a play therapy session. The rating looks at the continuum of cultural use of self, ranging from observation to direct engagement or intervention related to cultural issues or cultural identity. Cultural "use of self" is more than simply knowing yourself and being curious about other(s). It is also about human rights and social justice advocacy (Cevallos et al., 2021). A multicultural orientation considers systemic oppression and inherent power differentials that exist in society. Play therapists must be aware of their cultural selves and have a curiosity about their child clients and their families. Some children live in marginalized situations in which their voices are limited and self-concepts are negatively impacted. Consideration of empowerment on the play therapy stage is a cultural and socio-political part of increasing safety, support, and ultimately social connectedness in the play therapy setting.

The Closing Scene

Oscar Wilde (as cited in O'Sullivan, 2015) likely stated it best when he said: "I regard the theatre as the greatest of all art forms, the most immediate way in which a human being can share with another the sense of what it is to be a human being." The play therapy stage is where the verbal, emotional, physical, embodied, and cultural selves culminate. It is the grand act of "being with" another in the telling, listening, and re-telling of life stories. Nuanced play-based activities between child and therapist are core to the ventral vagal state of social connectedness.

Conclusion

The Polyvagal-informed play therapist aims to understand the interception and exteroception needs of clients, as well as the science of creating safe spaces to maximize both the speed and magnitude of therapeutic gains. Toys are selected, not collected, and they are placed in predictable arrangements within the physical space. A range of sensory experiences is provided as well as a variety of methods for blocking out sensory input, so that those clients who are sensory seeking, sensory defensive, or a complex presentation of both can make choices that enhance their neuroception of safety within the space. The influence of the "person" of the play therapist is emphasized, and therapists are invited into the assessment of the self in five main domains: 1) Verbal Use of Self; 2) Emotional Use of Self; 3) Physical Use of Self; 4) Self-System; and 5) Cultural Use of Self. Therapists then contrast their use of self with specific observations of the child's response(s), which directly inform the therapist in how to stay in the safe and connected space with the child.

🗑 Therapy Takeaways

- Polyvagal informed playrooms (both indoor and outdoor) require consideration related to size, sound, color, light, shape, space, and the chosen toys and tools themselves based upon the foundational value of providing the neuroception of safety for the play client.
- The neuroception of safety being experienced by the play therapist at any given moment in the therapy process is a powerful partner in the work, while as a neuroception of danger (or life threat) can be incredibly dysregulating for both the therapist and the client.
- Therapist use of self considers five main domains for reflection and self-rating: 1) Verbal Use of Self; 2) Emotional Use of Self; 3) Physical Use of Self; 4) Self System; and 5) Cultural Use of Self. This is critical to ensuring a ventral vagal condition in the play therapy setting.

References

Barfield, S., Dobson, C., Gaskill, R., & Perry, B. D. (2012). Neurosequential model of therapeutics in a therapeutic preschool: Implications for work with children with complex neuropsychiatric problems. *International Journal of Play Therapy*, *21*(1), 30.

Benton, D., & Young, H. A. (2015). Do small differences in hydration status affect mood and mental performance? *Nutrition Reviews*, *73*(Suppl 2), 83–96.

Blume, C., Garbazza, C., & Spitschan, M. (2019). Effects of light on human circadian rhythms, sleep and mood. *Somnologie*, *23*(3), 147.

Booth, P., Taylor, B., & Edmonds, C. J. (2012). Water supplementation improves visual attention and fine motor skills in schoolchildren. *Education and Health*, *30*(3), 75–79.

Cevallos, P. L., Post, P., & Rodriguez, M. (2021). Practicing child-centered play therapy from a multicultural and social justice framework. In E. Gill & A. Drewes (Eds.), *Cultural issues in play therapy* (pp. 13–31). Guilford Press.

Dana, D. (2018). *The Polyvagal theory in therapy: Engaging the rhythm of regulation*. Norton series on interpersonal neurobiology. W. W. Norton & Company.

Dana, D. (2020). *Polyvagal flip chart: Understanding the science of safety*. Norton series on interpersonal neurobiology. W. W. Norton & Company.

Edmonds, C. J., & Jeffes, B. (2009). Does having a drink help you think? 6–7-Year-old children show improvements in cognitive performance from baseline to test after having a drink of water. *Appetite*, *53*(3), 469–472.

Goodyear-Brown, P. (2009). *Play therapy with traumatized children: A prescriptive approach*. Wiley.

Goodyear-Brown, P. (2019). *Trauma and play therapy: Helping children heal*. Routledge.

Goodyear-Brown, P. (2021). *Parents as partners in child therapy: A Clinician's guide*. Guilford.

Goodyear-Brown, P. (2022). *Big behaviors in small containers: 131 trauma-informed play therapy interventions for disorders of dysregulation*. PESI.

Grant, R. J., Stone, J., & Mellenthin, C. (2020). What is the importance of regulation in your play therapy work: How is it best achieved? In J. R. Grant, J. Stone, & C. Mellenthin (Eds.), *Play therapy theories and perspectives: A collection of thoughts in the field* (pp. 91–101). Routledge.

Jennings, S. (2005). Embodiment-projection-role: A developmental model for the play therapy method. In C. Schaefer, J. McCormick, & A. J. Ohnji (Eds.), *The international handbook of play therapy: Advances in assessment, theory, research and practice* (pp. 65–76). Jason Aronson.

Jennings, S. (2014). Applying an embodiment-projection-role framework in group-work with children. In E. Prendiville & J. Howard (Eds.), *Play therapy today*. Routledge.

Kirby, J. N., Doty, J. R., Petrocchi, N., & Gilbert, P. (2017). The current and future role of heart rate variability for assessing and training compassion. *Frontiers in Public Health*, *5*, 40.

Knez, I. (1995). Effects of indoor lighting on mood and cognition. *Journal of Environmental Psychology*, *15*(1), 39–51.

Kong, Z., Liu, Q., Li, X., Hou, K., & Xing, Q. (2022). Indoor lighting effects on subjective impressions and mood states: A critical review. *Building and Environment*, 109591.

Liska, D., Mah, E., Brisbois, T., Barrios, P. L., Baker, L. B., & Spriet, L. L. (2019). Narrative review of hydration and selected health outcomes in the general population. *Nutrients*, *11*(1), 70.

Morton, L., Cogan, N., Kolacz, J., Calderwood, C., Nikolic, M., Bacon, T., Pathe, E., Williams, D.,& Porges, S. W. (2022). A new measure of feeling safe: Developing psychometric properties of the neuroception of psychological safety scale (NPSS). *Psychological Trauma: Theory, Research, Practice, and Policy*.

O'Sullivan, C., & Wilde, O. (2015). Drama and autism. *Encyclopedia of Autism Spectrum Disorder*, DOI10.1007/978-1-4614-6435-8_102102-1 pp. 1–13.

Porges, S. W. (2011). *The Polyvagal theory: Neurophysiological foundations of emotions, attachment, communication, and self-regulation*. Norton series on interpersonal neurobiology. Norton.

Porges, S. W. (2015). Play as neural exercise: Insights from the Polyvagal theory. The power of play for mind brain health. *Mindgains.org*, *GAINS*, 3–7.

Porges, S. W. (2017). *The pocket guide to the Polyvagal theory: The transformative power of feeling safe*. Norton.

Porges, S. W. (2021). Polyvagal theory: A biobehavioral journey to sociality. *Comprehensive Psychoneuroendocrinology*, *7*, 100069.

Porges, S. W., Bazhenova, O. V., Bal, E., Carlson, N., Sorokin, Y., Heilman, K. J., Cook, E. H., & Lewis, G. F. (2014). Reducing auditory hypersensitivities in autistic spectrum disorder: Preliminary findings evaluating the listening project protocol. *Frontiers in Pediatrics*, *2*, 80.

Porges, S. W., & Lewis, G. F. (2010). The polyvagal hypothesis: Common mechanisms mediating autonomic regulation, vocalizations and listening. In *Handbook of behavioral neuroscience* (Vol. 19, pp. 255–264). Elsevier.

Yasenik, L., & Gardner, K. (2012). *Play therapy dimensions model: A decision-making guide for integrative play therapists*. Jessica Kingsley Publishers.

Yasenik, L., & Gardner, K. (Eds.). (2018). *Turning points in play therapy and the emergence of self: Applications of the play therapy dimensions model.* Jessica Kingsley Publishers.

Yasenik, L., & Gardner, K. (2020). Therapeutic use of self and the play therapy dimensions model. In *Routledge international handbook of play, Therapeutic play and play therapy* (pp. 341–359). Routledge.

3
The Sounds of Safety in an Unsafe World

Recovering from Domestic Violence Through Polyvagal-Informed Play Therapy

Lorri Yasenik and Jennifer Buchanan

Overview

Through the case of Zoe, the reader is invited into a six-part play therapy journey weaving the use of sound, music, and movement into sessions. The Polyvagal power of sound, including singing, is exemplified. Stimulation of the vagus nerve through vocalizing and breathing can create feelings of calm, safety, and security. Face and head muscles are used when you listen to and produce music (Breit et al., 2018; Dana, 2020; Porges, 2010). Special considerations in the purposeful use of music, sounds, and voice are included in a summary as a guide for the play therapist.

Zoe

The sound of breaking glass shatters against the wall beside four-year-old Zoe. Her small body moves instinctively, avoiding the shards that scatter on the floor beside her. She stands frozen and in silence as the sounds erupt around her: high-pitched screams, more glass, and threats of harm as her mother and father lunge towards each other. Her mother has a knife. Her father's arm is bleeding. Taking in all the movement and sound around her, her eyes stay fixed on the bright red drops on the floor as her father holds his arm and shouts louder. Her mother shouts back. Zoe wants to move, but she can't. She wants to go to one of her parents. She wants to run. She is filled with fear and can't do anything. Zoe stands still, and she can't feel her body

DOI: 10.4324/9781003352976-3

anymore. The next day Zoe wakes up in her bed. She can't remember how she got there. She feels a sense of dread. In the kitchen her mother is clattering about, slamming cupboard doors. She goes to the kitchen, and the mess is cleaned up; a pile of broken glass is sitting beside the broom. Zoe remains very quiet. She notices her father isn't there. Maybe he went to work.

When Zoe was seven years old, her mother and father separated. This came after many visits by police and multiple interventions by child protection services. Zoe's day-to-day world changed, as she was no longer exposed to the ongoing violence between her parents. Zoe began to spend one week with each parent. Her parents continued to hate and antagonize one another, and transitions between her parents were fraught with conflict and allegations. The legal system became involved, and each parent had a lawyer. Each parent undermined the relationship Zoe had with the other. Zoe was referred to play therapy.

Zoe arrived in my office at the age of nine. Her life journey until recently had been one of chaos, uncertainty, and witnessing her parents' psychological and physical abuse (the spectrum of forms or combination of forms not easy to categorize) (Potter et al., 2020). Zoe was soft-spoken, and her long hair partially covered her face. Her mother presented as highly agitated and focused on me finding Zoe's father to be aggressive and abusive so that "Zoe wouldn't have to see him anymore." Zoe's mother's alarm system appeared constantly activated, and she claimed she wanted Zoe to be "protected." Zoe had "run away" from her father's house during visits, and she had begun to scratch her skin, leaving parts of her arms and legs raw and sore. When brought by her mother, Zoe echoed her mother's comments that her father "yelled a lot" and she was scared at his house, but some things did not add up so neatly.

Polyvagal theory posits that there are three primary circuits that provide neuro regulation of the autonomic or physiological state and are regulated by the ventral vagal, dorsal vagal, and sympathetic pathways (Porges, 2017). The ventral vagal pathway is the way to autonomic balance, which is when the system is non-defensive and can support mobilization and immobilization. Would I be able to mobilize Zoe's social engagement system (ventral vagal) and increase her ability to stay present? Additionally, would I be able to assist Zoe by engaging her social engagement system with the dorsal vagal circuit through using cues of safety? Could Zoe engage in play without becoming defensive and either shutting down or moving to aggressive play? Could I help her autonomic nervous system engage and relax at the same time so that she could experience a feeling of calm and rest? These were my questions.

Conceptualizing Zoe: Perceived Sounds of Danger

I learned about Zoe's responses and behaviors at both homes. Zoe was more reactive at her father's than her mother's home. Zoe had a stepbrother at her father's home, and sometimes he would be reprimanded. Zoe herself noted she didn't know why she got "so scared" when he was in trouble because after some exploration, the consequences and intensity or duration of the parenting interventions were actually in the normal/mild range of healthy parenting. Her father's raised voice and shift in tone didn't have to be targeted at her for Zoe to neurocept danger. In fact, compared to her mother's tone, her father was soft-spoken. Regardless, her autonomic nervous system either descended into a dorsal vagal state, where no one could reach her, and *she* didn't know where she "went" or she would flee and leave the house (sympathetic state) (Porges, 2017). If Zoe fled, she could later describe a feeling of danger, but she couldn't provide any actual anchors to justify her feeling. When younger, fleeing was not an option for Zoe. The trouble with faulty neuroception is that risk can be detected when there is none. Zoe was stuck with faulty neuroception. Recovery and return to a more socially connected state (ventral vagal) only happened with the passage of time. Zoe's internal radar was shaped and "pre-set" as Dana (2020) notes, which creates a mismatch between what the autonomic nervous system identifies as safety or risk (Porges, 2015).

Both households were now much calmer, more responsive, and non-abusive as each parent had re-partnered with new people, creating a less reactive experience for each parent (the parents continued not to like or trust the other, however). When Zoe would take flight to a nearby aunt's house when confronted with any raising voice volume, change in tone, or loud noises particularly coming from her father or her father's home, she would call her mother to come and pick her up. The conflict between her parents would escalate as her mother pointed towards her father as "abusive." The trouble with this conceptualization was that Zoe had no examples of harm and in fact reported good relational examples when spending time with her father. Moreover, Zoe's mother tended to reinforce, without evidence to the contrary, Zoe's faulty neuroception and reinforced messages of lack of safety related to her father. Her father was highly involved in the therapy process and seemed dedicated to helping Zoe recover from early exposure to violence between him and her mother. Her mother, however, was unwilling to join the process in the same way, as her feelings of alarm and accompanying defenses got in the way of learning more about the effects of Zoe's early childhood experiences. There are many impacts of domestic and family violence

on children, including poor health and educational outcomes, greater proba-
bility of impaired parenting (including inconsistency and parent irritability),
continued experiences of parental conflict after separation, and child behavioral and emotional outcomes (Kaspiew et al., 2017).

Polyvagal Theory Comes Alive in the Playroom with Zoe

Zoe tentatively entered the playroom. During the first few sessions, I focused
on safety in the play therapy space, safety in Zoe's body, and safety in our relationship together. In autonomic nervous system terms, Zoe and I explored
the play space by observing what was available and gaining a visual map of
what could be used, experimenting with the sounds, textures, and smells in
the room. Sound, sight, smell, taste, and experience of tactile features of
objects are all elements of our exteroception or awareness of what is in our
external world. The playroom exploration was Zoe's first step in making contact with the treatment environment. Zoe was drawn to musical instruments
with rhythmic sounds, soft fuzzy objects such as stuffed animals, puppets,
and anything that had texture such as miniatures with soft features. She
liked the sensory bin and explored various available scents. She could hear
the ticking clock in the room, which disturbed her, so it was removed. Zoe
demonstrated hypervigilance to small sounds, creaks, and distant voices; all
seemingly taken in as potential danger cues. I carefully provided an explanation for the various sounds.

Proprioception is the awareness of where our bodies are in space. I handed
Zoe a flowy scarf that matched my own. While humming softly I moved my
scarf in slow circles and looked at Zoe while doing so. Zoe began to copy my
movements. We joined in eye contact, and I continued to hum a song that
Zoe thought was silly but made her smile. Face/heart contact was initiated
(Porges, 2017). We began a lead-follow-lead series of movements, and our
bodies moved together in space and time. I started to say things about what
my body was feeling. I could feel my heartbeat, and I started to feel warm
all over. I said my breathing reminded me of the rain stick as I breathed in
and out during our movement game. Zoe said she could feel her heart too.
We put one hand on our hearts and continued to move the scarves with our
other hands. We began to work with interoception (the awareness of what
was going on in our bodies). We both dropped to the floor and ended our
game by taking turns using the rain stick and listening to the beads drop
when we turned it over and over. This was the beginning of our relationship
together.

Six Play-based Interventions Towards Safety and Awareness: Therapeutic Powers of Play

Once a predictable safe space and an interpersonal connection was made, the work began. Zoe loved miniatures and gravitated towards sand play and musical sounds. Each intervention spanned multiple sessions and reflected one or more therapeutic power(s) of play (Schaefer & Drewes, 2014).

Intervention 1

Zoe was introduced to the concept of the autonomic nervous system (ANS) through an interactive animated video, facilitating communication through direct teaching (Schaefer & Drewes, 2014). When the video ended, I said that maybe we could work with her ANS. Zoe looked directly at me and said, "No, we are working with mini- Zoe." The intuitive wisdom in that statement was immediately embraced. Zoe was asked to choose a character who could be her and one that could be mini-Zoe. Zoe chose two figures, a cat for her and the tiniest girl figure on the shelf for mini-Zoe. I asked Zoe to create a scene for big Zoe and mini-Zoe. Interestingly, the first scene included two figures that were identified as her mother and father, a scary dragon coming out of the water, a turtle, and a dog. Mini-Zoe was protected under an umbrella far away from the parent figures, turtle, dog, and the scary dragon. Mini-Zoe had begun to take on an observer role while the family members and the fear state (dragon) were represented in the scene. Big Zoe was able to begin talking to mini-Zoe, assisting her to create safe spaces and to deliver messages to the parent figures (fostering emotional wellness through confrontation, reenactment, and counterconditioning fears). In child therapy, providing distance through projective materials is what assists children to begin to develop accurate cues of safety and cues of danger.

Intervention 2

I invited Zoe to create an art map of her autonomic hierarchy. This art-making activity was a picture of three zones: ventral, sympathetic, and dorsal. Zoe wrote the three words, divided her picture into three zones, and then chose a color to represent each section. I gave Zoe some simple descriptions of each word/zone and brainstormed with her to choose words for each section (one at a time). For *ventral*, for instance, she chose the words *friends*, *happy*, *warm*, *laughter*, *good sleep*, *no worries*, etc. For each zone Zoe then chose a symbol to represent the accompanying feeling state. She chose a soft stuffed mini-lion for ventral, a character running and one hiding under jewels for sympathetic, and a glass turtle for dorsal. For dorsal she said, "I can't talk, can't answer. I'm in my room, I'm frozen, I want to be alone." This interactive art-making activity invited Zoe into a brief description of her vagal system. We then returned to the play metaphor with the figures she had chosen. She used the figures and created separate sand worlds for each—increasing her overall awareness of the hierarchical states. During the metaphorical use of the symbols chosen, we began to introduce sounds that went with each vagal state using the musical instruments in the playroom.

Intervention 3

I met with each of her parents and followed the same process. I showed each of them the video. With Zoe's permission, we invited each parent individually to meet with us, and Zoe led each parent through their own mapping of hierarchical states. Zoe's parents were also asked to use words, colors, and symbols to represent each state. Zoe was nervous but curious as to what each parent might say. They were also asked to choose a sound that went with each state. Zoe was clearly empowered during this intervention. The locus of control was with Zoe as her parents were asked to follow her instructions. The therapeutic power of increasing personal strength was witnessed here (Schaefer & Drewes, 2014). Additionally, Zoe's parents had an experience of knowing something about their nervous systems and now had language to address Zoe's system.

Intervention 4

Zoe brought mini-Zoe and the symbols representing each hierarchical state chosen by her and her parents into sand play. The percussion instruments were part of the process, and Zoe re-created three worlds: ventral, sympathetic, and dorsal worlds. Each world was assigned specific sounds. Zoe played with the intensity, volume, and rhythms of the sounds. She practiced repeating sounds she noted as safe, protective, happy, and connected. Zoe created secret doorways and pathways for mini-Zoe to pass through to get to her ventral vagal "happy" space. Zoe was working with the three key areas of trauma recovery: re-experience, re-sensitize, and re-connect (Malchiodi, 2020). Zoe continued to work with the therapeutic power of fostering emotional wellness and counter conditioning of her fears through the play. She was leading mini-Zoe (a part of self) to practice a felt-sense of safety through the play metaphor. Zoe was observing and narrating the journey of mini-Zoe, who she helped inform about various body sensations and particularly positive self-soothing body sensations as she linked what she called "happy" sounds to the journey of the character. Levine (2015) refers to a gradual process of coming to a felt-sense, and this was possible with the distancing technique of the externalized self mini-Zoe.

Intervention 5

We created a play list for mini-Zoe. This activity was interesting, as it allowed Zoe to choose music for the younger her. What would mini-Zoe like? I offered many tunes to choose from, and it was no surprise that Zoe chose a number of early childhood tunes that were not only easy to sing, but some were accompanied by motions and actions such as "Head and Shoulders, Knees and Toes," "Itsy Bitsy Spider," "The Wheels on the Bus," and a quite a few children's Christmas songs. Together we created a concert for mini-Zoe. We set mini-Zoe in an "audience" chair (it was hard to see her, she was so small), and we acted out the songs together. We used props and movement items. I found the music to play in the background. It was hard to get through a song without breaking down in laughter. Face and head muscles are used when you both listen to and produce music. The middle ear muscles support listening (Dana, 2020; Porges, 2010). Zoe was engaging in an autonomic activity that helped with breathing and heart rate. The therapeutic power of enhancing social relationships was observed here as Zoe built empathy towards a part of self, impacting self-empathy.

Intervention 6

An invitation was made to mini-Zoe to begin to create a series of pictures for big Zoe. Large paper, finger paint, and other messy materials were provided. Increasing internal communication between the parts of self, offering big body movement, and encouraging imagination were targeted. Expressive pictures full of bright color with no request to paint a "picture of something" seemed to engage Zoe, and she was able to enter the art-making and have an experience of flow. I had large paper as well, and we tracked back and forth making big shapes together. I was also painting for big Zoe. Together we entered into imagining what big Zoe liked and didn't like (all part of the exploration of "self") (Yasenik & Gardner, 2019) and looked into our paintings to find hidden pictures. Once the paintings were done, we decided what sounds went with the scenes and together created soundscapes (Dana, 2021) of wind, rain, sun, splashing water, and silence. Mini-Zoe was empowered with insight about big Zoe's ups and downs and could now tell how much of the time she was in a ventral vagal connected feeling space and when she departed from this space. The therapeutic power of increasing personal strengths could be observed as Zoe worked in the metaphor on self-regulation and self-esteem.

These interventions are considered a focus series weaving between directive and non-directive clinical activities. Most of the time, therapy occurred in a less-conscious space by remaining in the play metaphor, moving between the dimensions of non-directive (non-intrusive responding) and collaborative play (co-facilitation) (Yasenik & Gardner, 2012).

The Therapeutic Power of Music, Sound, and Voice

It is well understood that music evokes a wide range of emotions and can be used to create a sense of safety and security by being an effective tool for grounding and centering oneself, particularly in times of stress or emotional upheaval (Kawakami et al., 2014). From the first note heard in the womb to the final sounds accompanying our very last breath, the influence of music and sounds in our lives is well-documented. However, the therapeutic power of music is rooted, and most impactful, within the relationship between therapist and client, and the moments "in" the music.

Engaging in music-based activities such as listening, moving, singing, or playing an instrument with another can bypass the verbal and move efficiently to the limbic system, fostering a safe gateway to difficult feelings. This was observed in Zoe's play therapy process. Although preferences vary, music's calming effect on the body's nervous system is most evident when listening to music with a slow tempo and relaxed melodies that activate the parasympathetic nervous system, helping to reduce feelings of stress and anxiety. Singing, which requires vocalizing and breathing, both of which stimulate the vagus nerve, can create feelings of calm, and certain types of music associated with positive memories and experiences can contribute to feelings of safety and security (Breit et al., 2018). For example, a person may feel comforted by listening to, or singing with, music that was played during a happy and peaceful time in their life. It was therefore not surprising that Zoe chose early childhood songs to sing to her externalized younger part of self.

In the therapeutic context, knowing when, how, and what music to use can be quite nuanced, but there are some useful considerations that can help all therapists integrate music more successfully into their work.

Using Music in a Clinical Setting for Emotional Regulation

Neurologists have long known that there were areas of the brain specifically dedicated to processing music, and with advanced brain imaging technology, they've discovered that music's reach is far more complex than previously believed (Janata, 2015). Sound information is passed to the auditory cortex and instantaneously broken down into many different elements including, but not limited to, timing (tempo), pitch, and tone (Patil et al., 2012). Auditory information is also sent to other parts of the brain to be compared against historical associations and emotional responses (Do I like it or not? Do I remember it? Does it trigger a memory, positive or negative?) stimulating many parts of the brain in both hemispheres, resulting in a global brain process (Janata, 2015).

From a clinical perspective, understanding this link between music elements and the target goal—in this case, emotion regulation—helps the therapist make informed decisions about the therapeutic function of music (TFM). Hanson-Abromeit (2015) defines the TFM as "the direct relationship between the treatment goal and the explicit characteristics of the musical elements, informed by a theoretical framework and/or philosophical paradigm in the context of a client" (p. 130).

From a clinical perspective, certain music and music experiences should be avoided when trying to help a person regulate and shift their physiological and emotional state (Senna Moore & Hanson-Abromeit, 2015). Based on her suggestions, these include:

- avoiding music that is minor, dissonant, or considered unpleasant
- avoiding unexpected musical events (e.g., sudden dynamic changes)
- making frequent (and swift) chord changes
- listening to music with eyes closed

In other words, having a deeper understanding of how music affects a desired change informs the intentional, therapeutic use of music in clinical practice. In Zoe's case, music using percussion instruments and playing with rhythmic sounds were important in helping to re-set Zoe's faulty neuroception.

Our Voice of Understanding and Comfort

The sound of a person's voice can have a significant impact on how they are perceived and the sense of safety and trust that they are able to convey (Alcee, 2019). A voice that is warm, friendly, and confident can help to create a sense of psychological safety and encourage open communication. In contrast, a voice that is tense, anxious, or aggressive can create a sense of unease or discomfort and may make it more difficult to establish trust. Zoe's early experiences of the sounds of her parent's voices during violent outbursts later produced a hypervigilance to raising voice tones. She neuro-cepted impending danger when no danger was present. Her ANS had been set to the fight/flight side of sympathetic responding.

There are several factors that can influence the sound of a person's voice, including their emotional state, their level of confidence, and their level of relaxation. When a person is feeling calm and relaxed, their voice is likely to sound more relaxed and pleasant. In addition, the way that a person uses their voice—including their tone, pitch, and volume—can also affect how they are perceived and the sense of safety that they are able to convey. For example, using a softer, more moderate tone may be perceived as more approachable and friendly, while using a louder or more aggressive tone may be perceived as threatening or intimidating—especially when attached to childhood triggers as in the case of Zoe.

Watch and Listen for Sensory Overload

In the context of music, sensory overload can be caused by a variety of fac-tors, such as loud volume, fast tempo, complex melodies and harmonies, and intense or rapid changes in sound (Yuan et al., 2022). Sensory overload can be a temporary and harmless experience for some people, but for others it can be more intense and even lead to anxiety or panic attacks. If you experience sensory overload from music or other stimuli, it can be helpful to take a break and find a quiet place to rest and recover. It may also be helpful to try relaxa-tion techniques, such as deep breathing or humming, to help calm the mind and reduce feelings of overwhelm. Symptoms of sensory overload include:

- difficulty focusing due to competing sensory input
- extreme irritability
- restlessness and discomfort
- urge to cover your ears or shield your eyes from sensory input

- feeling overly excited or "wound up"
- stress, fear, or anxiety about your surroundings
- higher levels than usual of sensitivity to textures, fabrics, clothing tags, or other things that may rub against skin

Conclusion

Overall, play therapists can support their clients' ANS by increasing their awareness of the purposeful use of sound, voice, music, and rhythms by developing an auditory environment in the play therapy space. In the case of Zoe, sound was a salient sensory factor in working with her faulty neuroception. Zoe was immersed in an integrative play therapy process that offered both non-directive and co-facilitative activities, which led to a more stable sense of safety and ventral vagal connection.

Therapy Takeaways

- Assess your play therapy room's sound environment. When you sit in the middle of the room and close your eyes, what sounds do you hear?
- Consider the creation of soundscapes.
- Build the right music kit. Consider how you purposefully invite sound, rhythms, and song into the play space. This includes a device for playing a client's chosen music.
- Identify and practice your therapeutic voice. Practice your cadence, tempo (speed), and tone (warmth vs. sharp). Record yourself and play it back.

References

Alcee, M. (2019, January 1). Developing a therapeutic voice. *Psychotherapy.net*. Retrieved February 11, 2023, from www.psychotherapy.net/article/developing-a-therapeutic-voice#section-finding-our-voice

Breit, S., Kupferberg, A., Rogler, G. I., & Hasler, G. (2018). Vagus nerve as modulator of the brain–gut axis in psychiatric inflammatory disorders. *Frontiers in Psychiatry*, 9(44), 1–15.

Dana, D. (2020). *Polyvagal exercises for safety and connection: 50 client-centered practices*. Norton.

Dana, D. (2021). *Anchored: How to befriend your nervous system using Polyvagal theory*. Polyvagal Institute, Sounds True.

Hanson-Abromeit, D. (2015). A conceptual methodology to define the therapeutic function of music. *Music Therapy Perspectives, 33*(1), 25–38.

Janata, P. (2015). Neural basis of music perception. *Handbook of Clinical Neurology, 129*, 187–205.

Kaspiew, R., Horsfall, B., Qu, L., Nicholson, J., Humphreys, C., Diemer, C., Cattram, D., Nguyen, C. D., Buchanan, F., Hooker, L., Taft, A., & Westrupp, E. M. (2017). *Domestic and family violence and parenting: Mixed method insights into impact and support needs-final report* (Anrows Horizons 4, Government of Australia).

Kawakami, A., Furukawa, K., & Okanoya, K. (2014). Music evokes vicarious emotions in listeners. *Frontiers in Psychology*, 431.

Levine, P. (2015). *Trauma and memory: Brain and body in a search for the living past: A practical guide for understanding and working with traumatic memory*. North Atlantic Books.

Malchiodi, C. A. (2020). *Trauma and expressive arts therapy*. Guilford.

Patil, K., Pressnitzer, D., Shamma, S., & Elhilali, M. (2012). Music in our ears: The biological bases of musical timbre perception. *PLoS Computational Biology*, 8(11), e1002759.

Porges, S. W. (2010). Music therapy and trauma: Insights from Polyvagal theory. In K. Stewart (Ed.), *Symposium on music therapy and trauma: Bridging theory and clinical practice*. Satchnote Press.

Porges, S. W. (2015). Making the world safe for our children. Downregulating defence and up-regulating social engagement to 'optimize' the human experience. *Children Australia, 40*(2), 114–123.

Porges, S. W. (2017). *The pocket guide to the Polyvagal theory: The transformative power of feeling safe*. Norton.

Potter, L. C., Morris, R., Hegarty, K., Garcia-Moreno, C., & Feder, G. (2020). Categories and health impacts of intimate partner violence in the World Health Organization multi-country study on women's health and domestic violence. *International Journal of Epidemiology, 00*, 1–11.

Schaefer, C. E., & Drewes, A. (2014). *The therapeutic powers of play: 20 core agents of change* (2nd ed.). Wiley.

Senna Moore, K., & Hanson-Abromeit, D. (2015). Theory-guided therapeutic function of music to facilitate emotion regulation development in preschool-aged children. *Frontiers in Human Neuroscience, 9*, 572.

Yasenik, L., & Gardner, K. (2012). *Play therapy dimensions model: A decision-making guide for integrative play therapists.* Jessica Kingsley Publishers.

Yasenik, L., & Gardner, K. (2019). Turning points and the understanding of the development of self through play therapy. In L. Yasenik & K. Gardner (Eds.), *Turning points in play therapy and the emergence of self: Applications of the play therapy dimensions model* (pp. 15–42). Jessica Kingsley Publishers.

Yuan, H. L., Lai, C. Y., Wong, M. N., Kwong, T. C., Choy, Y. S., Mung, S. W., & Chan, C. C. (2022). Interventions for sensory over-responsivity in individuals with autism spectrum disorder: A narrative review. *Children, 9*(10), 1584.

4

The Genius of the Disembodied Self

Coping with Childhood Sexual Abuse

Paris Goodyear-Brown and Sueann Kenney-Noziska

Overview

Many of the child and teen clients who present as sexual abuse survivors carry deep shame. This shame is often tied to a set of "shoulds" that have been institutionalized at the highest levels of our legal and judicial systems. These shoulds represent macrosystemic misunderstandings of the autonomic nervous system's (ANS) response to overwhelming stress; the power differential between children, adolescents, and the perpetrators of their sexual abuse; and the consequent effects of powerlessness on the child's neuroception of danger and life threat. These harmful beliefs trickle down to the individual survivors of child sexual abuse and rob them of an understanding of the brilliant adaptations that our bodies may make on our behalf in moments of extreme threat. Sometimes the shoulds are personal: *I should have been able to fight back. I should have said no. I should have told someone the first time it happened.* Sometimes the shoulds have been culturally reinforced. Lawyers are allowed to ask teenage victims on the stand, "Did you say no? Did you struggle? Did you try to get away?" If the victim's answer to any of these questions is no, there is an insidious implication that if they had not wanted the sexual attention they would have *acted in* the moment or *acted on* the environment. What these responses have in common is the belief that the victim could have made a choice to act, that it was within their conscious control to do so, and that action would be the safest or most adaptive coping option. What if inaction or immobilization instead were the innate wisdom of the body (Porges, 2011, 2021)?

DOI: 10.4324/9781003352976-4

Immobilization is often accompanied by a sense of disconnection or dissociation. For the purposes of this conversation, *dissociation* is defined as the movement away from contact with one's own body, other people, or the environment at large, a separation of the core self from the embodied brain (Badenoch, 2017). To understand the innate wisdom of immobilization, the genius of the disembodied self, the evolutionary hierarchy of the mammalian ANS must be understood and then overlaid with the attachment needs of children. Until recently, the ANS was understood as being comprised of two branches, the sympathetic fight or flight response (often conceptualized as the gas pedal) and the parasympathetic system (often conceptualized as the brake). Stephen Porges, after mapping the pathways of the vagus nerve, posited that there are three potential pathways that might be taken when the stress response system is activated: immobilization, mobilization, and social engagement.

The dorsal branch of the vagus nerve runs down into our guts and is the most ancient stress response. A dorsal vagal shutdown or immobilization occurs when mammals neurocept life threat. This death-feigning, sudden stilling effect shuts down our digestion to conserve the body's energy and moves us into a state of collapse. The neuroception of life threat is a viscerally experienced, instantaneous, and non-conscious assessment that there is no room or time for choice, and choice and time are necessary for sympathetic activation (fight or flight) to be triggered. If a lion has stealthily crept up on a small creature in the wild, that small creature has no time to run away and will not be benefitted by fighting back, so pretending to be dead is the body's wisdom. Perhaps that lion only wants fresh meat and will move on. This is the immobilization or death-feigning response. Moving up the autonomic hierarchy, the mobilization response pumps blood to our heart and oxygen to our lungs, preparing our bodies for sympathetic states of fight or flight and is often triggered when we are neurocepting danger. The neuroception of danger implies choice. When a human sees the lion coming from a distance, there is time to react or mobilize, and the choice can be made to either run away, try to kill it, or fight back.

The really good news is that another branch of the parasympathetic nervous system, the ventral vagal branch, offers a face-heart connection and invites social engagement with one another. This ventral state occurs when mammals neurocept safety. The nuanced communication of safety provided through a soft tone of voice and face, warm eye gaze, and non-threatening proxemics can mitigate a person's descent down the autonomic ladder, helping them remain either safely still or safely able to work with their sympathetic arousal states. Humans seek safety in and with one another (Porges, 2009; Siegel, 1999). What happens, then, when some of these safety signals (such as warm eye gaze and prosodic voice) are paired with uncomfortable, inappropriate, painful, and unspeakable violations of the child's body? The authors suggest that the felt sense of incongruence that children endure when they are being sexually abused amplifies the neuroception of life threat. Moreover, the pairing of safety signals with unspeakable acts confuses the child about the whole concept of safety, often calling into question whether or not they can trust their embodied sense while also calling into question whether or not they can trust the grown-ups.

Sexual Abuse as Interruption

Almost all sexual abuse is perpetrated by a known, loved, and/or trusted adult, and 91% of perpetrators are known to the child (Center for Disease Control, 2022). If almost all abusers are also known and trusted by the parents of the child victim, imagine the layers of confusion and the risk of long-term relational consequence this causes for the child. Children come into the world neurophysiologically wired for connection. Attachment theory has taught us that children seek proximity to their caregiver for protection, for need meeting, and for nurture (Bowlby, 2008). From their secure base, they move out to explore the world. When a child is scared, their attachment system is activated, and they move back toward their caregiver for comfort. *But what if the caregiver is actually the source of their fear?* In childhood, the implicit agreement is that your attachment figure will protect you from all threats—but what happens when they are the source of threat? Childhood sexual abuse sets up exactly this powerful paradox, creating developmental derailment (Van der Kolk, 2015) of the neuroception of safety. Normalization of the dorsal vagal shutdown response must be contextualized in the power differential between adult and child and in the understanding of attachment needs in children and teens.

Amplified Dimensions of Polyvagal Theory

Take Sydney, the five-year-old little girl who endures her father's sexual violations once weekly for years. Running away from the threat is not possible, as her family is all she knows and provides her with food, shelter, and intermittent kindness or normalcy. She can't fight back, as her inner wisdom correctly assesses that fighting back against her father, who weighs four times what she does, would result in her being further hurt physically. Crying out for help would disrupt the family and risk awakening everyone to the abuse. Her father hints that her mother won't want her anymore if she learns of the abuse or threatens that she wouldn't be believed if she tells or that she'll be separated from her family forever. Sydney may be protecting another child in the home, enduring the abuse herself so that her younger sister isn't chosen to replace her.

Even more complicated is the scenario in which dad pairs nurture of various sorts with sexual violations. Sydney may perceive herself as special even while dreading each and every sexually exploitive act. Because she can't fight back and she can't run away (in effect, her choices have been removed), Sydney simply shuts down, moving into a state of immobilization during the sexual abuse. There may be blessed relief in her nervous system's response, as she may not feel the physical pain of the abuse as viscerally, hear the sexual grunting noises of the perpetrator as clearly, or have to white-knuckle her way to staying quiet and still. In the moment of hurt, her nervous system gives her the gift of shutting down. When this process of dorsal vagal shutdown (DVS) is normalized, victims of sexual abuse can undergo seismic paradigm shifts. They begin to see themselves as survivors and can celebrate the wisdom of the body's dissociative or numbing response.

Secondary Sympathetic Activation

I just wanted to get it over with. This phrase has been heard by both authors in cases where a child or teen's sexual abuse has happened repeatedly and with patterned chronicity. One thirteen-year-old explained that her stepfather would rape her whenever mom worked the graveyard shift. Mom's schedule was posted each Sunday on the refrigerator, so she would always know exactly when she was going to be sexually abused during the following week. The anticipatory anxiety can be more emotionally painful for the child, when they are enduring the excruciating waiting for the assault to begin, than the assaultive act itself. For this thirteen-year-old girl, her heart would start to race, and she would begin to sweat; she would take heaving breaths and felt like her heart would burst. She described these sympathetic activations as her body's reminders of the impending doom and confessed that these embodied anxiety responses felt "way worse" than the abuse itself. In fact, once the rape had begun, she would stare at the dots on her dropped ceiling, finding images, patterns, and constellations the way the non-abused child would play with finding shapes in the clouds. The victim might even instigate (unconsciously or consciously) a speedier start to the abuse in some way. This might include going to the perpetrator's room, pouring the offender another drink, or even picking a fight.

In cases of chronic sexual abuse, mobilization responses can also occur before and after the acute incident (the sexual assault itself). These peritraumatic responses may include signals that the child perceives prior to the abuse (such as a doorknob being turned or the clink of the whiskey bottle in the trash can) and signals the child perceives after the abuse (such as the sound of water running in the shower as the victim tries to wash away their abuse). Triggers associated with the assaultive sexual act itself may also provoke sympathetic activation—the smell of alcohol on a person's breath, a certain piece of clothing, or a particular piece of music being played. These triggers can engender a sympathetic ramp-up in the child's body (heart races, blood and oxygen move into the heart and lungs to gear up for danger) and may be discharged through fight or flight, particularly when they are experienced in a setting where more choice is available. For example, the foster child who was sexually abused at bath time may become enraged when his bewildered foster parent tells him it is time for a bath. These triggers can be confusing for parents.

TraumaPlay™, an attachment-based, neurophysiologically grounded, flexibly sequential play therapy model, works to help parents embody the three roles of Safe Boss, Nurturer, and Storykeeper. Caregivers are initially benefited by the therapist's role of Storykeeper as the clinician helps make sense of the big behaviors being seen now in light of their earlier CSA experiences. The therapist translates the parts of the ANS into a Polyvagal Zoo filled with animals that represent the neuroceptions of life threat, danger, and social engagement (see Goodyear-Brown, 2021, 2022 for a more thorough explanation). This metaphor is useful in offering a playful explanation of Polyvagal theory while providing a shared language for the family to return to as sexual abuse is processed. TraumaPlay therapists frequently help parents and children create zoos in the sand tray that represent their stress response states and use this metaphor throughout treatment (see Figures 4.1 and 4.2).

Even more nuanced is Porges' premise that one must move up the autonomic ladder to heal (Dana, 2018; Porges, 2018). Therefore, a period of sympathetic activation, especially from children who have coped with overwhelming stress through immobilization and dissociation, is expected as part of the healing process. This pattern has been experienced by both authors with countless clients. Offering co-regulating caregivers a Polyvagal understanding of their child's big behaviors (if/when they arrive) can shift a parent's

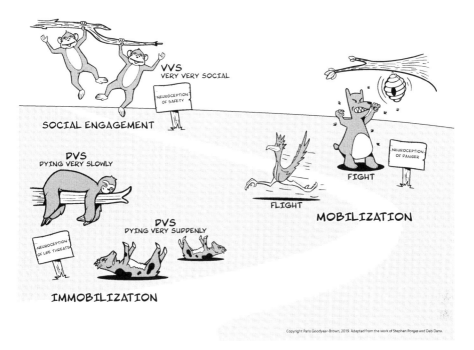

Figure 4.1 Polyvagal Pathways

Source: © Paris Goodyear-Brown (2019). Reprinted with permission.

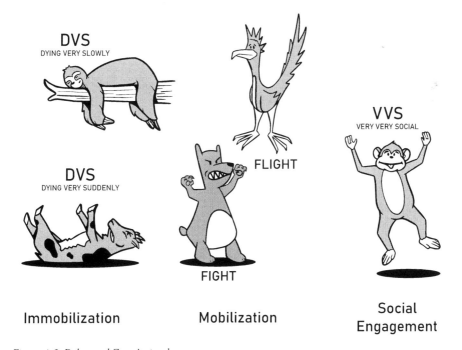

Figure 4.2 Polyvagal Zoo Animals

Source: © Paris Goodyear-Brown (2019). Reprinted with permission.

paradigm from a set of limiting shoulds ("My child has talked about the abuse, so they *should* be fine now" or "My child is physically safe now, she *should* feel safe") to an understanding that acting out, in certain contexts, is more healing than inaction or a perceived sense of calm.

Exosystems and the Nervous System

Helping professionals, including but not limited to police officers, lawyers, judges, doctors, nurses, teachers, and therapists, can collude with the consequences of our nervous system responses. The immobilization state, and the dissociation it represents, can lead to a decrease in explicit memories in the wake of disclosure. The little boy who endured his anal penetration while focusing his mind on the house he would later build in Minecraft may not be able to tell a detective what color the walls were in the room where the abuse happened. The teen who counts the ceiling tiles is unlikely to have explicit memories of the time of day, the exact number of times the abuse happened (if ongoing), how many windows were in the room where the abuse occurred, or which wall the dresser was on. Both authors have worked with children and adolescents who have been asked these sorts of explicit memory questions that our legal system approves as "proofs" of the assault. When a survivor is unable to recall these details or to report them consistently, they lose credibility with the decision-makers who deal with evidence.

Another Unlikely Outcome

Untreated survivors of CSA are at greater risk than others of misattributing a neuroception of safety to a person or situation that is truly dangerous. The child's neurophysiology chooses to lean away from the hurt during the most terrifying or painful moments of their experience. It does this through immobilization, numbing, disconnection, or disembodiment, wiring the child's embodied brain to a lifetime of dissociative leaning when things become painful in their bodies, in their relationships, or in their environment. Understanding the autonomic patterning that has been paired with eminent threat can help to explain revictimization as the lack of a primed fight or flight response. The numbed, potentially "watered down" response that might occur when a new sexual violation is threatened might be expressed as a misattribution of the neuroception of safety or a conflation of the child's or teen's most painful previous moments of experience with perceived peace during a new abusive experience.

Down-regulation responses of the autonomic nervous system become habituated, and the dissociative consequences can limit the child or teen's capacity to enjoy trust and relationships. A chronic pattern of immobilization might also lead to a habituated numbing or unfocused inattention to danger cues in the environment. If the victim gets out from under the immediate or ongoing threat, there is an opportunity for corrective emotional experiences. As the child grows and their agency increases, they may have opportunities to take risks relationally with friends, mentors, or romantic partners.

Perpetrators may use language like "I can tell this feels good to you. We could stop if you really want to. You didn't stop me." This language reinforces the victim's false belief that they let the perpetrator do it, they consented, or they actively participated. Using victim-first language in order to put the blame where the blame belongs, deconstructs the idea that the sexual activity was consensual—it wasn't.

Case Examples and Treatment Parameters

To clinically address the dorsal vagal shutdown, the authors recommend play therapists intentionally incorporate the following treatment parameters: (a) help the client return to their body, (b) shift the client's sense of blame and shame, which often requires some psychoeducation, (c) create opportunities for the client to take relational risks, and (d) facilitate the development of the neuroception of safety. The following case examples, shared with consent, highlight the application of the Polyvagal theory within the identified treatment parameters for two victims of childhood sexual abuse. (*Note: Case examples do not represent treatment in its entirety but highlight components of using a Polyvagal-informed lens in the treatment of sexually abused children and adolescents who experience DVS.*)

Case Example Juan: *"I was in the corner of the ceiling when it happened."*

Six-year-old Juan enters therapy with a typical clinical profile for victims of interpersonal sexual trauma—the "acting out," externalizing child with many "behavioral" issues. Previously, he was receiving treatment for Attention-Deficit Hyperactivity Disorder (ADHD) and Oppositional Defiant Disorder (ODD). It was not until he disclosed chronic sexual abuse at the hands of his stepfather that his big behaviors (Goodyear-Brown, 2022) could be re-storied as sympathetic activation related to his sexual abuse. He was then referred to a trauma-informed play therapist.

During Juan's forensic interview, he stated: "I was in the corner of the ceiling when it happened." From an investigative and forensic standpoint, this appears nonsensical and raises issues around credibility. From a dorsal vagal shutdown perspective, this is recognized as a protective mechanism for survival. In essence, Juan would "check out" of his mind and body during episodes of sexual abuse as a means to cope with the horror.

Treatment began with Child Centered Play Therapy (Ray, 2011) and an emphasis on establishing the neuroception of safety in the therapeutic relationship. Despite his history of interpersonal trauma, Juan engaged in the play therapy process without hesitation. During the first several months of treatment, he presented as a "hurricane" in the playroom. He appeared almost frantic as he moved through the room grabbing, tossing, and roughly playing with the toys. The room would be in complete disorder when he was done. Toys were scattered, shelves were in disarray, and the previously organized playroom was left in a disordered mess. Chaos and instability emerged as Juan's dominant play theme. As defined by Ray (2011), this theme reflects: "I am confused by my world. I don't know how to bring order to my world. It's out of my control" (p. 115). This theme offered insight and understanding of his young, six-year-old world of trauma—confusion, turmoil, betrayal, and panic.

As treatment progressed, Juan began to experience a new "safe" place with a safe relationship with an adult (Safe Boss)—a place and relationship that he had not experienced before. Gradually, his play became less frantic and more organized. Play themes reflected relationship, power/control, safety/security, and protection. (Refer to Ray (2011) for a detailed description of each theme.)

As play themes developed, posttraumatic play emerged in metaphor (Gil, 1991, 2011, 2017; Goodyear-Brown, 2009, 2019). In other words, play themes were reflective of childhood sexual victimization. Superimposing dynamics of childhood sexual abuse as delineated by Finkelhor and Browne (1985) and Summit (1983) over Juan's play revealed secrecy, helplessness, entrapment and accommodation, betrayal, and powerlessness. There was an unconscious link between Juan's play and his sexual trauma. Small, vulnerable animals would be harmed, nurturing characters would also be a source of hurt or injury, evil characters would be "banished" from the play only to return shortly after that, and attempts at safety and protection were absent.

Of particular significance was posttraumatic play reminiscent of entrapment and accommodation. Juan would consistently place vulnerable, smaller, or harmed characters outside of the play itself—as if the character were observing from the outside in. For example, over a series of sessions, Juan's play themes involved a forest/animal kingdom in which the baby bear would be harmed or injured in some way by other larger animals. Following the injury or harm, Juan would place the baby bear away from the play on a high shelf, windowsill, on top of the puppet stand, or on top of the toy tree, which was outside of the forest. The baby bear would "observe" from its high position and later return to the woods and be incorporated into the play theme. It was as if the baby bear "was in the corner of the ceiling" in a passive, depersonalized position. Through play, Juan was showing the genius of the disembodied self. Through play, he expressed: "I was in the corner of the ceiling when it happened."

The continuum of therapeutic responding within posttraumatic play themes and metaphors gently nudged Juan's posttraumatic play toward more adaptive, metaphoric resolutions (Kenney-Noziska, 2019). This included trauma-informed descriptive statements (i.e., "Oh, no! Here comes that snake again!"), trauma-informed reflection of emotions (i.e., "The little bear is so scared and confused."), giving voice to characters (i.e. being the voice of the baby bear saying, "I'm so little and scared."), wondering about possibilities within the play (i.e., whispering, "I wonder what can be done to keep baby bear safe?"), and inviting or offering options (i.e. "Maybe the big bear can protect the little bear or the police can stop the snake."). Juan gradually incorporated resolution, protection, and safety into the play. The baby bear was protected, the source of harm was cast out of the forest, and the baby bear remained fully present in the woods.

Cognitive-behavioral responding within play themes was additionally employed to shift blame and shame onto the offender and highlight the hierarchical and power differentials inherent in sexual victimization. This occurred within play metaphors to honor the play and remain in the brain's right hemisphere, where fragmented, traumatic memories are stored and accessed. Examples included responses such as, "The snake is not supposed to hurt the baby bear," "The baby bear is important and deserves to be safe," "This is all the snake's fault," and "The snake is responsible for hurting the baby bear and destroying the forest."

Juan incrementally took relational risks by increasingly involving the therapist in his play. He assumed the role of "director" and guided the therapist to take on specific roles, use certain character voices, and assist during times of protection and healing (e.g., pretending to be the doctor and placing band aids on the baby bear). Relationship, nurturing, reparation, and integration themes (Ray, 2011) emerged as treatment progressed and play themes evolved.

The sexually abusive environment Juan had endured trained his nervous system and designed his functioning during sexual victimization as freezing, fawning, or feigning. Hence, the dorsal vagal shutdown and his statement, "I was in the corner of the ceiling when it happened." In moments when the sexual abuse was not occurring, he functioned in a hyperaroused state where there was always impending doom. His neuroception of safety was repeatedly disrupted. Juan experienced an incremental neuroception of safety through the attuned play therapy relationship. Boundaries were clear; he was not enticed, threatened, or manipulated into any form of abuse or exploitation; and he experienced a Safe Boss (Goodyear-Brown, 2019).

Case Example Destiny: *"I would just lay there and let it happen."*

Destiny was 14 years old when she entered treatment for the first time. She had been a victim of childhood sexual abuse by her grandfather. The abuse began at age six and continued most of her life until she was 13 ½. Her sexual abuse was discovered after she confided in a peer who told a school teacher, and an official report was made. Because Destiny's childhood sexual abuse was "confided" versus actively "disclosed," she was cautious when she entered the assessment appointment.

In contrast to Juan, Destiny presented another common clinical profile for victims of childhood sexual abuse—the internalizing, depressed, withdrawn, numb, "checked-out" youth. The Trauma Symptom Checklist for Children (TSCC) (Briere, 1996) was utilized as a part of a comprehensive, trauma-informed assessment. The TSCC is a broadband, standardized measure of acute and chronic posttraumatic symptomatology for children and youth ages 8–16 that measures posttraumatic stress and related psychological symptomatology. Destiny's scores indicated clinical levels of depression, anxiety, and posttraumatic stress, with her highest clinical scores being dissociation, avoidance, and sexual concerns.

Destiny was very protective of her grandfather, who had been a father figure throughout her life. This protective dynamic is frequently seen in victims of childhood sexual abuse—particularly when a family member or relative has victimized them. Destiny's grandfather was "always there" for her, helped the family financially, and fulfilled other vital roles in her life. He lovingly referred to Destiny as his "little Mija," a Mexican term of endearment that translates as "daughter."

During the initial phase of treatment, Destiny was disengaged. She would slouch in her chair, keep her head down, and frequently respond with a shoulder shrug, "I don't know," or "I don't care." Over several sessions, she was offered a variety of expressive media (i.e., play, art, sand tray) to share about or express herself but to no avail. Sometimes, we sat in silence for the majority of the session. The therapeutic silence communicated: "I see you and can provide a safe space when you're ready." It was an attempt to create a neuroception of safety through the silence.

Eventually, it happened. Destiny took a risk and asked if she could have pretzels from the bag on the therapist's desk. As she reached for the bag, her attention turned toward a piece of paper with the template for the intervention, "I'm fine" (A. Vigil, personal communication, July 15, 2019). The template is an outline of a person with the word *FINE* written across the mouth and empty cartoon thought bubbles drawn above the head. She asked: "What's that?" The therapist explained it was one of the ways teenagers shared their true thoughts when they said, "I'm fine." Destiny picked up the template, took the box of colored pencils, and quietly worked on the activity. The therapist honored her process and served as a silent witness as she worked. When she was done, Destiny turned to the therapist, handed over the paper, and said: "Here." Inside the thought bubbles, she had written *distant*, *numb*, *damaged*, *avoid*, and *worthless*. She shared her experience of living in an immobilized dorsal vagal state.

Be it ever so slight, this was the opening into her world. Treatment slowly started to inch forward. Play, art, and sand approaches were integrated within the frameworks of core components of trauma treatments (National Child Traumatic Stress Network, 2022), treatment targets of Trauma-Focused Cognitive Behavioral Therapy (TF-CBT) (Cohen et al., 2006, 2017), and the flexibly sequential TraumaPlay™ components (Goodyear-Brown, 2019, 2022). Destiny and the therapist began to gently brush up against the sexual trauma using expressive approaches in an intentional, trauma-informed manner.

Psychoeducation, emotional expression, and augmentation of coping, both active and cognitive, were intertwined in the therapeutic process. As Destiny experienced a more accurate, genuine neuroception of safety, she incrementally invited the therapist deeper and deeper into her inner world of suffering. Color Your Heart (Goodyear-Brown, 2002), an intervention whereby Destiny quantified emotions regarding her sexual abuse, included *guilt, shame, regret, damaged, tired,* and *depressed.* This is a textbook description of the hypoarousal state of the dorsal vagal shutdown.

Shortly after, Destiny was invited to create a sand tray with the therapeutic prompt: "Create a scene in the sand that shows what your world was like after people found out about the sexual abuse." Her effort and energy focused on a skeleton chained to a bench and carefully balanced on the ledge of the corner of the tray. In the center of the tray, she carved out a divot in the sand and placed a globe with a figure of an older adult standing next to it.

The tray was metaphorically processed by dialoguing about the images and the world she created. The therapist avoided direct comments or questions connecting the tray to Destiny's history of abuse. In other words, the tray was explored by maintaining the symbolic imagery and accessing right hemispheric trauma memories (Goodyear-Brown, 2009, 2022). For example, "Tell me about the skeleton" and "How does the skeleton feel?" versus "Are you the skeleton?" "Is the figure in the middle your grandfather?" As she shared a portion of her "story," Destiny described the skeleton as the "watcher" who sits and passively observes what is happening and explained that the adult figure was the "provider" and "protector of the world."

When asked, "How does the skeleton feel about the provider and protector of the world?" Destiny responded: "The skeleton misses him. He was my whole world." (Note: The client chose to pull the processing out of the metaphor in her last statement.). The tray was left intact when Destiny left the session with the caveat that it would not be there for her following sessions as others use the sandtray room. A picture of the completed tray was taken and used for processing points in subsequent sessions.

Initial processing maintained the metaphor. Destiny carefully unpacked bits and pieces of her trauma narrative as processing went deeper. She identified the adult male figure as her grandfather. Use of the sand tray was a respectful titration of trauma (Goodyear-Brown, 2019) and invited Destiny to share pieces of her story. Eventually, she identified herself as a "floating skeleton" during incidents of sexual victimization. Destiny described being "outside" of her mind and body as the abuse occurred. She described checking out by stating: "I would just lay there and let it happen."

Destiny describes a dorsal vagal shutdown during times of sexual abuse. Simply put, she was trapped. She could not fight her offender, nor could she flee. She experienced physical and psychological safety by "shutting down" during the ongoing episodes of sexual victimization. However, Destiny perceived the genius disembodied self as "consent" for her sexual abuse. Cognitive distortions included: "I would just lay there and let it happen," "I let him have sex with me," "We had sex," and "I never ever tried to stop him."

Given these distortions around blame and responsibility, as well as the importance of helping her understand the hierarchy and power differential inherent in childhood sexual abuse, a portion of therapy was dedicated to identifying and reframing faulty, distorted cognitions related to causality and responsibility. This work relied heavily on concepts from Cognitive-Behavioral Play Therapy (CBPT) (Knell, 1993, 2009, 2011) modified for adolescents via directive play therapy approaches. Blameberry Pie (J. Shelby, personal communication, July 15, 2015), an intervention whereby causes of sexual victimization are written on paper strips and placed inside a pie pan to create a "blameberry" pie, allowed Destiny to share her internal dialogue around causality for the abuse. Each strip placed in the pan was removed and expanded for accuracy. Real causes for sexual victimization remained in the pie of blame (i.e., My grandfather caused the abuse). Incorrect thoughts were removed and put in tort tins with the clarification that these statements were misattributions of responsibility and were about different things versus being causes of sexual abuse (i.e., *I didn't stop it from happening*) went into a tort tin about her grandfather abusing trust and power).

Although the immobilization response empowered Destiny to survive during moments of sexual abuse, it came with poor long-term outcomes. The dorsal vagal shutdown resulted in fragmented memories and disconnection from her body. It resulted in a young adolescent chronically functioning in a hypoaroused state—feeling numb, zoning out, shutting down, and withdrawing. The dorsal vagal shutdown also created a false neuroception of safety as her Safe Boss (grandfather) was the source of harm while simultaneously serving in the role of a false, disingenuous Nurturer (Goodyear-Brown, 2019). Destiny's baseline for safe social engagement with others and her neuroception of safety had been derailed.

Reconnecting Destiny with a sense of self and re-joining her mind and body was gradual. Concrete skills such as deep breathing, grounding, and meditation were incorporated into treatment. Structured, directive interventions were used, including Feelings in My Body. In this activity, Destiny placed different colored stickers inside the outline of a body to identify where her emotions were felt and experienced in her body.

The most important piece of work was Destiny's social connection in the play therapy relationship and a shift in her neuroception of safety. The therapeutic relationship served as an optimal ventral vagal state with an autonomic balance of the sympathetic nervous system and the dorsal vagal pathways. Chronic childhood sexual abuse disrupted Destiny's social engagement system. However, these disruptions were partly repaired in the therapeutic relationship, including repairs in physiological states through the social interactions and cues of safety offered in the therapeutic relationship.

Conclusion

Employing a polyvagal perspective when conceptualizing cases of childhood sexual abuse helps providers better understand the internalizing and externalizing symptoms we frequently encounter. Juan was not a "bad" child needing behavioral modification as his primary treatment. Destiny was not a "resistant" teenager who wasn't "ready for treatment." Both had disruptions in their senses of felt safety. They needed protection from further sexual victimization and to experience healthy social engagement and connection simultaneously.

While Polyvagal theory does not capture all treatment needs for victims of childhood sexual abuse, it certainly aids in our case conceptualization. It changes the manner in which we value the play therapy relationship in trauma treatment. It also provides a valuable tool for helping caregivers, teachers, and others understand what is disrupted when childhood sexual abuse occurs.

 Treatment Takeaways

- Polyvagal theory, the science of safety, helps us understand the physiological and psychological response of the autonomic nervous system in children and adolescents who have experienced dorsal vagal shutdown to survive. A shutdown response in the moment of a sexually abusive act perpetrated on a child or adolescent by a trusted caregiver or adult is adaptive.
- Long-term outcomes may include functioning in a hyper- or hypoaroused state, a misattributed neuroception of safety, or an inflated neuroception of safety or life threat.
- Macrosystemic misunderstandings of the human ANS system are benefited by being educated about the potential for children to dissociate during their abuse, therefore the resulting injustice of expecting

convictions of perpetrators to be based on a child's explicit recollections and consistent recounting of events policies, procedures, laws, and judicial processes needs to expand for victim survivors of child sexual abuse.

- When a child or teen has coped with sexual abuse through immobilization and a dorsal vagal shutdown response, it is likely that they will experience some sympathetic activation and be perceived by their grown-ups as dysregulated or hyperaroused. Safe Boss grown-ups can benefit from Storykeeping the child's trauma experiences as they interpret the child's big behaviors.
- Conceptualizing treatment from a trauma-informed, Polyvagal lens with consideration of the dorsal vagal shutdown is an essential perspective for play therapists who work with sexually abused children and adolescents.

References

Badenoch, B. (2017). *The heart of trauma: Healing the embodied brain in the context of relationships (IPBJ)*. Norton.

Bowlby, J. (2008). *Attachment*. Basic books.

Briere, J. (1996). *Trauma symptom checklist for children (TSCC): Professional manual*. Psychological Assessment Resources.

Center for Disease Control. (2022, April 6). *Fast facts: Preventing child sexual abuse*. www.cdc.gov/violenceprevention/childsexualabuse/fastfact.html

Cohen, J. A., Mannarino, A. P., & Deblinger, E. (2006). *Treating trauma and traumatic grief in children and adolescents*. Guilford.

Cohen, J. A., Mannarino, A. P., & Deblinger, E. (Eds.). (2017). *Treating trauma and traumatic grief in children and adolescents* (2nd ed.). Guilford.

Dana, D. (2018). *Polyvagal theory in therapy: Engaging the rhythm of regulation*. Norton.

Finkelhor, D., & Browne, A. (1985). The traumatic impact of child sexual abuse: A conceptualization. *American Journal of Orthopsychiatry, 55*(4), 530–541.

Gil, E. (1991). *The healing power of play: Working with abused children*. Guilford.

Gil, E. (2011). Children's self-initiated gradual exposure: The wonders of posttraumatic play and behavioral reenactments. In E. Gil (Ed.), *Working with children to heal interpersonal trauma: The power of play* (pp. 44–63). Guilford.

Gil, E. (2017). *Posttraumatic play in children: What clinicians need to know*. Guilford.

Goodyear-Brown, P. (2002). *Digging for buried treasure: 52 prop-based play therapy Interventions for treating the problems of childhood*. Paris Goodyear-Brown.

Goodyear-Brown, P. (2009). *Play therapy with traumatized children: A prescriptive approach*. Wiley.

Goodyear-Brown, P. (2019). *Trauma and play therapy: Helping children heal*. Routledge.

Goodyear-Brown, P. (2021). *Parents as partners in child therapy: A clinician's guide*. Guilford.

Goodyear-Brown, P. (2022). *Big behaviors in small containers: 131 trauma-informed play therapy interventions for treating disorders of dysregulation*. PESI.

Kenney-Noziska, S. (2019). Integrating directive and posttraumatic play therapy to address childhood trauma. *Play Therapy Magazine, 14*(2), 12–15.

Knell, S. M. (1993). *Cognitive-behavioral play therapy*. Routledge.

Knell, S. M. (2009). Cognitive behavioral play therapy: Theory and applications. In A. A. Drewes (Ed.), *Blending play therapy with cognitive behavioral therapy: Evidence-based and other effective treatments and techniques* (pp. 117–133). Wiley.

Knell, S. M. (2011). Cognitive-behavioral play therapy. In C. E. Schaefer (Ed.), *Foundations of play therapy* (2nd ed.). (pp. 313–328). Wiley.

National Child Traumatic Stress Network. (2022, December 12). *Core components of trauma-informed interventions*. Retrieved December 12, 2022, from www.nctsn. org/treatments-and-practices/trauma-treatments/overview

Porges, S. W. (2009). The Polyvagal theory: New insights into adaptive reactions of the autonomic nervous system. *Cleveland Clinic Journal of Medicine, 76*(Suppl 2), S86.

Porges, S. W. (2011). *The Polyvagal theory: Neurophysiological foundations of emotions, attachment, communication, and self-regulation (IPNB)*. Norton.

Porges, S. W. (2018). Polyvagal theory: A primer. In S. W. Porges & D. Dana (Eds.), *Clinical applications of the Polyvagal theory: The emergence of polyvagal-informed therapies* (pp. 50–69). Norton.

Porges, S. W. (2021). *Polyvagal safety: Attachment, communication, self-regulation (IPNB)*. Norton.

Ray, D. C. (2011). *Advanced play therapy: Essential conditions, knowledge, and skills for child practice*. Routledge.

Siegel, D. (1999). *The developing mind: How relationships and the brain interact to shape who we are*. Guilford.

Summit, R. C. (1983). The child sexual abuse accommodation syndrome. *Child Abuse & Neglect, 7*(2), 177–193.

Van der Kolk, B. (2015). *The body keeps the score: Brain, mind, and body in the healing of trauma*. Viking.

5
Healing Attachment Ruptures with Safety and Connection Through Play

Jackie Flynn and Bridger Falkenstien

Introduction

Attachment has been central to the field of psychotherapy since the inception of our discipline; something about the connections we share as humans has continued to captivate our attention and clinical focus throughout the centuries. However, although attachment has been so intimately influential to us as therapists and healers, it is among the most underappreciated and misunderstood concepts in our field, both in its formation and function (Crittenden & Landini, 2011), as well as what role attachment plays in therapy and how we should work with it (Hart, 2011). Often conceptualized from the outside-in by linking behavioral patterns to theoretically consistent "attachment styles," recent scholarship has looked at attachment from the inside out by observing the formation and regulation of the neurobiological "attachment system" as it matures throughout the lifespan, developmentally giving way to the identity of the core self, and our various mental states and their accompanying behavioral patterns (Hill, 2015; Schore, 2021); this is where our conversation must begin, from the inside out. Attachment from this perspective brings the relational history of the client (and the therapist) into the heart of the therapy room, where affect regulation and distress tolerance create a winding rollercoaster along the dance of psychotherapy (Cozolino, 2017). The nature of our relational history includes the individual experience of acceptance, challenge, grief and loss, sexuality and desire, rejection, guilt and shame, joy, fear, anger, love, and play, as well as the perceived appraisal of these experiences from our attachment figures and the surrounding interpersonal environment (Panksepp & Bivens, 2012). This

DOI: 10.4324/9781003352976-5

parallel process creates our internal world, including our window of affect tolerance (Schore & Sieff, 2015), our concept of self (Damasio, 2010; Schore, 2019), and our experience of others and our relationship to them (Crittenden, 2016). From this perspective, our experience of attachment moves beyond the constructs of "secure" and "insecure" as we see its essential link to how we make sense of the world, regulate our body's various nervous systems to survive, and strive for safety in connection. Relationships are essential to our survival and therefore instrumental to the development of our physiology and psychology; to struggle with or lose relational attachments is a direct threat to our short-term safety and our long-term development, health, and survival (Hill, 2015; Schore, 2011). With such an intimate importance to our development and long-term wellness, how can we work with attachment and its rupture in therapy? Our answer is both simple and complex: *play.*

This chapter will explore the impact of attachment rupture and loss on our developing autonomic nervous system (ANS) through the lens of the Polyvagal theory (PVT; Porges, 2011, 2021), as well as how we can embrace the healing power of the ANS to heal attachment wounds with play therapy and the therapeutic powers of play (Schaefer & Drewes, 2013). The chapter is designed to give a grounded and practical window into PVT case-conceptualization and application in the play therapy space through a case study. Through this case study, we will meet a client through their presenting intake information and then apply a PVT case-conceptualization through the play therapy process to observe the outcome. Remember to stay curious throughout your reading of the chapter and imagine what it would be like for you to implement conceptualization like this into your play therapy practice.

Case Study

Meet Anna. Anna is an 11-year-old female, internationally adopted from China when she was three years old. Not much is known about Anna's life before she was adopted as she was too young to recall any memories consciously, and not much was reported to the adoption agency including any information about her biological family and living environment. This is not uncommon, as many international adoption cases have limited information about the adopted child and their background. However, Anna's adoptive parents suspect that Anna was sexually abused as they've observed her "doing inappropriate things with her dolls" at home. Anna experiences frequent emotional outbursts and seeks to disconnect from others during times of distress, especially when disciplined, with noticeable changes in affect and disorientation to present circumstances. Her parents also report that Anna has been "stealing and hoarding" food from the kitchen during the night, often hiding it in her closet laundry basket. Reports from Anna's pediatrician describe encopretic symptoms, shifting from constipation to uncontrolled fecal soiling. Her parents are also concerned about Anna's struggles academically, as Anna often forgets assignments, lessons, and other important events and information pertaining to school once she's home. Report card comments from Anna's teachers often describe her as daydreaming, not paying attention, and engaged in off-task behaviors while in class.

Based on this initial case description, priority areas of concern were sexualized play, power dynamics, and aggression. Additionally, the case description also includes some relevant information for our Polyvagal conceptualization, including a reportedly frequent state of dysregulation, swinging from sympathetic activation in her emotional outbursts and off-task behavior at school to her experiences of dorsal shutdown with her "checking out," disconnecting from others when overwhelmed, forgetfulness and daydreaming, and her encopretic symptoms. From a clinical perspective, initial treatment for Anna's case entailed a non-directive approach through child-centered play therapy with parent consultation and in-session participation. Here's Jackie's description of her initial consultation with Anna's mother:

> "When I first spoke with Anna's mother during an initial parent intake session, I could hear the desperation in her voice as she described their situation. Tears streamed down her cheeks, with momentary glances away, as she shared painful details involving Anna's theft, lying, sexualized play, and school struggles. During the conversation, she nervously moved her body looking uncomfortable on my couch. Her body language communicated to me feelings of worry, embarrassment, and shame. I felt a sinking feeling in my gut when she shared how Anna would go several days, sometimes weeks, without having a bowel movement, then 'poop her pants' shortly after getting in the car in the carline after school. When I described how trauma can sometimes be at the root of digestive and other body issues, Anna's mother seemed shocked, letting out a deep breath and loud sigh. Over the course of our conversation, her appearance and affect softened, and her breathing shifted from pressured and short to a more natural and regulated pattern. I told her about the therapeutic benefits of play therapy and described what therapy may entail for Anna. She commented with concerns about Anna's reluctance to participate in therapy. After speaking with the parent, I also felt concerned, wondering if Anna would be resistant to therapy based on what the parent described. Perhaps she'd struggle with connecting to me and the therapeutic experience. Regardless of our shared uncertainty, we decided to move forward with scheduling her first play therapy session."

In play therapy, the parent-child relationship is considered to have substantial influence on the child's overall wellbeing. Accordingly, parent consultation is an integral part of play therapy. From this initial consultation, so much is being added to the initial case description. On the surface, Anna's mother is expressing deep attachment distress, confusion, fear, and desperation. Like so many, just talking about the struggles of her child brings strong activation into the room and creates an opportunity for attunement between the mother and the therapist. As Jackie shared, even in hearing about Anna's struggles, she sensed a dorsal activation in herself with a "sinking feeling in my gut," describing an autonomic attunement to the mother's desperation, confusion, and fear, as if Jackie's somatic response might be a window into the everyday reality for Anna's mother. In essence, Jackie's attunement with Anna's mother created a safe invitation for Anna's mother to share the vulnerable information necessary for a comprehensive treatment approach. Aware of the power of autonomic attunement and the benefits of providing context, choice, and connection (Dana, 2018), Jackie spoke with compassionate leadership with the mother about what possibilities there might be to use the therapeutic powers of play in play therapy (O'Connor et al., 2016; Schaefer & Drewes, 2016) to work with Anna. As Jackie described, it seems that this description, coupled with Jackie's confidence in the effectiveness of play therapy, provided enough safety for them both to feel brave in beginning therapy. Here's more from Jackie on her first time being with Anna and her mother together:

> "I wasn't sure what to expect when I first met Anna. After my conversation with her mother, I shared some of her concerns about Anna, but I also remembered that when a client realizes that we are playing during our time together, their anxieties and discomfort tend to progressively slough away the more we meet. When Anna arrived for her first session, a seemingly happy, calm little girl strolled into my office and politely sat on the couch with her hands on her lap. As with many of my clients over the years, Anna presented much differently than her mother initially described. This difference is not uncommon for many adoptees in my experience, as with any new person they meet, they've learned to hide away their vulnerable and authentic self in favor of a defensive strategy to people please; they seem to act in a way that attempts to preemptively please those in their environment to reduce any potential for rejection or other negative responses. While on the surface Anna seemed like everything was fine, I sensed something deeper going on inside her. I could feel the incongruence of her appearance with what my system perceived in her. She seemed uncomfortable with it all. While likely unconscious to Anna, she fidgeted in her chair. Her voice was shaky and quiet. Through her facial expressions, I felt what seemed to be fear, mixed with a desire to please. The lack of familiarity in the playroom and with me felt like huge cues of danger. So, exploring the space and playing together was a priority for me to establish safety."

In her description of this opening session, Jackie wonderfully demonstrates the foundation to a Polyvagal-informed play therapy session by tuning into her own neuroceptive awareness before and during her interaction with Anna. Deep attunement like this can establish trust and a supportive environment for the development of co-regulation, an essential component of play therapy. By giving voice to her internal dialogue leading up to the session, we have a window into Jackie's neuroception; before meeting Anna, Jackie anticipated an incongruence and complexity in Anna's presentation, a challenge for Jackie's nervous system which she was keen to explore. In moments of uncertainty, particularly wherein we may interact with other social mammals, our anticipatory threat detection system has the potential to fill us with sympathetic activation, preparing us as much as possible for what might happen (Porges, 2021). Anna likely experienced a similar anticipatory activation as her nervous system was also challenged with an uncertainty of what to expect as well as the activation surrounding the circumstances that brought her to treatment. In synergetic play therapy, this co-experiencing of somatic responses related to the client's felt emotionality is referred to as the "set-up" for a positive play therapy experience (Dion, 2018). As Jackie described her subverbal attunement to Anna's incongruence and autonomic dysregulation, the choice of how to first interact becomes more informed. Let's see how Jackie chose to begin her first direct interaction with Anna:

> "After Anna and her mother sat down, I spoke first: 'Hi there, I'm Jackie. I'm so glad we get to be together like this. Would you like to play a game of 'Don't let the balloons hit the floor' with me?' I slowly took three balloons from the cabinet, blowing them up and tying them carefully to allow time for Anna to get a good look at me and how I moved. 'Okay,' I said, 'Let's do this.' Then all three of us, Mom, Anna, and I, playfully moved around the space attempting to keep the balloons up. It started off rather slow as many of these first sessions do, but as the reciprocity of play and our shared sense of connection increased, Anna and her mother quickly warmed up as we started laughing and moving around the room following the balloons, periodically bumping into each other and exchanging quick glances and laughter."

While this icebreaker activity may seem mundane and straightforward, let's take a deeper look at what's going on. First, using the neuroceptive awareness Jackie cultivated in the first moments of their interaction, Jackie chose to speak first. With a sensitive tone and soft cadence, this compassionate leadership invites everyone involved to join together in the activity (a likely cue of safety or neutrality), making it more likely that collaboration will continue. The alternative, demanding or forcing Anna through something (which might be neurocepted as cues of danger or threat), could make it more likely that activation will flood the space and defensive strategies will emerge in sympathetic and dorsal form. Second, after introducing herself to Anna and her mother (invitation to familiarity and safety), Jackie's first verbal invitation to Anna was not a demand for Anna to do something by herself (a likely cue of danger or threat) but rather to join Jackie in doing something together. Invitational language is essential throughout the duration of the therapeutic relationship as it provides an important cue of safety in combining context, choice, and connection. It's important also to remember that what is a cue of safety to one may be a cue of danger or threat to another; a careful sensitivity to your intention and action as the therapist, and the client's response, is essential. As therapists we can often miss the importance of this first invitation being collaborative rather than performative, even by first asking a question like "How are you?" or "So how do you feel about coming in to see me today?". While well-intentioned, the implicit autonomic translation of these invitations could be "You're on your own here, and you better do it the right way." Instead, Jackie introduced herself (a likely cue of safety), shared how she was feeling about their first meeting (a likely cue of safety), and invited collaboration right away where she would take the lead instead of making Anna feel pressure to perform (a likely cue of danger or threat).

> As Jackie continued to lead the session and begin blowing up the balloons, Anna is continuously at the center of Jackie's focus, where the goal is to promote cues of safety more than that of danger or threat, and to perpetually provide opportunity for context, choice, and connection. Additionally, Anna getting to watch an adult blow up balloons provides a spontaneous novelty for Anna's system, already beginning to stretch her autonomic flexibility and invite her into a playful state. Allowance and space for our clients' need to assess the situation by closely observing their therapist before engaging increases our chances of creating a safe enough invitation to connect. Finally, Jackie had full awareness of the importance of attachment in Anna's case, evidenced by Jackie's perpetual inclusion of Anna's mother in the activities of the session. While Anna's mother seems to have provided consistently for Anna's basic needs, opportunities to play together open up a completely new world of possibilities for Anna's mother to see Anna's core self emerge and for there to be an invitation to safety in connection with this novel experience of authenticity and spontaneity. What at first glance may appear to be a slow start to therapy, this way of working can actually speed up the healing process while simultaneously cultivating a deeper and more attuned rapport with our clients. This playful, mixed state of safety and the felt sense of danger found in all new experience is an excellent opportunity for Anna to increase her autonomic flexibility, add comfort and confidence to her attachment with her mother, and provide a non-threatening environment for Anna and her mother to deepen their attachment with

memories of play and attunement available for later recall. Let's see how Jackie utilized these opportunities as the session continued:

"After about 3 minutes, the attuned movement offered a sense of comfort and connection that we all seemed to experience. It was clear, we all felt more connected; no longer were we mere strangers to each other. In just over 10 minutes of play, we strengthened our relationship in a way that wouldn't have occurred without playing together. Slightly out of breath, I looked at Anna and said, 'Would you like a tour of this place?' Anna smiled and shook her head yes. Together with her mother, we walked around the play and art room to familiarize ourselves to the area. 'In here, you can play and use anything in here in almost any way you'd like. Sometimes, I will choose what we do, and sometimes you will choose what we do. Sometimes we will meet with just you and I, while other times, your mom may join us. How does that sound?'"

Moving through mixed autonomic states of sympathetic activation and ventral safety in connection, Jackie created a space for the three of them to play, stretch their autonomic flexibility, and familiarize themselves with the various autonomic cues of the therapy setting. After this simple icebreaker activity, the therapy room has held space for a wide range of autonomic activation. This included sympathetic and dorsal activation in the initial anticipatory fear and perceived incongruence, as well as a mixed state of sympathetic activation and ventral safety in connection during the introduction and balloon icebreaker that got them up and moving together. Now that the therapy space can be experienced by each of them as safe enough to hold this wide range of autonomic experience, familiarity with and attunement to one another in such a dynamic environment can continue to increase autonomic flexibility and trust with one another. Without this playful icebreaker activity, and Jackie's willingness to participate and model a way of being in the therapy room, it's unlikely that Anna would feel safe enough to be brave in exploring the office with her mother and Jackie. Additionally, because the icebreaker activity included both Anna and her mother, Anna's mother can continue to be a supportive resource and cue of familiarity for Anna throughout the next activity, as well as a point of connection for Jackie to guide Anna in experiencing dorsal, sympathetic, and ventral activation throughout each session. While attachment may not be the explicit focus of the session, this case study illuminates how attachment is constantly utilized and shaped.

It's important to remember the role of attachment in social mammals as not an outside-in behavior but an inside-out reality of how safe, resourced, and capable we feel from moment to moment in the face of a world that isn't always safe. Because Jackie is intentionally providing novel experiences for Anna and her mother that include an ever-widening range of autonomic activation, Anna and her mother have an equally abundant opportunity to strengthen their attachment toward security where "all of me is safe with all of you." In the play therapy room, Anna gets to see the imperfect and playful parts of her mother, Jackie, and herself, where the myths of perfectionism and expectation are left at the door. Making space for our human imperfections in an attuned and safe environment through the reciprocity of play often generalizes to other areas of the client's life that otherwise remain rigid, leaving them feeling inadequate and unworthy. It is likely the case that many of Anna's behavioral struggles and autonomic activation stem from her felt sense of isolation, rejection, social threat, scarcity mentality, and performance anxiety as every day at school confirms these fears (Porges, 2021; Sieff, 2015). However, in the play therapy space, Anna is invited into a disconfirming experience (Ecker et al., 2012) that has the power not only to heal and strengthen her attachment with her mother but also to generalize to the world outside the therapy room as a new resource to promote a felt sense of safety in (remembered) connection (O'Connor et al., 2016). It is the hope of the Polyvagal-informed play therapist that these disconfirming experiences transcend the boundaries of the play therapy room and reshape the client's perception of self, felt sense of safety with caregivers, and increase their willingness to be spontaneous and self-expressive. Consistent with the therapeutic powers of play, Jackie continues to promote these desires in play therapy with Anna in how she perpetually provides intended cues of safety, context, choice, and connection. Jackie also consistently makes space for Anna's distress without any expectation that Anna feel differently. This combined presence of safety and distress essentially infuses ventral energy into the experience, supporting a shift toward connected attunement and healing, and accessibility to heal deeper ruptures rooted in Anna's early attachment experiences. Let's see how Anna responds to her own autonomic shifts during the icebreaker activity as the session continues and concludes:

> "After a brief pause in response to what context I'd given, Anna nodded her head and curiously explored the room as her mother and I followed along. Her face lit up as she opened the art supply cabinet, asking questions about various materials, asking if I had stuff to make slime. She giggled when she noticed a teddy bear missing an ear. Slowly, the intonation of her voice reflected more safety as she moved around the room. Her fascination with the sand tray in the center of the room was evident as she scooped up sand, poured it into the funnel, and watched it flow. It was

as though she was waking up through our play together. She pulled games from the shelves, hugged stuffed animals, and tackled the bop bag. She even crawled into the tent in the corner of my room where she stayed for about 10 minutes or so. As the session progressed, I could visibly see her body start to soften more and more as her affect moved more towards regulation. When it was time to end the session, she offered a slight smile and leaned in for a hug as she thanked me. I felt her feel safe for the first time. While we were still in the initial stages of our work together, Anna and her mother experienced the power of play that seemed to shift their lived reality and bring them closer together; an experience and hope they both desperately needed."

Building on the familiarity, predictability, spontaneity of attuned movement, and the felt sense of safety in the reciprocity of play in the session, Anna continued to strengthen her autonomic flexibility, bravely explore the playroom, and increasingly interact with her surroundings, as opposed to collapsing into a shutdown dorsal vagal state. As social mammals, humans don't do these things without first feeling safe enough to be brave. All these moments are great indications that Anna is feeling more and more safe, as well as a deepening sense of safety in connection with everyone in the room. Without safety, healthy and attuned attachment is unattainable. Play therapy offers safety to our autonomic nervous system in a way that can't be taught, only neuroceived through the felt sense of the body. This is what Porges (2021) means by "play as a neural exercise" (p. 61) wherein the outcome of an attuned experience of play, particularly with a caregiver, can foster a more robust autonomic flexibility, enabling them to transition between active and calm states more efficiently and adaptively together, this being the functional utility of co-regulation. Consistent experiences of this nature are also likely to rapidly reshape social learning and increase the resilience of self and our confidence in the safety of connection with others (Schore, 2021). With an attuned Polyvagal-informed play therapist like Jackie, Anna's struggles at school, her copretic symptoms, and even her hoarding of food can be addressed in session and supported through her mother's involvement with play therapy. This approach to play therapy sees behavioral struggles as expressions of attachment needs and a flailing in isolation and performance anxiety for a dependent nervous system that has no anchor. By including Anna's mother in her experiences of the various states of activation throughout the session, Anna is invited into co-regulation with her mother wherein a healthy and secure attachment relationship can form, for it is through regular and predictable experiences of co-regulation that safety in connection and secure attachment are built (Porges, 2022).

Conclusion

Attachment is not merely a measure of interpersonal wellness or satisfaction, but instead an indicator of one's felt sense of safety and preparedness in a world of mixed signals. Accordingly, attachment ruptures pose a debilitating threat to our developing autonomic nervous system in our neuroception, autonomic hierarchy, and our ability to co-regulate. From early life experiences of attachment rupture, our neuroception can become complicated and filled with more cues of threat than cues of safety. Our autonomic hierarchy can become locked in chronic states of activation with little ability to rest in ventral safety in connection, making co-regulation feel impossible and a threat to be avoided. However, with an attuned play therapist, every session can become an opportunity to reshape and regulate these attachment ruptures and ultimately strengthen the client's resilience, autonomic flexibility, and felt sense of safety in connection to be generalized outside of the therapy room through internalized co-regulation.

As with many traumatized children suffering from relational trauma rooted in early childhood attachment ruptures, clinical applications of the Polyvagal theory in play therapy can create the safety in connection necessary for deep, long-lasting healing with the potential to change the lives of those we work with and their families. As with Anna and her mother, play therapy can make a world of difference. Consider the following takeaways from Anna's case:

1. Anna's traumatic experiences affect her internal sense of regulation and her external sense of safety within her relational resources. Our approach then must integrate work with the body, her relationships, and the environment.
2. Establishing familiarity, clear expectations, and relational continuity across the various interactions Anna has can go a long way. Through parent consultation sessions and working with Anna's school, we can help to set a foundation for context, choice, and connection whenever possible.
3. Reciprocity and co-regulation are key areas to work on with Anna if we want her to be able to discover safety in the classroom and at home. Additionally, exercises that incorporate these two elements can establish a predictable rhythm of context, choice, and connection that Anna can then look for in her world outside the play room.

References

Cozolino, L. (2017). *The neuroscience of psychotherapy: Healing the social brain* (3rd ed.). Norton.

Crittenden, P. M. (2016). *Raising parents: Attachment, representation, and treatment* (2nd ed.). Routledge.

Crittenden, P. M., & Landini, A. (2011). *Assessing adult attachment: A dynamic-maturational approach to discourse analysis.* Norton.

Damasio, A. (2010). *Self comes to mind: Constructing the conscious brain.* Pantheon.

Dana, D. (2018). *The Polyvagal theory in therapy: Engaging the rhythm of regulation.* Norton.

Dion, L. (2018). *Aggression in play therapy: A neurobiological approach for integrating intensity.* Norton.

Drewes, A. A., & Schaefer, C. E. (2016). The therapeutic powers of play. In K. J. O'Connor, C. E. Schaefer, & L. D. Braverman (Eds.), *Handbook of play therapy* (34–59). Wiley.

Ecker, B., Ticic, R., & Hulley, L. (2012). *Unlocking the emotional brain: Eliminating symptoms at their roots using memory reconsolidation.* Routledge.

Hart, S. (2011). *The impact of attachment.* Norton.

Hill, D. (2015). *Affect regulation theory: A clinical model.* Norton.

O'Connor, K. J., Schaefer, C. E., & Braverman, L. D. (2016). *Handbook of play therapy.* Wiley.

Panksepp, J., & Bivens, L. (2012). *The archaeology of mind: Neuroevolutionary origins of human emotions.* Norton.

Porges, S. W. (2011). *The Polyvagal theory: Neurophysiological foundations of emotions, attachment, communication, and self-regulation.* Norton.

Porges, S. W. (2021). *Polyvagal safety: Attachment, communication, and self-regulation.* Norton.

Porges, S. W. (2022). Polyvagal theory: A science of safety*Frontiers in Integrative Neuroscience, 16*(871227), 1–15.

Schaefer, C. E., & Drewes, A. A. (2013). *The therapeutic powers of play: 20 core agents of change.* John Wiley & Sons.

Schore, A. N. (2011). Foreword. In P. M. Bromberg (Ed.), *The shadow of the tsunami and the growth of the relational mind.* Routledge.

Schore, A. N. (2019). *Right brain psychotherapy*. Norton.

Schore, A. N. (2021). The interpersonal neurobiology of intersubjectivity. *Frontiers in Psychology, 12*(648616), 1–19.

Schore, A. N., & Sieff, D. F. (2015). On the same wave-length: How our emotional brain is shaped by human relationships. In D. F. Sieff (Ed.), *Understanding and healing emotional trauma: Conversations with pioneering clinicians and researchers* (pp. 111–136). Routledge.

Sieff, D. F. (2015). *Understanding and healing emotional trauma: Conversations with pioneering clinicians and researchers*. Routledge.

6
Neurodivergencies and Polyvagal Theory

Incorporating Polyvagal Theory

Karen Stagnitti

Tommy

Tommy was three years old. He arrived screaming. His face was red and scowling, and he was furious. He didn't want to see this new lady. Last time he had seen 'a new lady' he was given a shot, and it hurt. His mother confirmed this to me as she pushed her screaming son in his stroller into the playroom. Clearly, Tommy's social engagement system was not activated, and his defensive systems were in full fight and flight.

As the phylogenetically newer circuit, the social engagement system is myelinated and part of the parasympathetic nervous system (ventral vagus) associated with feeling safe (Geller & Porges, 2014). This newer circuit supports a state of calm (Geller, 2017; Geller & Porges, 2014). Tommy needed to feel safe, experience a state of calm, and only then would his defensive systems be lowered. In order to create a feeling of calm and safety, I invited Tommy's mum, with Tommy still in his stroller (a familiar space for him), into the playroom, and I sat with an open posture as far away from Tommy as was possible in the room. I didn't look at Tommy, but rather looked away, said nothing, and waited for his mother to attend to him. I was the threat, and to reduce Tommy's sense of threat, I needed to be non-threatening. So I didn't talk to him, I did not try and calm him, and I physically moved away from him.

As I heard Tommy's screams and cries quiet, I looked over near him. He stayed in his stroller, and I did not instruct his mother to remove him or to do anything different from what she was already doing. She knew he was upset, and having an upset child come to therapy can also be distressing for

DOI: 10.4324/9781003352976-6

parents (Andrews et al., 2013). When Tommy quieted a little, I rolled a ball over near him without moving from my seat. This was a signal to him that there were no needles here, but there were toys. I also had a puppet, and the puppet popped up and waved its arm in Tommy's direction. Tommy looked. The puppet came a little closer as I moved the puppet in a way to say, "I'm a bit scared". Tommy smiled. I chatted with his mum when she finally sat down near me, having settled her son.

Neurodiverse Children

Tommy had a diagnosis of autism and Attention Deficit Hyperactive Disorder (ADHD), and his mother had brought him in for a pretend play assessment. Understanding a child's ability in pretend play is the first step in Learn to Play Therapy. Learn to Play Therapy aims to build a child's ability to self-initiate spontaneously their own ideas in pretend play with pleasure and joy (Stagnitti, 2021). Children with autism have shown increased ability in self-initiated pretend play with accompanied joy when engaging in this therapeutic play approach (Davidson & Stagnitti, 2021; Stagnitti & Pfeifer, 2017; Stagnitti, 2021). It took two sessions before Tommy's play assessment was completed. The second time he came in, he was screaming. However, this time he only screamed for half the session, settled more quickly and began to manipulate and explore the toys I had placed on the floor of the playroom. By the fourth session (which now had progressed to his second Learn to Play Therapy session), Tommy was running into the room with a big smile on his face. His mum said he had been asking over the past three days when he could come and play. His defensive systems were dampened, and his social engagement system was activated. He felt safe.

Children with autism experience a chronic hyperarousal of a sense of danger in social situations with unfamiliar adults. Some children with autism and intellectual disabilities may experience a sense of danger with familiar and unfamiliar people (Patriquin et al., 2019). The social world requires constant monitoring, interpretation, and appropriate responses that are ever changing (Muscatello et al., 2022). This is stressful to children with autism and autistic people because understanding social situations with social reciprocity and communication puts high demands on them, as diagnostic characteristics can include selective difficulties in social, communicative and imaginative abilities (Jaarsma & Welin, 2012; Muscatello et al., 2022). For Tommy, the new situation of seeing 'a new lady' when his experience had included experiences of pain (i.e., a needle) was highly stressful.

Children with autism are neurodiverse, as are children with ADHD, Fragile X, Dyspraxia, Dyslexia, Dyscalculia, Dysgraphia, Tourette's syndrome, Meares-Irlen Syndrome, Hyperlexia, and Synaesthesia. The term *neurodiversity* was first used by Judy Singer in 1998 (Baron-Cohen, 2019: Jaarsma & Welin, 2012; Leadbitter et al., 2021). The Neurodiversity Movement, which has been driven by articulate autistic adults, is impacting practice and research and is moving language from person-first (e.g., person with autism) to identity first (autistic person) (Jaarsma & Welin, 2012). In this chapter, I will be focussing on a child with autism and ADHD and using the term *child with autism*, as young children are not yet able to fully evaluate whether identity-first language is how they understand themselves (Harter, 2012).

Neurodiversity Movement

Those in the Neurodiversity Movement have argued that there is a natural variation in neurological development and functioning and that autistic individuals should be accepted and appreciated for "who they are" and *not normalised* (Baron-Cohen, 2019; Hughes, 2021; Jaarsma & Welin, 2012). The values of the Neurodiversity Movement have generated much discussion on the heterogeneity of neurodiversity within the autistic population with arguments that there are autistic people who do require support (for example, Baron-Cohen, 2019; Costandi, 2019; Hughes, 2021). The impact of the Neurodiversity Movement is shifting thinking on how professionals engage with autistic people and children with autism because it "offers a corrective to the historical dominance of medical approaches to autism, opening up other ways of thinking about the interests and rights of autistic people" (Hughes, 2021, p. 48).

In response to the debate and as a result of the Neurodiversity Movement, Leadbitter et al. (2021) advocated for interventions within early childhood that: a) did not cure or normalise children with autism; b) improved a child's 'goodness of fit' within their social and physical environment; c) supported resilience, happiness, and joy; and d) promoted autonomy. Such interventions and research would improve mental health and quality of life of autistic people, work towards identifying causes of distress and intolerance of uncertainty, and reduce anxiety. Learn to Play has put out a statement responding to this shift in thinking (www.learntoplayevents.com/wp-content/uploads/2022/04/The-Neurodiversity-Movement-and-Learn-to-Play-Therapy.pdf).

Feeling Safe and Learn to Play Therapy

Let's now return to Tommy and his Learn to Play Therapy sessions. Creating a feeling of safety in the child and parent/carer is core to Learn to Play Therapy because if children do not feel safe, they do not engage in emotionally meaningful play. This is based on Porges' Polyvagal theory, but it is also the starting point in working with children with autism to reduce anxiety and promote autonomy, joy and happiness so the child experiences a deeper sense of self within their social environment. To state the obvious, "Therapy is not effective if the child or parent/carer does not feel safe within Learn to Play Therapy sessions" (Stagnitti, 2021, p. 64). The therapist's therapeutic presence, through neuroception within and between the therapist, child and parent, promotes a safe therapeutic environment and positive relationship.

> This bidirectional communication (neuroception) usually operates outside our awareness (Allison & Rossouw, 2013; Geller & Porges, 2014; Siegel & Bryson, 2012). . . . Neurobiologically, our therapeutic presence is the right brain to right brain interaction between us and the children we work with (Allison & Rossouw, 2013; Geller, 2017). . . . This, in turn, allows the social engagement system of the child to function. Play cannot happen if a child is not engaged.
>
> (Stagnitti, 2021, pp. 64–65)

In Learn to Play Therapy, the first session is an assessment of a child's pretend play ability (e.g., Pretend Play Enjoyment Developmental Checklist, Stagnitti, 2017; Child-Initiated Pretend Play Assessment 2, second edition, Stagnitti, 2022). The administration of the Pretend Play Assessments used in Learn to Play Therapy are underpinned by Axline's principles (Axline, 1974) and begin by the therapist inviting the child to play with toys and objects while the therapist passively and comfortably observes the child. To help the child feel at ease and safe, the therapist sits to the side of the child with the toys between the therapist and child. If the child is anxious, the therapist moves further away to give the child physical space and mental space to orient to the toys (Stagnitti, 2021).

Through the play assessment the therapist builds understanding of what interests the child, what abilities the child has in play and how the child responds to and interacts with the therapist. Tommy was very interested in how the toy ice cream and cone connected. He was not interested in any characters or puppets, he only used single repetitive actions in his manipulation of the toys, his play did not reflect events in his own life (for example, eating, drinking) and he only used the objects in a literal way. He was not interested in communicating with me. Even though he was engaged and interested in how the ice cream and cone went together, he did not display a deep pleasure of joy in playing. The play assessment informed me that Tommy's pretend play had not started to develop. His emotional engagement and joy in play were a priority in the early sessions.

Joy and Engagement in Play at the Child's Level of Play

Eberle (2014) argues that the elements of play are anticipation, surprise, pleasure, understanding, strength and poise, with examples of kindred terms such as *curiosity, excitement, joy, knowledge, drive* and *spontaneity*. Play is pleasure, joy and emotional engagement. Panksepp called one of his seven identified affective systems, which are genetic and motivational systems, PLAY, that being social joy (Panksepp & Biven, 2012). The PLAY system is situated within the subcortical region in an area rich in opioids, along with ascending dopamine systems, which are important for joy, laughter and positive emotions (Kestly, 2014; Panksepp & Biven, 2012). In Learn to Play Therapy, understanding the child's level of play development and engaging with the child at their understanding of play informs the therapist of which play activities will be more likely to engage the child (because they understand), lessen the child's stress (because it may be of interest) and provide positive opportunities to begin to enjoy the play. The selection of play activities is also designed to activate the child's social engagement system, so they are more curious and interested to engage in play.

For Tommy, sessions began with play activities such as peek-a-boo (building anticipation of where the object was hiding) and throwing and catching a ball with a large doll. This latter activity allowed Tommy to move around, throw the ball however he liked, and have the ball returned to him by a large doll. The first few sessions began with ball throwing, and the longer Tommy was engaged, the more he laughed, and the more the doll interacted with him. At one stage the doll tried to pull the ball from Tommy. He crouched down giggling, holding the ball tightly. He was emersed in the play with pleasure. His window of tolerance (his level of tolerance to process various intensities of emotion while still remaining calm and coping, Siegel, 2012) was widening. He was experiencing the Therapeutic Power of Play of positive emotions (Parson, 2021; Schaefer & Drewes, 2014). His social engagement system was active, and he was beginning to interact with the doll as a living, breathing, being. The doll would talk to him and be naughty, and the more he played, the more he looked at the doll's face and talked back to the doll.

Doll/teddy play is a play skill within Learn to Play Therapy that is targeted from the first session. Playing with a toy character is decentering from self, where the child imposes thoughts and meaning onto the toy (Stagnitti, 2021, p. 215). For neurodiverse children, this play skill is often missing in their play, and the toy character gets treated as an object with no assigning of emotional meaning. The use of the toy character together with pleasure and joy in play opens the child to the realization that the character is 'alive'. The character is also less threatening to a child, and the child will often listen to the character and not the therapist! Tommy began to interact with the toy character as a living being, and he transferred this skill to other characters that would join him in play activities. This ability to decenter from self also opened up the possibilities to Tommy of being more aware of others and what others may be thinking and feeling. This ability translates into greater social awareness and ultimately enhancing social relationships, the latter being another Therapeutic Power of Play (Parson, 2021; Schaefer & Drewes, 2014).

Engaging with Children to Build Pretend Play Ability

On his play assessment it was observed that Tommy was interested in pulling toys apart and putting them together (i.e., the ice cream and cone). Selection of toys for play activities in the early sessions of Learn to Play Therapy included toys like wooden food that are connected by Velcro®. Each piece of wooden food has two halves, and a toy knife is used to pry the two connecting pieces apart. Tommy loved this activity because he was exploring how the pieces fit together. This tapped into his one strong interest in play: exploring how things connect. As he cut the toy food, I quickly put the pieces back together so he could keep cutting the food apart. When he had been involved in this play activity for 10 minutes, I pretended to eat one of toy food pieces. He looked at me with bewilderment. He didn't know he was cutting up food. He was only interested in how the toy pieces fit together. Over the following three sessions, Tommy continued to engage in cutting the wooden food, and I 'ate' more pieces of 'food' and also offered some of these to a large doll. By the fourth session, Tommy offered the large doll a piece of 'food'. The toy doll thanked him and with slurping noises 'ate' the food. He smiled and thought this was fun. He also shifted in how he cut the wooden food by cutting it carefully as though he was cutting real food. The play with this toy now increased in complexity, with Tommy cooking the food in a pot on a stove and preparing picnics with the toy characters.

Moving children's play ability from single actions and little understanding of the meaning in the play to a sequence of logical play actions with meaning and understanding is a technique used in Learn to Play Therapy called 'repetition with variation' (Stagnitti, 2021). Repetition with variation is used a lot in the beginning sessions of Learn to Play Therapy (Davidson & Stagnitti, 2021). As the therapist co-plays with the child, at the child's level of play, the therapist repeats the play actions in the play, and in response to the child, starts to shift the play by adding variations to the play. These can be small variations (for example, have a cup of tea and blowing on the empty cup to signify 'hot') or larger variations (for example, as teddy goes to sleep repeatedly, the teddy reads a book and then goes to sleep). With Tommy, repetition with variation was used by firstly pretending to eat the wooden food only once in the first session (and observing Tommy's bewildered glance at what I was doing), to Tommy offering the doll food, to cutting up the food to cook. Repetition with variation is used to build play skill complexity in a way where the child feels safe, not rushed, and maintains their social engagement. Repetition with variation can be used to simplify the play (if the child is becoming overwhelmed), extend the play and consolidate understanding of the intention in the play.

The play assessment and further observations of Tommy, as the Learn to Play Therapy sessions began, revealed that Tommy didn't know how to play with toys. This is not uncommon with neurodivergent children who have not developed pretend play ability. Tommy did not know how to play with a truck. In one of the early sessions, I gave Tommy a large truck. I had a truck, and together we pushed the truck and stopped the truck. This was a physical play activity that involved lots of movement. Tommy giggled, laughed, continually smiled and found great pleasure in this play activity. When Tommy and I had had enough of pushing the trucks around, his mother said, "He doesn't get it". "Yes, I noticed that too", I said. It took two sessions of pushing and stopping trucks for Tommy to understand that to play with a truck involves 'driving' and 'stopping'. Once he understood how to play with a truck, I then introduced play activities that involved the teddy going for a ride in the truck. By the eighth session, Tommy was playing with several small cars and parking them in a toy garage.

Tommy could engage in one play activity for 25 minutes now. At this stage of therapy, I was working on building Tommy's ability to add several logical play actions together as well as introducing object substitution into the play. Object substitution is the use of symbols in the play, and it begins with physically similar objects used in substitution, for example, a box for a bed

(Nicolich, 1977). During his play with the garage, Tommy spontaneously put a small character in a small car and parked the car in the garage. He took the cars to the gas pumps and filled his cars up with gas, then he parked them. He also integrated a shoebox lid into his play as a ramp for his cars to drive up. The ramp was introduced by his mother, who joined in the play.

As Tommy's pretend play increased in complexity, he began to build constructions out of blocks and Lego® bricks. He included characters in his play and created play scenes using props and objects. He imposed meaning on his play, and as his sequences of play actions became longer, he created short stories in his play. Outside of the playroom, Tommy had friends over to play at his house. Staff at his daycare center reported that Tommy often led the play, as he knew how to play with the toys and create stories in his play. The staff also commented that they now needed to provide Tommy with more toys to play with. The therapeutic powers of play that were observed through Tommy's interactions with the toys, his mother and me, and reported from outside the playroom were: increased personal strengths with creative problem solving and self-regulation; enhancement of his social relationships with social competence; and a fostering of emotional wellness with positive emotions and stress reduction.

Increasing complexity in pretend play ability has a robust relationship to language, where children also increase in taking the lead in communicating and conversing with adults (Creaghe & Kidd, 2022; Davidson & Stagnitti, 2021; Quinn et al., 2018). Over the Learn to Play Therapy sessions, Tommy increased his verbal interactions with the toy characters, his mother and me. He took the lead during the sessions. He would run into the playroom with a large smile. He knew how to play with the toys, and he could choose which toys he wanted to play with during a session. Tommy's social engagement system was active, and reports from outside the playroom also indicated that he was more likely to be socially engaging with others rather than being overcome with fear and anxiety.

Conclusion

The aim of Learn to Play Therapy is to build a child's spontaneous, joyful engagement in the pleasure of pretend play. Pretend play ability empowers children with the skills needed to play in the metaphor. By providing a safe play environment with a feeling of safety, the child's defence systems are dampened, and their social engagement system is activated. Over Learn to Play Therapy sessions, as the child's ability to play is fostered, children take the lead in the sessions as they understand the intention and meaning in the play. Throughout the session the therapist is co-regulating with the child at the child's level of understanding play, creating a sense of safety within the child's window of tolerance within the zone of proximal development (Stagnitti, 2021; Vygotsky, 1934/1997).

As the child's social engagement system is activated, the therapist, at the pace of the child, may use repetition with variation to challenge the child's play ability to a more complex level of play (Stagnitti, 2021). If the child is overwhelmed with this complexity, the therapist brings the play to an earlier level, or if the child disengages in the play, the therapist responds by re-engaging the child through the use of a character or an interest. "True play is pleasure and enjoyment. The child's play is not a behaviorally learnt response. . . . It is a responsive process to build capacity to play in a child who finds play difficult" (Stagnitti, 2021, p. 70). For neurodiverse children, such as children with autism, the ability to understand the intention of the play and to play beyond the literal empowers the child with skills that are transferred from the playroom to their day-to-day life. Life, then, is less stressful as children's social engagement system is activated more regularly. Learn to Play Therapy aims to build neurodiverse children's capacity to engage intentionally, meaningfully and joyfully in play.

 Treatment Takeaways

- Children need to feel safe in order to engage in play.
- The therapist creates a feeling of safety through smiling, open posture and being physically and emotionally responsive to the child, within the child's window of tolerance.
- Understanding a child's pretend play ability and play interests informs the selection of play activities that do not overwhelm the child.
- To be able to truly play involves joy, pleasure and an understanding of the intentionality of the play.

References

Allison, K. L., & Rossouw, P. J. (2013). The therapeutic alliance: Exploring the concept of "safety" from a neuropsychotherapeutic perspective. *International Journal of Neuropsychotherapy, 1*, 21–29.

Andrews, F., Griffiths, N., Harrison, L., & Stagnitti, K. (2013). The expectations of parents on low incomes and therapists who work with parents on low incomes of the first therapy session. *Australian Occupational Therapy Journal, 60*(6), 436–444.

Axline, V. (1974). *Play therapy*. Ballantine Books.

Baron-Cohen, S. (2019). The concept of Neurodiversity is dividing the autism community. It remains controversial but it doesn't have to be. *Scientific American*. Blog.

Costandi, M. (2019). *Against neurodiversity. The movement has good intentions, but favours the high-functioning and overlooks those who struggle with severe autism*. Aeon.

Creaghe, N., & Kidd, E. (2022). Symbolic play as a zone of proximal development: An analysis of informational exchange. *Social Development*, 1–19.

Davidson, D., & Stagnitti, K. (2021). The process of learn to play therapy with parent—child dyads with children who have autism spectrum disorder. *Australian Occupational Therapy Journal*, 68, 419–433.

Eberle, S. G. (2014). The elements of play. Toward a philosophy and definition of play. *Journal of Play*, 6, 214–233.

Geller, S. M. (2017). Neurophysiology of therapeutic presence. In S. M. Geller (Ed.), *A practical guide to cultivating therapeutic presence* (pp. 43–60). American Psychological Association.

Geller, S. M., & Porges, S. W. (2014). Therapeutic presence: Neurophysiological mechanisms mediating feeling safe in therapeutic relationships. *Journal of Psychotherapy Integration*, 24, 178–192.

Harter, S. (2012). *The construction of the self* (2nd ed.). The Guilford Press.

Hughes, J. (2021). Does the heterogeneity of autism undermine the neurodiversity paradigm? *Bioethics*, 35, 47–60.

Jaarsma, P., & Welin, S. (2012). Autism as a natural human variation: Reflections on the claims of the Neurodiversity Movement. *Health Care Annual*, 20, 20–30.

Kestly, T. A. (2014). *The interpersonal neurobiology of play*. Norton.

Leadbitter, K., Buckle, K. L., Ellis, C., & Dekker, M. (2021). Autistic self-advocacy and the neurodiversity movement: Implications for autism early intervention research and practice. *Frontiers in Psychology*, 12, 782.

Muscatello, R. A., Kim, A., Vandekar, S., & Corbett, B. A. (2022). Diagnostic and physical effects in parasympathetic response to social evaluation in youth with and without autism spectrum disorder. *Journal of Autism and Developmental Disorders*, 52, 3427–3442.

Nicolich, L. M. (1977). Beyond sensorimotor intelligence: Assessment of symbolic maturity through analysis of pretend play. *Merrill-Palmer Quarterly of Behavior and Development*, 23(2), 89–99.

Panksepp, J., & Biven, L. (2012). The archaeology of mind. Neuroevolutionary origins of human emotions. Norton.

Parson, J. (2021). Children speak play. Landscaping the therapeutic powers of play. In E. Prendiville & J. Parson (Eds.), *Clinical applications of the therapeutic powers of play. Case studies in child and adolescent psychotherapy* (pp. 3–11). Routledge.

Patriquin, M. A., Hartwig, E. M., Friedman, B. H., Porges, S. W., & Scarpa, A. (2019). Autonomic response in autism spectrum disorder: Relationship to social and cognitive functioning. *Biological Psychology, 145,* 185–197.

Quinn, S., Donnelly, S., & Kidd, E. (2018). The relationship between symbolic play and language acquisition: A meta-analytic review. *Developmental Review, 49,* 121–135.

Schaefer, C., & Drewes, A. (2014). *The therapeutic powers of play: 20 core agents of change* (2nd ed.). Wiley.

Siegel, D. (2012). *The developing mind: How relationships and the brain interact to shape who we are* (2nd ed.). The Guilford Press.

Siegel, D., & Bryson, T. (2012). *The whole brain child: 12 revolutionary strategies to nurture your child's developing mind.* Bantam Books Trade Paperbacks.

Stagnitti, K. (2021). *Learn to play therapy: Principles, process and practical activities.* Learn to Play.

Stagnitti, K. (2022). *Child-initiated pretend play assessment 2* (2nd ed.). Learn to Play.

Stagnitti, K., & Pfeifer, L. (2017). Methodological considerations for a directive play therapy approach for children with autism and related disorders. *International Play Therapy Journal, 26*(3), 160–171.

Vygotsky, L. S. (1997). *Thought and language* (Alex Kozulin, Trans. and Ed.). MIT Press. (Original work published 1934)

7
Plagues, Pandemics, and the
Polyvagal Theory in the Playroom

Natalie Hadiprodjo and Judi Parson

Overview

> *Ring-a-ring o' roses*
> *A pocket full of posies*
> *A-tishoo! A-tishoo!*
> *We all fall down.*
>
> —traditional

It is well established that children naturally use play to explore and make sense of the world around them. During the coronavirus pandemic, children's play reflected the rapid changes that swept the world. Children were observed to introduce hand sanitizer into their shop play, to pretend to be the teacher of a virtual classroom, and to adapt traditional games to reflect their current reality, for example, a game of 'Duck, Duck, Goose', was observed to be transformed into a game of 'Covid, Covid, Clean'. This game of chase, an apt metaphor for the elusive coronavirus that dodged attempts at eradication. This capacity by children to weave community-wide events into their play is not new. The game 'Ring Around the Rosie' is reputedly linked to the bubonic plague in London in the 1600s. While the evidence to support this is debated, it has been suggested that the ring reflected the rash that accompanied the plague, the posies kept the smell of death at bay, the sneezing a symptom, and the fall, death. Some online commentators observe that it is macabre to think of children playing about death in such a frivolous manner, but the play therapist understands that play is not frivolous but of great importance. Play provides a developmentally suited means through which children can 'play with' the frightening and even the morbid, in a way that alleviates anxiety, increases feelings of mastery, and aids wellbeing—at both a psychological and physiological level.

DOI: 10.4324/9781003352976-7

For many children, this normative play takes place in the backyard or the playground, and no further intervention is required. Other children may need the support of a therapist to assist in activating the therapeutic powers of play within the safety of a therapy relationship to assist them in working through their fears and anxieties. Play therapists are responding to increased referrals for children experiencing anxiety in the wake of the COVID-19 pandemic. As we face potential future pandemics, the Polyvagal theory sheds light on the physiological mechanisms that may underlie the therapeutic powers of pandemic play, both in the playground, and in the therapist's playroom.

What Are Plagues and Pandemics?

Plagues are caused by the Bacterium *Yersinia Pestis* in which sufferers may develop rapid onset fever, chills, headache, and exhaustion (Gideon Informatics & Berger, 2021). There are three types of plague: bubonic, pneumonic, and septicaemic. The bubonic plague has additional symptoms including painful and swollen lymph nodes (buboes), and the pneumonic form includes coughing, chest pain, and difficulty breathing (Gideon Informatics & Berger, 2021). Both forms can progress to the septicaemic form whereby the infection enters the bloodstream. The bacterial infections that cause the plague can be treated with antibiotics but can become an epidemic or pandemic.

An epidemic is where an infection occurs in a large population or community at a particular time, whereas a pandemic means that it spreads to other countries around the world (Herring & Swedlund, 2020). Pandemics can be caused by other bacteria such as mycobacterium tuberculosis (TB) as well as viruses such as the influenza (flu) viruses (Centers for Disease Control and Prevention, 2022). The ongoing COVID-19 pandemic is caused by a particular virus strain—Severe Acute Respiratory Syndrome Coronavirus 2 (SARS-CoV-2) and has been described as a tragedy, where many people lost loved ones or jobs and life became increasingly uncertain (Zoumpourlis et al., 2020).

Pandemic Play and the Polyvagal Theory

Polyvagal theory is a theory of how relationships regulate the fear response of the autonomic nervous system (ANS) via the functioning of the vagus nerve. The theory emphasizes the importance of feeling safe as a prerequisite for social connection and has been dubbed the 'science of safety' (Porges, 2022).

The theory focuses on the many or 'poly' functions of the vagus nerve. The vagus nerve is a component of the parasympathetic nervous system (PNS) and is theorized to be responsible for both states of social connection as well as states of immobilization (Porges, 2011). Social engagement is governed by the myelinated part of the vagus nerve, the ventral vagus. States of immobilization are governed by the unmyelinated part of the vagus nerve, the dorsal vagus (Porges, 2015a). States of mobilization remain the responsibility of the sympathetic nervous system (SNS), however, the vagus nerve can also influence the SNS through its influence on the heart. A decrease in the influence of the vagus nerve on the heart allows the SNS to have a greater influence, resulting in an increase in heart rate and states of mobilization (Porges, 2015a). In this way the vagus nerve acts like a brake; it has an inhibitory influence on the heart that allows for states of calm social connection. When this brake is released, it allows for active mobilized states (Porges, 2015a).

The state of the nervous system is determined by a process called neuroception, an unconscious process through which the nervous system evaluates if something is safe, dangerous, or a threat to life (Porges, 2022). When there is a neuroception of safety the social engagement system is activated, and our defence systems suppressed. The vagal inhibition on the heart increases, heart rate slows, facial muscles relax, the voice becomes melodic, and the ear is tuned to hear the human voice (Porges, 2011). When our social engagement system is online, we feel safe, calm, and connected (Porges, 2011). When there is a neuroception of danger, vagal inhibition of the heart decreases, heart rate increases, pain thresholds increase, facial expressions flatten, and the middle ear muscles tune to low frequency or 'predator' sounds rather than the human voice (Porges & Lewis, 2010). We become less available for social connection and may move into a mobilized fight or flight response. Immobilization is the last line of defence and only occurs when there is neuroception of life threat. This results in a decrease in heart rate and behaviours that may include withdrawal from social connection, avoidance, shut down, feigning death, dissociation, or freeze (Porges, 2015a).

There are however exceptions; an individual can experience states of immobilization and mobilization without fear. Immobilization without fear includes experiences such as reproduction, childbirth, and nursing. In these unique states the social engagement system co-ops the immobilization system (the dorsal vagus) to allow for calm states of immobilization (Porges, 2011). Alternatively, play is an example of mobilization without fear. During active play, such as in games of chase or rough and tumble play, the social engagement system co-opts the mobilization system—the SNS (Porges, 2011). The fact that it is play prevents activation of the fight or flight response. Play therapist Theresa Kestly observes that children may also experience low arousal play states that may be described as immobilized play without fear, such as pretend sleep and nurturing play (Kestly, 2016).

Not only is play a unique autonomic state, but it also plays a unique role in regulating the nervous system. Porges identifies play as a neural exercise that strengthens the vagal brake and supports mental and physical health (Porges, 2015b). Play enhances an individual's capacity to deal with stress. The observed game of 'Covid, Covid, Clean' may illustrate Polyvagal play or mobilized play without fear. In this game a group of children are socially connected. They are sitting in a circle, in a calm state, then shift to vigilance as they anticipate being tapped on the head as the next 'Clean'—at which point they mobilize as they chase 'Covid' around the circle. The game is typified by play signals such as eye contact, laughter, and smiles that indicate they are 'just playing', keeping their levels of arousal within their autonomic window of tolerance. Through this play children are exercising their vagal brake, as they move between states of calm, vigilance, and mobilization as they wait, chase, and return to a seated position on the ground and back to a state of calm. In the same way, 'Ring Around the Rosie' follows a similar pattern of mobilization and then physical collapse and calm. This game has the further addition of rhyme, which may also play a role in calming the nervous system (Porges & Lewis, 2010). These games mirror early attachment games such as 'peek-a-boo' that assist children to neurally navigate through a sequence of autonomic states (while in relationship) that strengthens the vagal break and supports the capacity of the social engagement system to down-regulate defensive responses (Porges & Daniel, 2017).

The capacity to transition smoothly between physiological states of mobilization and then calm is key to mental health and wellbeing (Porges, 2022). These games are examples of how children use everyday play to harness the neurobiological powers of play to exercise and finetune their autonomic nervous system in relationship. At the same time, these games are metaphorical and give voice to the anxieties children are seeking to master, including collective events such as pandemics and plagues. Through play, children may gain both a physiological and symbolic mastery over their fears, worries, and anxieties.

The Pandemic Paradox

The Polyvagal theory draws attention to a paradoxical challenge that accompanied the COVID-19 pandemic (Porges, 2020). A pandemic poses a threat.

From a Polyvagal perspective the most adaptive means of dealing with threat is via social connection. However, social restrictions enforced during the pandemic limited access to connection with others as a means of calming physiological responses. Children also had fewer opportunities for play. Thus, social restrictions limited access to autonomic resources most relied upon by children to manage threat. We also know that children must feel safe to play and that play may be inhibited by events that elicit negative emotional states (Panksepp & Biven, 2012). As Panksepp and Biven observe, "Play only occurs when one is safe, secure and feeling good, which makes play an exceptionally sensitive measure for all things bad" (2012, p. 355).

The first response to threat is mobilization and activation of the SNS that may be expressed as anxiety or irritability (Porges, 2022). Prolonged mobilization may eventually lead to an immobilized state reflected in withdrawal, despair, and depression (Porges, 2022). Children who faced trauma and adversity prior to the COVID-19 pandemic may have already been struggling with poor autonomic regulation, placing them at greater risk for mental health difficulties in the wake of the pandemic. Polyvagal concepts deepen our understanding of protective defences and how they may present in therapy (Ryland et al., 2022). Children referred to play therapy are likely experiencing autonomic dysregulation. Children with anxiety may by operating with high sympathetic tone. Those who present as withdrawn and depressed may be operating with high dorsal vagal tone. A primary goal of therapy is to assist a child to move into an autonomic state that supports safety and connection (Porges, 2022). An ability to respond to challenge and return to a state of autonomic safety and homeostasis is likely what constitutes resilience (Porges, 2022) and arguably a successful therapeutic intervention.

Polyvagal Theory and the Therapeutic Powers of Play

Play therapists must create the right conditions for healing and growth at both a psychological and physiological level (Prichard, 2016). The therapeutic powers of play and the Polyvagal theory may be viewed as two sides of the same coin. The therapeutic powers of play could be viewed as the psychological or therapeutic powers required for growth. The Polyvagal theory provides a framework for conceptualizing the physiological mechanism that may underlie the therapeutic powers of play. These may be viewed as the physiological conditions for growth that a therapist aims to facilitate.

The specific therapeutic powers of play are generated in and through play to facilitate therapeutic change. The original 14 therapeutic powers of play were first identified by Charles E. Schaefer in 1993 and were reviewed and

Therapeutic powers of play

Facilitates communication	Fosters emotional wellness	Enhances social relationships	Increases personal strengths
• Self-expression • Access to the unconscious • Direct teaching • Indirect teaching	• Catharsis • Abreaction • Positive emotions • Counter-conditioning fears • Stress inoculation • Stress management	• Therapeutic relationship • Attachment • Social competence • Empathy	• Creative problem solving • Resiliency • Moral development • Accelerated psychological development • Self-regulation • Self-esteem

Figure 7.1 List of the 20 Specific Therapeutic Powers of Play
Source: Schaefer & Drewes (2014)

expanded as 20 core agents of change by Schaefer and Drewes and catego-rized into four sections: facilitates communication; fosters emotional well-ness; enhances social relationships; and increases personal strengths (see Figure 7.1) (Schaefer & Drewes, 2014). Whilst the list is comprehensive, ongoing debate challenges additional specific therapeutic powers of play and some consider that the therapeutic relationship is a foundational element that underlies the therapeutic powers of play. For a summary of all the ther-apeutic powers of play and clinical examples see Parson (2021a) and Melita and Parson (2022).

Pandemic Play and the Therapeutic Powers of Play

When selecting and integrating the therapeutic powers of play, the more powers available, the more likely therapy will be effective. Play also simulta-neously overlaps many specific therapeutic powers of play. Using the Schaefer and Drewes (2014) categories as listed, several therapeutic powers of play will be explored in the context of pandemic play and the Polyvagal theory.

Enhances Social Relationships

The *therapeutic relationship* is foundational to therapy and the first therapeu-tic power of play that must be activated within a therapeutic intervention.

Polyvagal theory supports the importance of relationships in helping children cope with threat. Through the lens of the Polyvagal theory, the therapeutic relationship requires activation of the social engagement system and an associated neuroception of safety. Children must feel safe at the level of the ANS to engage in therapy. The person-centred conditions espoused by Rogers, such as empathy, unconditional positive regard, and genuineness align with the Polyvagal theory and may be central to creating a sense of safety (Ryland et al., 2022). The therapist's use of their own bodies, such as the tone of their voice, their facial expression, use of eye contact and physical proximity, must also be used to create a sense of autonomic safety (Porges, 2022). Supporting a child's social engagement system in therapy is vital to help down-regulate their defence systems (Daniel, 2019). This also allows a child to then engage in mobilized and immobilized play without activation of the threat response system. From this socially engaged and playful state other therapeutic powers of play may then come to the fore.

Facilitates Communication

The incorporation of COVID themes into pretend play provides children with the opportunity for *self-expression* as they make sense of their own experience of the pandemic. For example, a child may use a medical kit to check whether toys are sick and/or to nurse a sick doll back to health. Throughout the pandemic play-based games and rhymes were also used as a form of *direct teaching* to encourage children to follow hygiene measures such as hand washing. The play therapist may also utilize *direct teaching* to aid mastery over stressful medical procedures such as nasal swab testing and COVID vaccinations by showing a child how these procedures work using a doll or teddy, after which the child may actively enact the procedure (Parson, 2021b). This in turn may also foster emotional wellness, in particular *stress inoculation* as it helps children manage their anxious feelings in relation to future events.

Fosters Emotional Wellness

In keeping with Rachman's (1977) three pathways to fear acquisition (i.e., direct experience, or indirect experience through modelling, or information transmission), Radanovic et al. (2021) investigated via an online survey of 376 children (7–19 years) and their parents in the Republic of Serbia the direct and indirect pathways to children's fear during COVID-19. The study found that the more the parents were fearful of COVID-19, the more they expressed it, which led to an increase in the children's fear of COVID-19.

Additionally, children's exposure to negative information relating to COVID-19 through media, friends or educators also contributed to the level of children's fear. The results indicated the importance of caregivers' behaviour during the global health crisis to *counter condition fears* through positive modelling and reducing the negative impacts of media and social communications. Interestingly, a further study by Thibodeau-Nielsen and colleagues (2021) found that frequent pandemic play served as a protective factor that buffered children against COVID-19 stressors, reducing the adverse contribution of caregiver stress on a child's distress.

As explored earlier in the chapter, pandemic play is also proposed to aid *stress inoculation* and *stress management* as it allows a child to exercise their vagus nerve to down-regulate their defense systems and develop a more resilient nervous system. The science of play is also intricately linked to the science of emotion. Jaak Panksepp, an affective neuroscientist, identified play as one of seven emotional systems in the brain including: SEEKING, RAGE, FEAR, LUST, CARE, PANIC, and PLAY. The PLAY system has its own unique neural circuitry and lies within the thalamus, a part of the brain rich in opioids and the reward neurotransmitter dopamine—which is why play, including pandemic play, is such a pleasurable experience that facilitates *positive emotions,* marked by joy and laughter (Panksepp & Biven, 2012).

Increases Personal Strengths

According to Vygotsky (1978) play creates a zone of proximal development that helps a child play beyond his age "as though he were a head taller than himself" (p. 102). From a Polyvagal perspective, play also extends a child's zone of autonomic arousal. Within play, in relationship, children have the capacity to play with mobilized and immobilized states without activation of the stress response system, which builds a child's capacity to *self-regulate* their response to stress. Research also demonstrates that pretend play in response to difficult life experiences, such as the COVID-19 pandemic, helps children to cope with stressful experiences (Thibodeau-Nielsen et al., 2021). Furthermore, play has the potential to serve as a protective factor against a range of adversity for diverse populations of children (Yogman et al., 2018).

Caregiver Involvement

As for any therapy intervention, caregiver involvement is key for effective therapy. In the first instance the play therapist may need to take a psychoeducational approach and support caregivers in understanding the importance of normative play and allay fears regarding pandemic themes in play. Caregivers may need to be reassured that they do not need to stifle a child's pandemic play, but that this play is vital in helping children make sense of difficult life experiences and has a positive influence on a child's autonomic regulation. In the first instance the caregiver may be supported to create opportunities for normative play for their child where they are allowed to 'play with' those events, both positive and negative, that impact their world.

Caregivers may also need support to look after their own autonomic nervous systems. Caregivers play a vital role in assisting children to regulate their nervous systems. If a parent is struggling to stay in a ventral vagal state of connection and safety, this will also impact on the child's capacity to utilize their connection with their caregiver to calm their ANS. As Badenoch and Kestly (2015) observe, "We have such powerful resonance systems that whatever is unfolding in the nervous system of the parents is experienced also by the children, and the less it is talked about, the more children inherit the felt sense patterns without being able to understand them" (p. 529). The paradox of the COVID-19 pandemic meant that many caregivers were less able to access their own social supports to sooth their own ANS, which in turn may have impacted on their capacity to co-regulate and sooth the ANS of their child and help them integrate their experience of the COVID-19 pandemic. A key role of the play therapist is to then support the caregiver to resume the role of a co-regulator.

Case Examples

Jack Transitions to Online Play Therapy During the Pandemic

Jack (pseudonym), a 12-year-old boy, was referred to play therapy for anxiety and depression following a traumatic bereavement. Jack was having difficulty sleeping and nightmares about death and dying. Throughout the initial in-person sessions, Jack processed some of his grief through play using a wide range of toys and creative resources. He particularly enjoyed expressing his thoughts and feelings whilst using the air-drying clay. The sensory experience of massaging the clay seemed to have a calming effect on Jack. Jack also used the clay tools to create detailed expressions on several clay figures.

It was in this early stage of therapy that lockdown impacted healthcare service provision in Australia in conjunction with the World Health Organization (WHO) activating social distancing and self-isolation protocols to protect human life and wellbeing (Renshaw & Parson, 2020). This meant that Jack's play therapy sessions required a rapid transition to tele-play ther-apy. This was a key challenge of the pandemic to which many play therapists had to quickly adapt. The very nature of the global health crisis amplified Jack's state of anxiety and grief response. A meeting was set up with Jack's parents to check internet connectivity, digital accessibility, and alternative communication to continue the play therapy sessions safely. A play kit was sent to Jack's home to be used in tele-play therapy sessions. Photos of the clay characters were printed off and included in the kit.

Jack's mother was also in a state of heightened anxiety with the additional responsibilities of home-schooling Jack, and his younger sister, whilst work-ing from home full-time. Jack's father was an essential worker who could not work from home. Additional psychoeducation for Jack's mother was provided to aid her own regulation and help her to support her children. A range of family play activities were provided to help the family connect and play and provide stress relief.

During the tele-play therapy sessions, the therapist used a range of technology such as whiteboard screen play and digital games to engage Jack while creating a sense of autonomic safety through the therapist's use of self. The therapist was cognisant of her use of facial expressions, tone of voice, and proximity to the screen to activate the social engagement system. In the transition to tele-play therapy, Jack reverted to early forms of attachment play and adapted hide-and-seek to the virtual world. He would show one of his toys and hide himself off screen whilst the toy engaged with the therapist; then the toy would leave, and Jack would surprise the therapist by popping back in front of the camera announcing "Boo!" Jack delighted in the therapist's reaction, responding with a surprised facial expression and associated vocalisations. As noted earlier, these types of games assist children to 'neurally navigate' through a sequence of autonomic states and down-regulate defensive responses (Porges & Daniel, 2017). Jack had found a way to engage in this play through the screen. These virtual sessions continued for several months as a means of maintaining con-nection with Jack and to support him during the additional challenges of the pandemic until he could return to the playroom.

Jill Gets Vaccinated with a Little Help from Directive Medical Play Therapy

Jill (pseudonym), a five-year-old girl, was referred to play therapy because of her fear of needles and the COVID-19 vaccination. Play therapy was arranged to support stress inoculation and counter conditioning of her fears in relation to the forthcoming vaccination. A calico doll was introduced to Jill, and she was provided with a range of colourful felt-tip markers. She created a doll called Sally. Initially Jill stayed away from the medical kit, but this was slowly and tactfully introduced by the therapist via another calico doll Ally, who showed Sally how to play with the medical toys.

Following a show and tell by the doll Ally, Jill selected a range of animals and placed them in multiple fenced areas or pens—all the pigs were in one pen, the cows in another fenced area, the lions and tigers were on an island, and all the other animal groupings were segregated, which seemed reminiscent of the stay-at-home orders. Jill then went to the medical kit and pulled out a needle and proceeded to inject all the animals in quick succession and afterwards said, "Phew . . . that's done. They're safe now". Jill then pretended to give injections to the therapist, instructing the therapist to stay still but yell, and then asked the therapist to give Jill her own vaccination during which Jill stayed still, but yelled. Jill instructed the therapist on how to put on a plaster (bandage) and care for her following the vaccination as she returned to a state of calm. Through this sequence of play the symbolic distance was lessened as the play moved closer to the self. Sitting still for a vaccination requires immobilization without fear. Through these play sessions, Jill was able to experiment with moving through various autonomic states and was able to 'play' with giving and receiving vaccinations, which helped her down-regulate her defence patterns and allowed her to sit calmy and tolerate her real vaccination. She proudly reported to the therapist that she sat still but yelled loudly during her COVID-19 vaccine. As observed by Porges (2022), this ability to respond to challenge (in this case a vaccine) and then return to a state of autonomic safety is a key feature of resilience.

Conclusion

The Polyvagal theory sheds light on the physiological mechanisms that may underpin the therapeutic powers of pandemic play, both on the playground and in the therapist's playroom. Play provides children a developmentally sensitive means through which they can 'play with' frightening events, including plagues and pandemics, in a way that aids mastery and wellbeing, both psychologically and physiologically. Play therapy harnesses play as a 'neural exercise' within a therapy relationship to finetune and strengthen the autonomic nervous system.

Treatment Takeaways

- Play therapists are advocates for play and educating the wider society regarding the role of play in aiding development and supporting emotional wellbeing, especially in the wake of community challenges such as pandemics and plagues.
- The Polyvagal theory provides therapists with a framework for understanding protective behaviours in children who may present to therapy and provides a theory for conceptualizing the physiological mechanisms that may underly the therapeutic powers of play and effective therapy.
- The play therapist must be aware of the state of their own nervous system in the playroom. A therapist must portray cues of safety using their voice, facial expressions, and gestures. Knowledge of the Polyvagal theory can help a therapist manage their own emotional regulation so they can better attune and aid in the regulation of their child clients.
- A key goal of therapy is to assist a child to move into an automatic state that supports feelings of safety and connection so they can explore difficult experiences without their ANS becoming overwhelmed. A play therapist assists a child to 'neurally navigate' through a range of autonomic states. Through play and the therapeutic relationship, the play therapist can assist a child to explore mobilized and immobilized states without fear, which in turn can train a child's ANS and build both physiological and psychological resilience.

References

Badenoch, B., & Kestly, T. (2015). Exploring the neuroscience of healing play at every age. In D. A. Crenshaw & A. L. Stewart (Eds.), *Play therapy: A comprehensive guide to theory and practice* (pp. 524–538). Guilford.

Centers for Disease Control and Prevention (CDC). (2022). *Types of influenza viruses*. www.cdc.gov/flu/about/viruses/types.htm

Daniel, S. (2019). Play therapy and Polyvagal theory. Towards self-regulation for children with paediatric medical trauma. In P. Ayling (Ed.), *Becoming and being a play therapist: Play therapy in practice* (pp. 234–246). Routledge.

Gideon Informatics, I., & Berger, S. (2021). *Plague*. Gideon Informatics, Incorporated.

Herring, A., & Swedlund, A. C. (2020). *Plagues and epidemics: Infected spaces past and present.* Routledge.

Kestly, T. A. (2016). Presence and play: Why mindfulness matters. *International Journal of Play Therapy, 25*(1), 14–23.

Melita, F. M., & Parson, J. A. (2022). Play in therapy and the therapeutic powers of play. In J. A. Parson, B. J. Dean, & N. A. Hadiprodjo (Eds.), *Integrating therapeutic play into nursing and allied health practice* (pp. 17–30). Springer.

Panksepp, J., & Biven, L. (2012). *The archaeology of mind: Neuroevolutionary origins of human emotions* (1st ed.). Norton.

Parson, J. A. (2021a). Children speak play: Landscaping the therapeutic powers of play. In E. Prendiville & J. A. Parson (Eds.), *Clinical applications of the therapeutic powers of play: Case studies in child and adolescent psychotherapy* (pp. 3–11). Routledge.

Parson, J. A. (2021b, December 5). Is your child frightened of needles? Here's how to prepare them for their COVID vaccine. *The Conversation.* https://theconversation.com/is-your-child-frightened-of-needles-heres-how-to-prepare-them-for-their-covid-vaccine-170791

Porges, S. W. (2011). *The Polyvagal theory: Neurophysiological foundations of emotions, attachment, communication, and self-regulation.* Norton.

Porges, S. W. (2015a). Making the world safe for our children: Down-regulating defence and up-regulating social engagement to 'optimise' the human experience. *Children Australia, 40*(2), 114–123.

Porges, S. W. (2015). Play as neural exercise: insights from the polyvagal theory. The Power of Play for Mind Brain Health. Mindgains. org, *GAINS*, pp. 3–7.

Porges, S. W. (2020). The COVID-19 pandemic is a paradoxical challenge to our nervous system: A polyvagal perspective. *Clinical Neuropsychiatry, 12*(2), 135–138.

Porges, S. W. (2022). Polyvagal theory: A science of safety. *Frontiers in Integrative Neuroscience, 16*, 1–15.

Porges, S. W., & Daniel, S. (2017). Play and the dynamics of treating pediatric medical trauma. Insights from Polyvagal theory. In S. Daniel & C. Trevarthen (Eds.), *Rhythms of relating in children's therapies: Connecting creatively with vulnerable children* (pp. 113–124). Jessica Kingsley Publishers.

Porges, S. W., & Lewis, G. F. (2010). The polyvagal hypothesis: Common mechanisms mediating autonomic regulation, vocalizations and listening. *Handbook of Behavioral Neuroscience, 19*, 255–264.

Prichard, N. (2016). Stuck in the dollhouse: A brain-based perspective of post-traumatic play. In D. Le Vay & E. Cuschieri (Eds.), *Challenges in the theory and practice of play therapy* (pp. 71–85). Routledge.

Rachman, S. (1977). The conditioning theory of fear acquisition: A critical examination. *Behaviour Research and Therapy, 15,* 375–387.

Radanovic, A., Micic, I., Pavlovic, S., & Krstic. K. (2021). Don't think that kids aren't noticing: Indirect pathways to children's fear of COVID-19. *Frontiers in Psychology, 12,* 635952.

Renshaw, K., & Parson, J. (2020). APPTA response to COVID-19 (Coronavirus). Australasia pacific play therapy association (APPTA). https://appta.org.au/wp-content/uploads/2020/03/APPTA-Reponses-to-COVID-19-March-2020.pdf

Ryland, S., Johnson, L. N., & Bernards, J. C. (2022). Honouring protective responses: Reframing resistance in therapy using Polyvagal theory. *Contemporary Family Therapy: An International Journal, 44*(3), 267–275.

Schaefer, C. E., & Drewes, A. A. (Eds.). (2014). *The therapeutic powers of play: 20 core agents of change* (2nd ed.). Wiley.

Thibodeau-Nielsen, R. B., Palermo, F., White, R. E., Wilson, A., & Dier, S. (2021). Child adjustment during COVID-19: The role of economic hardship, caregiver stress, and pandemic play. *Frontiers in Psychology, 12,* 716651.

Vygotsky, L. S. (1978). *Mind in society: The development of higher psychological processes.* Harvard University Press.

Yogman, M., Garner, A., Hutchinson, J., Hirsh-Pasek, K., Golinkoff, R. M., & Health Committee on Psychosocial Aspects of Child and Family Health and Council on Communications and Media. (2018). The power of play: A pediatric role in enhancing development in young children. *Pediatrics, 142,* 2018–2058.

Zoumpourlis, V., Goulielmaki, M., Rizos, E., Baliou, S., & Spandidos, D. A. (2020). The COVID-19 pandemic as a scientific and social challenge in the 21st century. *Molecular Medicine Reports, 22*(4), 3035–3048.

8
Reclaiming a Feeling of Safety in Natural Disasters

Preparatory and Advanced Interventions Using Play and Play Therapy

Claudio Mochi and Isabella Cassina

As the 4 × 4 advanced effortlessly on the hairpin bends, I (Claudio) rejoiced that I maintained my position: I would not start any staff training or support any activities of the "centres" until I had visited them all. From the top of the first peak, the view was impressive. Along with the vastness of the mountainous scenery, I was struck by the signs of the earthquake that left numerous fractures in the rock and the gleam from hundreds and hundreds of metal roofs of the temporary shelters. I had participated in several post-disaster interventions before, and one of the things I had grasped was that every situation has some common elements along with a lot of unique needs. These unique demands of each disaster site make it impossible to create a one-size-fits-all pre-packaged program. The organization that hired me had managed to set up centres in the most remote areas affected by the earthquake. It was a great investment of energy to reach them all and to spend time there, but the experience of interacting with new colleagues and children was invaluable. I learned several important idiosyncrasies of this community's response to the disaster, one of which was critical to my understanding. To protect physical safety, the centres were very carefully set up. The grounds were well-demarcated and free of hazards, while the tents for the activities inside were securely fastened to withstand any event, including the wind that blew with great vigour in those areas. Nevertheless, when the gales broke through, they almost always created a strong moment of disorientation, especially when they produced very loud noises, sometimes real roars that joined the sound produced by the sheets of the adjacent temporary structures. When the wind whistled loudly, everything became disrupted, and the flow of activities was

DOI: 10.4324/9781003352976-8

interrupted. Some children would jump in surprise while others would stiffen or freeze altogether. What struck me most, however, was the reaction of the adults: no one remained indifferent. While the expression of many became serious, almost suffering, for a few others the gaze became absent if only for a few moments.

Several adults were alarmed by a set of stimuli perceived as threatening. This was important because a state of alarm is not only unpleasant but limits all our social capacities and inhibits the ability to self-regulate and co-regulate others (Porges, 2021). My local colleagues' state of alarm also affected the children with whom they interacted, making it more difficult for them to regain a feeling of safety and begin the process of recovery. Despite their best intentions, my colleagues, who also survived the disaster, could do nothing about it. Feeling in danger is minimally influenced by our cognitive processes. The state of alarm is a physiological reaction intended to defend the organism and triggered by a completely unconscious assessment of the dangerousness of the context, a process Porges calls *neuroception*. Overall, the way the centres were structured had many merits—above all, the creation of very accessible spaces where children could have predictable and physically safe opportunities to interact with each other and play, and the involvement of local adults.

Effective One-size-fits-all Crisis Intervention Does Not Exist

The situation described concerns the 2005 Kashmir earthquake in Pakistan. A natural disaster of vast proportions that is estimated to have killed 87,000 people, including 19,000 children (Reliefweb, 2006), destroyed hundreds of thousands of homes and public buildings, including schools, and killed almost a million farm animals. It affected approximately 500,000 families. This catastrophe, even though it is considered one of the great natural disaster scenarios, has many aspects in common with other critical events (such as wildfire, flood, hurricane, tornado, earthquake, tsunami, etc.): more or less suddenly, they destroy the lives of individuals and entire families; wipe out property, common resources and productive activities; and disrupt the safety and dreams of life known up to that moment. The life that remains will never be the same again.

Unfortunately, in almost all cases, this first traumatic event is compounded by a multitude of subsequent stressors. Often with limited access to a variety of basic needs, the most fortunate must come to terms with their material losses and the uncertainty of what will happen in the future. For others, this is combined with the overwhelming grief of losing loved ones, the mourning that follows and/or the suffering caused by the physical injuries sustained. In addition, for some groups each of these elements is compounded by the weight of previous physical, mental and social vulnerabilities.

From the catastrophic event to the accumulation of additional difficulties, it is easy to imagine that each element has the potential to challenge the coping skills of any individual with the risk of causing disruption to one's sense of balance, give rise to symptom formation and create a series of enduring personality changes (Cassina & Mochi, 2023). According to Perry (2007), children exposed to traumatic events have a higher rate (from 15% to 90%) of developing PTSD than the general population. Moreover, the residual emotional, behavioural, cognitive and social sequela of childhood trauma persist and appear to contribute to neuropsychiatric problems throughout life. Yet, considering statistics and experience on the ground, the certain outcome of a given event cannot be predicted. Not only are events objectively different for each individual, but also, they are experienced differently. The impact of the situation is influenced by the protective and vulnerability factors of each individual and their support system, by personal history and by the chain of events leading up to the disaster, including what happens during and after the traumatic event. Even at the community level, the same disaster has different impacts and reactions.

In essence, while every disaster event is united by many critical issues and has the potential to generate a high level of suffering even in the long term, each critical event is objectively and subjectively different for both the individual and his, her, their community. This is a relevant aspect to consider when designing an intervention. In fact, each programme should be sufficiently articulated to respond quickly to the identified needs while managing to maintain a level of flexibility that allows adaptation to the uniqueness of the context. In addition to the damage caused by unplanned events (IASC, 2007), over-structured interventions also run the risk of failing, particularly by neglecting two fundamental dimensions of support: time and space.

Responsiveness is very important in an emergency as is attunement. In each context there are different time factors to consider. Schedules that are too tight or too rigid will fail to adjust to the need of the moment. It takes time to understand what the most pressing needs are, and it takes time for the most profound needs to emerge. Time is also essential to create a sense of connectedness, to motivate the wish to engage and to prepare the ground for the application of different interventions since for "any treatments to be effective and efficient it is necessary to keep the autonomic nervous system out of a state of defence" (Porges, 2017, p. 24). As anticipated, another key element is space. Closed protocols and very structured programmes leave little or no space for active participation, initiatives and solutions from local partners and community members. In Kashmir it was very clear that it was not the local personnel who had to adapt to the programme, but the other way around.

Coping with the Present While Building for the Future

To know me is to breathe with me, to breathe with me is to listen deeply, to listen deeply is to connect.
—Ungunmerr in Foundation for Indigenous Sustainable Health, 2022

Post-disaster scenarios require planning interventions in which the majority of the work takes place outside the typical therapeutic settings. One of the greatest challenges for professionals is to export certain skills and therapeutic factors outside the playroom. The catastrophic event, unlike other traumatic events, is characterized by a unique combination of conditions:

• The individual is exposed to sudden and numerous sources of suffering and worry, some of which persist over time.
• Very often events affect the entire community including the support system.
• Co-regulating professionals may be dysregulated themselves and in need of support.
• It is rarely the client who seeks assistance but rather the professional who needs to approach the survivors.
• Disaster interventions impose the challenge of integrating seemingly distant necessities and activities.

In general, post-disaster support should provide the conditions to be able to create connections, safety and involvement in a way that is in tune with the context and needs expressed. It is crucial to respond to (and sometimes anticipate) emerging needs while maintaining a coherent and organized but also flexible and revisable structure. Disaster work cannot be restricted to the application of a single protocol or methodology but requires a process-oriented approach tailored to the unique conditions of the event. A process-oriented approach "assumes that chaining of actions and different phases are necessary to understand the variety of needs and resources available, adaptation to the evolving aspects of the context, and engagement and cooperation with the local support system" (Cassina & Mochi, 2023, p. 12).

In our years of field work in a number of disasters and critical circumstances, we developed an approach called "Coping with the present while building for the future" (CPBF) (Cassina & Mochi, 2023). CPBF is not a predefined plan; it is more like an old MAP (Mochi, 2022), a collection of reference points in chronological order that help support local partners and professionals to acquire a feeling of safety, orientation and understanding in times of danger and confusion. It is a tool that sets the base for co-construction and guides the steps of the entire disaster intervention. In the coming pages we introduce some of the main reference points.

The Safest Possible Environment

When risks are assessed and the environment perceived as safe, we have the potential to recruit the most advanced neural circuits that "support connectedness, health, growth and restoration" (Porges, 2021). Based on this consideration, the common denominator of any interaction in a disaster context should be to sustain the feeling of safety, to create what we refer to as the Safest Possible Environment (SaPE).

In disaster scenarios, the fear of the event, the additional post event stressors, the constant reminders of what happened, the signals of unsafety produced by other survivors may all nourish a state of constant defensiveness. Continual exposure to threatening signals can turn a defensive state into a permanent condition. As Porges (2018) describes, "Life threat could retune the autonomic nervous system to lose resilience and to remain in defense states" (p. 67). One consequence is that individuals perceive risk even when there is none (Porges, 2011, 2021). This is one of the main reasons why promoting safety in disaster scenarios is a goal that accompanies the entire process.

According to Polyvagal theory our system provides two pathways to downregulate defensive systems and promote safety. One is *passive* and responds without conscious awareness to cues of safety such as prosodic voice, warm and welcoming facial expressions and gestures of accessibility. The other pathway is *active* and requires voluntary behaviours to trigger mechanisms that change physiological state such as breathing, vocalization, posture movement, etc. The *active* way provides "neural exercise" to optimize the regulation of the physiological states. In planning a psychosocial support programme, it is very important to consider that the *passive* way promotes the initial feeling of safety that allows the access to the *active* pathways.

In situations such as the Kashmir earthquake or the scenarios described in Chapter 9, increasing an organism's experience of safety cannot rely only on the work done inside the playroom. Many situations require as much safe exercise as possible. The SaPE expresses the effort to multiply the number of safety experiences. Cassina (2015) introduced the idea of the world as a giant playroom describing the intent to export outside the therapeutic room some of the most effective elements that are part of the play therapy experience to the largest possible number of individuals. This vision might sound grandiose, but it is actually the essence of any successful intervention in disasters areas. Following this perspective, a post-disaster program should focus primarily on maximizing the chances to stimulate a feeling of safety at every stage. The CPBF approach, for instance, is a multilayered intervention in which "each level has its specific goals and additional aims such as establishing a more solid sense of safety and trust in the relationship and collecting more accurate information about the needs of the survivors and local partners" (Mochi, 2022, pp. 47–48).

Figure 8.1 illustrates how each phase of the intervention is permeated by the effort to progressively nurture a neuroception of safety. Shaping the SaPE starts with the way we approach the first activities such as needs assessment

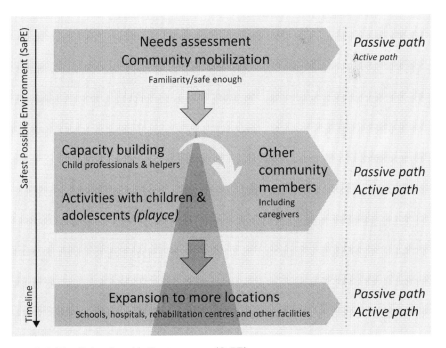

Figure 8.1 The Safest Possible Environment (SaPE)

and community mobilization. The initial contact usually is directed to adults and focuses mainly on recruiting the *passive* pathway. The entire ground-work phase is dedicated to providing multiple chances to convey messages of safety and creating a sense of familiarity.

Neural exercise starts when this initial stage has created the basic conditions of safety, relationship and knowledge to engage adults and children on a regular basis. Adults directly involved in the program start the capacity building process to support and implement activities for children. The activities for children usually take place in a *playce* (a physical space used to carry out different types of activities in a patterned, predictable way, according to the times and needs of the participants, which also promotes the application of the Therapeutic Powers of Play). These are subsequently expanded in more contexts such as schools, hospitals, rehabilitation centres and other facilities dedicated to children (Mochi & Stagnitti, 2023). The progress of these activities, together with the relentless work of community mobilization, nurtures curiosity and a sense of trust, gradually predisposing adults to become more and more involved in therapeutic initiatives including all activities that voluntarily stimulate the regulation of physiological states.

Kashmir: Moving Toward the Safest Possible Environment

In Kashmir, the construction of the SaPE started with the involvement of the staff of the centres. After relieving them of the imposition of a new curriculum to be introduced in the centres, the work was as follows: we started by building greater mutual awareness by participating in ongoing activities; then we began working on expanding attention and awareness of one's own body and emotional states, experimenting with different exercises for self-regulation and co-regulation; finally, we worked together to identify skills and techniques that could be exported to work with the children.

We would like to share some of the moments that characterized this process. After a brief introduction of each participant, we engaged the groups in a quiz play. The themes were less related to local context and traditions, and more related to reactions to critical events for adults and children, and the value of the Therapeutic Powers of Play (Schaefer & Drewes, 2014) in supporting pathways to wellbeing. We also involved the contestants in simple juggling games to encourage movement, fun and teamwork. The aim of these first activities was to exchange information, create a non-threatening atmosphere and solicit the active participation of colleagues. Pursuing the same objectives, we started talking about some basic emotions, representing them first graphically and then with facial expressions. Each colleague had a paper frame for this activity, which he placed around his head, transforming the face into a painting that highlighted the various feelings.

After this round of activities and a pleasant and nourishing break, we moved on to the "Body Outline" activity with the intention of identifying in the drawings of bodies where certain emotions are felt. The same activity repeated several times with reference to various circumstances offered the opportunity to start contacting the experiences that aroused the strongest reactions. This step allowed me to share psychoeducational information and also coping strategies. Being an active participant myself, I (Claudio) suggested my preferred modalities. As a Play Therapist and Qi Gong scholar, many of my techniques had to do with play, the use of breathing and postures (Mochi, 1998). Practicing the various activities provided an opportunity to broaden one's knowledge and spend time together listening to poetry, religious verses or music using musical instruments, singing and above all, developing creative combinations of all these modalities.

The combination of play, information, active participation, space for everyone's initiative and neural training had an unexpected positive effect. Many of my colleagues who grew up in adverse contexts would never have admitted that they were struggling and needed to exercise to get better if they had not found the space and time to do so. They, too, were surprised at how much the knowledge they had accrued prior to the trauma, drawn from traditional customs and resources, had neural reinforcement potential. These activities could become a routine for the adult helpers and offer fun ideas to practice with children.

The Grounding Phase

Porges (2011) cautions us that "attempts to engage a person with a trauma history, rather that eliciting spontaneous social behavior, may trigger defensive and aggressive behaviors" (p. 171). Post-disaster interventions are, in fact, extremely time and space sensitive and should include a preparatory and an advanced phase. The first lays the ground for the success of the second. The approach CPBF respects the hierarchy of needs (food, shelter and physical security are more pressing than psychotherapy) and follows a progression of actions that starts from the less-specialized activities addressed to the larger population, to the most refined forms of treatment addressed to smaller groups. The grounding phase includes need assessment, community mobilization and any other activity that supports the building of safety and trustful relationships such as participation in different meetings, religious functions, etc.

In the development of a post-disaster intervention, each action informs and structures the next by following the pattern "need-goal-activity" (or "N-G-A") (Cassina & Mochi, 2023). The constant assessment and monitoring of the activities helps to identify more specific needs, define new goals, and select the most suitable set of activities to pursue them. This way of proceeding aims at involving the highest number of people in the safest way, avoiding rushing and exerting pressure while preparing the ground for more specialized interventions. As in other crisis interventions, even in the aftermath of a natural disaster the final goal is to develop "something tangible that helps to build new possibilities and directions towards an improvement of life conditions" (op. cit., p. 14). For this reason, the entire process should grant constant space for inputs, adjustments and new directions.

The Role of Play in Post-disaster Contexts Stage by Stage

> Expressive arts therapies [including play therapy] help reconnect implicit and explicit memories of trauma, improve the capacity to self-regulate affect and set the stage for integration and recovery.
> Yasenik & Gardner, 2017, p. 61

It was in Iran, in 2004, in the clinic built for the treatment of the most severely traumatized children that I (Claudio) witnessed children playing earthquake for the first time. Back then, I did not know how to use play as therapy. We had several rooms in containers equipped with some toys, mostly to make the spaces more attractive for children and to be used as a warm-up. I noticed that children enjoyed building different kinds of structures and would break them down with excitement while making clamouring noises and repeat the activity over and over. The disaster was massive and killed almost half of the population in the city, and I was surprised to realize that children were enjoying playing out this sequence. I did read about post-traumatic play (Terr, 1983), but I had never witnessed the force behind this kind of play and what it could do for children.

Schaefer (2009) indicated as spontaneous therapeutic play activity in which children use the Therapeutic Powers of Play to alleviate their own difficulties or to gain mastery over them. Play is a natural healing tool (Gil, 2006; Crenshaw et al., 2015; Schaefer & Drewes, 2014) that requires certain conditions to be activated and used in order to promote growth and wellbeing. "Children in play, reconstruct, reenact and reinvent their stressful experiences in order to understand them, assimilate their reality, and achieve mastery over them" (Schaefer, 1994, p. 302). Also, according to the Polyvagal theory, play has "functions as a neural exercise that improves the efficiency of the neural circuit that can instantaneously down-regulate fight/flight behaviors" (Porges, 2021). Pako's story is not representative of all children but not unusual and illustrates some relevant elements in this regard.

> Pako was 8 years old, he loved attending school and playing football with the other children. After the earthquake that devastated Haiti in 2010 and the sudden death of his father, everything had changed. Several months had passed and Pako still had not left the tent. We had set up play initiatives together with the teachers in which most of the children took part, but not Pako. With time, however, my (Isabella's) presence intrigued him and he began to attend the conversations I had in the tent with his mother and in the street with the neighbours. One day his mother invited him again to visit what we would now call the "playce" when no one was there. Looking back, the space was poorly equipped and not particularly attractive, but Pako still seemed intrigued and asked to play a game he had seen me play with his mother. It was a traditional play similar to Shanghai and the new, colourful sticks exerted a special fascination for him. This activity remained his favourite in the few meetings we had together before he decided to join the other children. The transition to the playce took much longer for him than for the other children and required constant and gentle involvement from his mother.

Applying the Therapeutic Powers of Play in highly critical circumstances such as natural disasters requires a comprehensive process. Play opens possibilities, allows potentials to emerge and offers repetition to build resiliency but, as any other exercise, to be effective a single episode is not sufficient but a process that aims at building play sanctuaries and a culture of play that would remain long after the intervention is concluded (Mochi, 2022).

Breathing exercises are a very powerful practice to recruit *active* pathways as it is the combination of dynamic movements and still postures. However, in the long time we have been practising yoga (Isabella) and Qi Gong (Claudio), we rarely could use related activities with participants/our clients without playing before, during and after them. Impersonating a balloon that inflates quickly and deflates slowly is more engaging, as well as doing the contest of the biggest bubble. Playing "Opera Talk" is also quite effective to practice long expirations, exercise creativity and group work, especially when children can decide the scenario they want to dramatize. This activity requires some modelling, but allows children to have fun, express freely, progressively raise the voice, make the words last as long as possible and accompany everything with wide theatrical gestures. Another exercise is performing postures, movements and breathing of big animals such as elephants, hippos and whales: "Children, let's move like an elephant, now look around, run like an elephant would do, stop, jump, hear carefully, breathe deeply like an elephant . . .". The playfulness and atmosphere encourage people to repeat the experience and accept something new with ease.

These kinds of activities usually work in different contexts and can introduce explanations about breathing and other useful practices. However, they need some level of preparation and groundwork. How would you react if somebody invited you to suddenly play elephant or to talk opera in the most terrifying moments of your life? These psychosocial activities (see "Advanced stage" in Figure 8.2) aim to ameliorate mild psychosocial problems through the empowerment of resilience capabilities, positive social interactions, the practice of co-regulation and expand coping skills, all while having fun. These activities also serve the purpose of identifying children who need specialized treatment to address more severe problems.

In the approach CPBF to make the intervention engaging, sustainable and safer, the use of play is articulated in three main stages. Each stage reflects what is actually manageable, the objective of play at this point in the recovery process and the optimal level of activation for children. Figure 8.2 reflects the concept of CPBF chart by including more people in the early stages and then decreasing the number of people as the intervention becomes more specialized. (This is the meaning of the inverted pyramid you see in the first column on the left.) In the initial stage, recreational activities can be implemented to *involve* as many people as possible. In the advanced stage, psychosocial activities are directed to *empower* selected groups of children. In the specialized stage, play therapy interventions focus on the *treatment* of a smaller number of children and families who need this kind of involvement.

In developing the specialized stage of the intervention, it is ideal to involve caregivers as the main sources of external safety and regulation. Caregivers can learn, for example, new modes of neural exercise and practice them with their children. Various approaches such as Family Play Therapy (Gil, 1994), Dynamic Play Therapy (Harvey, 2006) and attachment-based play therapy models such as Theraplay (Munns, 2000) are ideal for working effectively with the whole family. In methodologies such as Filial Therapy (VanFleet & Guerney, 2003) and Child-Parent Relationship Therapy (Landreth & Bratton, 2006), moreover, it is the caregiver who assumes the role of primary change agent and conducts therapy sessions with their child. All these modalities offer valuable references for developing experiences of co-regulation,

Stage	Objectives	Activities
Initial stage Recreational activities The power of play is used for recreation, connection and assessment.	**Children:** experience a safe context, distraction, fun, release of tension, predictability, socialization with possibility to connect with peers and adults which are active in the project and the community. **Helpers:** involve children in the project. Play helps to build relationships with children and is used as initial identification of psychosocial needs.	Traditional and popular. Lighthearted, fun or sport group activities. Planned and organized by the project team or volunteers. Children can also organize them under team supervision.
Advanced stage Psychosocial activities Play based group activities to promote abilities in children and ameliorate mild psychosocial problems.	**Children:** identification and expression of emotions, self-regulation, coping skills, stress management, etc. **Helpers:** strengthen positive relationships and deeper needs assessment.	Age-specific group activities also extrapolated from different Play Therapy group activities. Each addresses a specific goal. Every session is followed by a report to document the process and results.
Specialized stage Play Therapy Different approaches to prevent or resolve psychosocial problems and psychological disorders and achieve optimal growth and development.	**Children and families:** addressing specific psychosocial needs, post-traumatic or other stress reactions, and multiple problems not improved with psychosocial activities.	Individual, group or family format using Play Therapy methodologies.

Figure 8.2 The Stages of a Crisis Intervention: Focusing on the Role of Play

Source: Figure reprinted with permission from Beyond the Clouds by Claudio Mochi, copyright (c) 2022 from Loving Healing Press.

strengthening relationships, attunement and understanding of the state and needs of others. By promoting better relationships, mutual support and creativity in family members, these methodologies are ideal. Unfortunately, however, they are not always practicable. In disaster scenarios (both natural and human-made), caregivers as well as professionals can be hit hard and find themselves in the position of first having to be helped themselves to recover a state of feeling safe. For this reason, as shown in Figure 8.1, dedicated interventions to support children where possible are complemented by dedicated work with adults contributing over time to the creation of the SaPE.

Conclusion

Natural disasters have the potential to suddenly induce in individuals and large sectors of the community a state of fear, helplessness and disconnection. Three aspects are fundamental to consider when conceptualizing post-disaster interventions: firstly, Polyvagal theory urges the practitioners involved to broaden their perspective by recognizing that the pursuit of health and restoration depends on the detection of cues of safety in the environment and in relationships. Secondarily, an effective crisis intervention should extend beyond the playroom and promote as many opportunities as possible to enjoy interactions and activities that produce safety, connection and resilience. Thirdly, based on the same principles set forth by Porges, in order to respect each individual's needs and timing, the therapeutic offer should include accessible programmes that ensure involvement, empowerment and treatment through adequate groundwork.

References

Cassina, I. (2015). Il mondo sarà un'enorme, rassicurante e ben equipaggiata stanza dei giochi, National contest, *News dal futuro. Il mondo nel 2030*, Helvetas Clip Award, Switzerland.

Cassina, I., & Mochi, C. (2023). Applying the therapeutic power of play and expressive arts in contemporary crisis work. A process-oriented approach. In I. Cassina, C. Mochi, & K. Stagnitti (Eds.), *Play therapy and expressive arts in a complex and dynamic world: Opportunities and challenges inside and outside the playroom* (pp. 6–27). Routledge.

Crenshaw, D. A., Brooks, R., & Goldstein, S. (2015). *Play therapy interventions to enhance resilience*. Guilford Press.

Foundation for Indigenous Sustainable Health. (2022). *Daddiri by Miriam Rose Ungunmerr*. www.youtube.com/watch?v=Pahz_WBSSdA.

Gil, E. (1994). *Play in family therapy*. Guilford.

Gil, E. (2006). *Helping abused and traumatized children: Integrating directive and nondirective approaches*. Guilford.

Harvey, S. A. (2006). Dynamic play therapy. In C. E. Schaefer & H. Kudson (Eds.), *Contemporary play therapy* (pp. 55–81). The Guilford.

IASC Inter-Agency Standing Committee. (2007). *IASC guidelines on mental health and psychosocial support in emergency settings.* IASC. www.humanitarianinfo.org/iasc/content/products.

Landreth, G. L., & Bratton, S. C. (2006). *Child parent relationship therapy (CPRT) treatment manual: A 10-session filial therapy model for training parents.* Routledge.

Mochi, C. (1998). *Integrazione mente-corpo attraverso lo studio del Qi Gong* [Unpublished dissertation, Laurea in Psicologia Clinica e di Comunità, Università La Sapienza Roma].

Mochi, C. (2022). *Beyond the clouds: An autoethnographic research exploring the good practice in crisis settings.* Loving Healing Press.

Mochi, C., & Stagnitti, K. (2023). Learn to play therapy in high-risk countries: The example of Nigeria. In I. Cassina, C. Mochi, & K. Stagnitti (Eds.), *Play therapy and expressive arts in a complex and dynamic world: Opportunities and challenges inside and outside the playroom* (pp. 96–119). Routledge.

Munns, E. (2000). *Theraplay: Innovations in attachment-enhancing play therapy.* Jason Aronson.

Perry, B. D. (2007). Stress, trauma and post-traumatic stress disorders in children. *The Child Trauma Academy, 17,* 42–57.

Porges, S. (2011). *The Polyvagal theory: Neurophysiological foundations of emotions, attachment, communication, and self-regulation.* Norton.

Porges, S. W. (2017). *The pocket guide to the Polyvagal theory: The transformative power of feeling safe.* Norton.

Porges, S. W. (2018). Polyvagal theory: A primer. In S. W. Porges & D. Dana (Eds.), *Clinical applications of the Polyvagal theory: The emergence of polyvagal-informed therapies* (pp. 50–69). Norton.

Porges, S. W. (2021). *Polyvagal safety: Attachment, communication, self-regulation* (IPNB). Norton. www.amazon.com.

Reliefweb. (2006). The Kashmir earthquake of October 8, 2005: Impacts in Pakistan. OCHA. https://reliefweb.int/report/pakistan/kashmir-earthquake-october-8-2005-impacts-pakistan#:~:text=Approximately%2038%2C000%20were%20injured%20and,affected%20more%20than%20500%2C000%20families

Schaefer, C. E. (1994). Play therapy for psychic trauma in children. In K. J. O'Connor & C. E. Schaefer (Eds.), *Handbook of play therapy advances and innovations* (pp. 297–318). Wiley.

Schaefer, C. E. (2009). *Foundations of play therapy [101], workshop.* Play Therapy Training Institute.

Schaefer, C. E., & Drewes, A. A. (2014). *The therapeutic powers of play: 20 core agents of change* (2nd ed.). Wiley.

Terr, L. C. (1983). Play therapy and psychic trauma: A preliminary report. In C. E. Schaefer & K. J. O'Connor (Eds.), *Handbook of play therapy* (pp. 308–319). Wiley.

VanFleet, R., & Guerney, L. (2003). *Casebook of filial therapy.* Play Therapy Press.

Yasenik, L., & Gardner, K. (2017). Counseling skills in action with children, adolescents and adults. In E. Prendiville & J. Howard (Eds.), *Creative psychotherapy. Applying the principles of neurobiology to play and expressive arts based practices* (pp. 59–80). Routledge.

9
Polyvagal-Informed Practice to Support Children and Caregivers in War

Toward the Creation of a Huge and Reassuring Playroom

Isabella Cassina and Claudio Mochi

The costs of war are inestimable from many perspectives, including the psychosocial impact, and can last for generations. Our work has taken us to areas of open conflict where the sound of bombs was in the background along with the cries of parents and the shy laughter of children playing. But war is not just open conflict; it also includes those moments of uncertainty, tension and fear before the first bomb exploded, and those where the worst seems to be over but in fact nothing is back to the way it was. War is not an isolated episode; it is a destructive process that lasts over time and affects all areas of people's lives. Some people living in war zones move within the borders of the country (we speak in this case of Internally Displaced People (IDPs)), while others seek refuge in other countries. The UN Refugee Agency estimates that 100 million people left their homes in 2022 because of conflicts, violence, human rights violations and persecution (United Nations, 2022a). Of these people, approximately 36.5 million are children. To this figure must be added the children who were forced to move because of natural disasters and those who have recently been displaced because of the Russian invasion of Ukraine (United Nations, 2022b).

War is a complex phenomenon and must be approached as such. The Avalanche Metaphor (Cassina, 2023), originally developed to represent the progressive accumulation of risk factors and the drastic reduction of protective factors that originates from a process of forced migration, supports us in

DOI: 10.4324/9781003352976-9

understanding the devastating potential of war for children and adults. The constant perception of threats can result for children in: "1) a pervasive pattern of dysregulation; 2) problems with attention and concentration; and 3) difficulties getting along with themselves and others" (van der Kolk, 2014, p. 160), and this can permanently alter their neuro systems (Porges, 2021). At the same time, the whole support system (i.e. nuclear family, extended family, school, friends/community, culture/religion) is deeply affected. According to the metaphor mentioned, we could say that an avalanche sweeps over everyone and everything it encounters.

Reaching a war-free region or country unfortunately does not coincide with a sudden end to the psychosocial difficulties accumulated and consolidated over time, nor does it mean feeling immediately safe. From a Polyvagal perspective, being safe is "a biobehavioral state determined by the nervous system, often independent of awareness and actual threat. Thus, removal of threat may not change physiological states or enable an individual to feel safe" (Porges & Carter, 2017, p. 223). An avalanche does not magically dissolve when it meets the plain. It may take years before the support system can return to play its full role, and there are serious risks of intergenerational trauma (Menzies, 2010; Sangalang & Vang, 2017; Castro-Vale et al., 2019). Unfortunately, as humanitarian workers we cannot prevent avalanches/wars from occurring, but we can provide interventions to alleviate the suffering they cause. This chapter introduces a number of considerations supported by the Polyvagal theory on the migration process and intergenerational trauma as relevant psychosocial consequences of war. Focus is on the possibility of restoring a feeling of safety for children and caregivers through the Therapeutic Powers of Play inside and outside the playroom.

Aiming to a World as a Huge, Reassuring and Well-Equipped Playroom

In 2006, I (Claudio) was working in Palestine in the midst of ongoing conflict to develop psychosocial centres for children. One of the activities provided was free playtime. "During one of these playtimes, we heard a loud explosion. All of the children stopped playing at once, and I stopped too. I was sitting on the ground and, as far as I remember, the children all looked suddenly at my colleague M. I still have goosebumps when I revisit the scene in my mind. M. did not blink, he did not appear nervous or worried, and continued with the activity he had been engaged in. After a few moments, all the children resumed their play. I did not know back then of Porges and the Polyvagal theory, but it was so clear for me that as referent adults, our relationship is a safety bank for children.

The moment children saw M. calm and at ease, they realized the place was safe for them; they got the "green light" to resume their play.
(Mochi, 2022, p. 33)

Unlike natural disaster scenarios (more on this in Chapter 8), human-made disasters are intentional. They enhance conditions of uncertainty, stress and fear on a long term and are entrenched in the everyday life of both children and adults with no clear prospects for improvement (Mochi, 2009). Moreover, traumatic episodes accumulated over time by caregivers can have additional consequences on children's wellbeing resulting in psychiatric symptoms, health issues and limited ability to deal with stress (Sangalang & Vang, 2017). In 2015, I (Isabella) took part in a Swiss national competition to develop projections for the future and went as far as to say that the world in 2030 should have become a huge, reassuring and well-equipped playroom. Unrealistic as it was, this vision contained a couple of principles that Claudio and I firmly believe in and apply in our work. First, "crisis intervention should aim to be a sustainable process in which the individual is not involved in a single therapeutic intervention but in a multitude of positive interactions and healthy activities" (Cassina & Mochi, 2023, p. 21) taking place inside and outside the playroom. The more extended the intervention, the better.

Second, safety always comes first. The approach "Coping with the present while building for the future (CPBF)" (Cassina & Mochi, 2023) represents the authors' MAP (Mochi, 2022) for crisis intervention and offers practical guidance for the development of a process-oriented approach. CPBF includes safety both among the principles of "good practice", together with respect and effectiveness, and among the elements of the grounding phase of crisis interventions, together with assessment, community mobilization and relationship. Only, in fact, "once the individual feels safe, he is ready to begin the course to regain psychic equilibrium and process his trauma, integrating traumatic memories, slowly recovering his self-regulation, re-establishing social connections, retrieving previously practised coping skills or learning new ones" (Mochi, 2009, p. 77).

Conveying a feeling of safety is crucial and preliminary to further clinical and non-clinical interventions and must be done extensively, reaching family, school, rehabilitation and recreational contexts. Polyvagal theory confirms the relevance of developing the Safest Possible Environment (SaPE) as defined in Chapter 8 even in those places where physical safety cannot be guaranteed. In the process of developing the SaPE in war zones, we consider that "the human nervous system provides two paths to trigger neural mechanisms capable of down-regulating defence and enabling states of calmness that support health, spontaneous social behaviour, and connectedness" (Porges & Carter, 2017, p. 222). One path is *passive* and refers to neuroception, a neural process that evaluates risk without requiring cognitive awareness (Porges, 2017, 2021). The episode in Palestine shows how the reference adult conveyed to children cues of safety via his facial expressions, vocal intonation and gesture, allowing them to have a sense of connectedness, co-regulate them, maintain a state of calm and resume playing. In addition, according to Polyvagal theory, indications of safety are reinforced by the characteristics of the space.

In Palestine the room could not be isolated from surrounding noise but included colourful toys and a variety of creative and expressive materials, and it offered the possibility to move freely in the space and to sit comfortably on the carpet. Another path is *active* and "requires conscious voluntary behaviors to trigger specific neural mechanisms that change physiological state" (Porges & Carter, 2017, p. 222). In this regard, it is worth emphasizing that play is an ideal neural exercise that allows children to alternate states of calm, uncertainty, alert, and calm again. In this way, play "improves the efficiency of the neural circuit that can instantaneously down-regulate fight/flight behaviors" (Porges, 2021). Moreover, "as the neural regulation of our social engagement system improves, we gain resilience in dealing with disruptions in our lives" (op. cit.). Equally important is to remember that "play itself is a process that mitigates the felt potency of trauma material" (Goodyear-Brown, 2010, p. 25). Among the most relevant Therapeutic Powers of Play (Schaefer & Drewes, 2014) in war contexts are self-expression, access to the unconscious, catharsis, abreaction, counterconditioning fears, stress inoculation, stress management and creative problem solving.

Understanding that play is the natural means of expression of children (Landreth, 2002) and their most instinctive and dynamic process of self-healing, the approach "Recovering lost play time (RLPT)" (Cassina, 2023) reminds us that forced migration, and war in general, can significantly limit children's ability, inclination and concrete possibility to play. Porges (2021), underlines "the effectiveness of the social engagement system to down-regulate fight/flight behaviors requires practice", and not all types of playful activities have the same value. Isolated play episodes, carried out individually and sometimes guided by electronic means, do not allow face-to-face regulation of the neural circuits that interrupt fight/flight behaviors. This makes it all the more significant to create the SaPE that can support children in reactivating, expanding and affirming their precious inclination to play through multiple, frequent and relevant sources such as caregivers.

The Challenge of Involving Caregivers to Enhance Children's Wellbeing

It was a September afternoon in 2009; the air was hot in the suburbs of Belgrade, Serbia. I (Isabella) was working for a local non-governmental organization providing humanitarian aid in shelters for Internally Displaced People. I was coming out of the last wooden one-room shack where a family of seven, spanning three generations, had been living for over twenty years. Power cables dangled from the roof and connected to a pole across the street. There was a smell of burnt plastic mixed with barbecued meat. "Do you know that everyone hates us here? It will be very difficult for me to find a job". Ivan was eight years old. We had known each other for a few weeks. While talking to me he looked into the void and made a repetitive movement with his right hand. "They dropped bombs on us, luckily they didn't hit us but they might try again, I don't trust anyone". To the rest of the world the Balkan Wars ended before he was born, but for him and his family it was as if time had stood still. In the shelters, adults and children talked about the same episodes from the past over and over again. They were always alert and chronically stressed. Their expressions were at times blank, frightened, angry and mistrustful. The number of people suffering from PTSD, anxiety, depression and psychosis was very high. It would have been very useful for me then to have my MAP (Mochi, 2022). I know today that I was only at the beginning of my awareness process.

Consequences of war and migration can last for many years after resettlement (Blackmore et al., 2020) and be transmitted for generations. The episode in Serbia gives us an idea that "the role of parental communication about the event and the nature of family functioning appear to be particularly important in trauma transmission" (American Psychological Association, 2022). A parent who has not had a chance to deal with the trauma may unintentionally pass it on to the next generation (Phillips in Menzies, 2010). Studies have found that trauma transmission can occur through attachment patterns (Castro-Vale et al., 2019). "When one experiences lack of attachment to one's primary caregivers, one can perceive oneself to be chronically in danger" (Porges, 2021). Although this makes the intervention more complex in terms of content, human resources and timing, it is further confirmation that the adult population, specifically caregivers, must have a primary role in shaping the SaPE for children.

In this regard, a first consideration is that "past trauma often leads to biased neuroception that detects risks when there is no risk" (Porges & Carter, 2017, p. 234) as happened in Serbia, and this limits the individual's ability to connect and co-regulate. It can take a long time before a relationship of trust can be established with caregivers, and the possibility to co-construct and undertake a process of wellbeing for the child becomes real. The interactions of humanitarian workers should be respectful of the process of stopping to give proper time and attention. Before directly involving caregivers in the playroom with children, it is essential to provide them with moments of sharing among adults, distraction and relaxation. The episode in Palestine illustrates that only when we activate our social engagement system and send safety cues can we become able to support others (Mochi, 2022). Over time, the encounters with caregivers will become more oriented towards direct support of children while maintaining a focus on adults' psychosocial wellbeing.

A second consideration is, as described for children, the spaces for caregivers and workers that receive them (e.g. professionals employed in shelters for refugee families in war zones or other destination countries) must be welcoming and reassuring to activate the *passive* path. To trigger the *active* path, a range of activities can be incorporated gradually according to the needs and rhythms of the individual and the group, considering cultural and gender aspects and any psychophysical difficulties. Activities can be playful (traditional and non-traditional), artistic and creative, musical, movement-based and breathing exercises. Play and expressive arts are powerful healing tools that "can provide children and their families and friends with a creative avenue for exploring their worries and psychological suffering induced by traumatic events" (Gil et al. cited in Byers, 2014, pp. 290–291).

Activity: "The Four Corners" by Isabella Cassina

The activity was developed initially for professionals working in crisis settings but proved to be effective as well in programs addressed to caregivers especially from an intermediate stage, when participants feel safe enough to consider a future perspective and are able to focus and open up with the practitioner and/or other participants. The activity, including the discussion, lasts about 45 minutes and can go up to 90 minutes or more with groups. In order to maintain a level of intimacy and give proper attention to the participants, we recommend not exceeding six persons.

Provide caregivers with blank sheets of paper and coloured pencils or markers. Invite them to identify a circumscribed challenge/difficulty they are experiencing at that moment and to represent it graphically, by means of a simple drawing or a selection of symbols, in the lower left-hand corner of the sheet. Once finished, invite them to think about their internal resources and represent them in the top left corner. Likewise, ask them to identify their external resources and to draw them in the bottom right-hand corner. The fourth corner, the top right corner, will be dedicated to areas for improvement: qualities and skills that could be nurtured and strengthened should be represented graphically.

The last space to fill is the centre of the sheet. Invite participants to think about the initial difficulty and represent the desirable solution in the middle of the sheet, considering all the elements already represented (i.e. internal and external resources and areas for improvement). Finally, you will ask the participants to share verbally what is depicted on the sheet to the extent they feel comfortable. A small variation can be suggested when handing over the blank sheet of paper at the beginning: folding the four corners to create hidden spaces in which to draw. Participants can decide whether to keep the corners closed during verbal sharing or to reveal one or more of the contents by opening the corners.

This activity allows the caregivers to have an insight into a current challenge. It can be the starting point for a personal reflection facilitated by the group leader, a moment of sharing, connection and mutual support between

Figure 9.1 An Example of "The Four Corners" Activity

participants. However, it can also be a guide for initiating change, moving from a passive to an active and empowering state (Levine, 2010). The activity can be repeated after some time to reflect on the representation and extent of the challenge, but also on the awareness and actual state of the person's internal and external resources.

Case Study: Dalia Recovering Her Lost Play Time

Dalia was three years old when she arrived at the reception centre for asylum seekers and refugees with her parents and two younger siblings. From the first meeting the educators had reported aggressive behaviour with peers and hyperactivity. Dalia was in a constant state of agitation and absolutely unable to concentrate. She played a sequence of two play actions at most before looking for another toy. Her mother showed signs of high anxiety and stress; she was physically and mentally exhausted and constantly on alert. She and her husband had lived in open conflict for years. They had decided to flee their home country when they were pregnant with their first child, Dalia. They reached the centre a few months after the birth of their third child. The journey had lasted over three years, during which the family had stayed in precarious conditions.

At first sight, the husband seemed to be less affected by the migration experience than his wife. He laughed in the corridors when he recounted blood-curdling episodes or vigorously explained to the other residents of the shelter his views on gender roles and the use of violence to settle scores. Dalia was almost always with him. I (Isabella) have always wondered about the line between the authentic self and the character he had sewn himself into in order to make sense of the atrocities he and his family had to face.

At the centre, a project aimed at psychosocial support for families called "Recovering Lost Play Time (RLPT)" (Cassina, 2023) had been in operation for a couple of years, which envisaged a series of possibilities including play therapy sessions. After sharing careful considerations, the multidisciplinary team proposed targeted support to the family. The mother seemed distant but relieved while the father was surprised and uneasy to be involved. He said he was not concerned about Dalia's aggressive behaviour; he felt she expressed character. Instead, he was upset that "she did not follow his directions and did not stand still for a moment".

For the planning and monitoring of the process we applied the RLPT chart (op. cit.) developed in 2013. The chart has four columns: in the first, the conditions, resources and limits of the child and family are indicated; in the second are the objectives for the child and family according to the observations made; the third lists "indicators", which are a series of quantifiable observations that allow the progress of the objectives inside and outside the playroom to be verified (indicators are very useful for sharing with the parents, to maintain their involvement and motivation in the process); in the fourth column, any other important information that can influence the family dynamics and wellbeing is listed.

Table 9.1 does not represent the totality of the information gathered in this case example but intends to make it understandable and to serve as an example for further applications. It is advisable to compile a chart at the beginning of the process and to insert any possible updates in a different colour.

It was not the time to include caregivers in the playroom. The mother was exhausted, stressed and scared, and the father did not seem fit yet. He was agitated and caught up in a thousand other thoughts. However, for the wellbeing of Dalia and her siblings, they both had to contribute in forging the SaPE. The child's most pressing needs and the parents' limited availability made us apply child-centered play therapy (more on this methodology in Chapter 14) with Dalia and develop a tailored parallel program for parents. Based on the indications included in Table 9.1, we consider it relevant to share two non-directive sessions.

In the second session Dalia enters the room with determination and walks towards the medical kit. She takes a bandage and tries to wrap it around her ankle then changes her mind and tries to put it on my wrist with little conviction. She takes a deep breath and drops to the floor dramatically, making a thud and exclaiming: "Ah!". I have the feeling that this is an invitation to play: "Oh, no! Something has happened! Let's see if I can find something I can help you with!". I approach her arm and pretend to fix something. Dalia says nothing, sits up again, looks me in the eye and suddenly falls back down in the same way. "Oh, no! This time I'll put a bandage on this foot!". Dalia stands up, looks around and throws herself back down on the floor with the same emphasis: "Ah!". I rescue her again with the medical kit, but she, without speaking, points to another tool, and I proceed accordingly. In this session Dalia will throw herself to the ground and allow herself to be rescued dozens of times, always with the same intensity and conviction and the same attention to my movements and rescue attempts. In the last couple of minutes, Dalia takes a stuffed snake almost two metres long, makes it slither across the room and then brings it close to my cheek making the sound of a kiss.

Table 9.1 Recovering Lost Play Time Chart (RLPT Chart)

Observations	Goals	Indicators	Other
Dalia (3 yrs.): – Good mastery of her body, movements and confidence in spaces – Poor verbal and non-verbal communication skills – Hyperactivity and lack of attention – Repetitive play and no more than two play actions in sequence – Lack of self-regulation and aggressive behaviour with peers and siblings **Mother:** – Highly stressed and exhausted (mainly takes care of the two younger siblings) – Strong reactions to noises (always on the alert) **Father:** – Spends a lot of time with Dalia in adult contexts where rhythms and content are not child-friendly – Promotes aggressive and violent behaviours as symbol of strength	**Dalia:** – Down-regulate her mobilized defence system – Improve verbal and non-verbal communication skills – Increase attention skills – Develop imaginary play – Decrease aggressive behaviour – Express and process strong emotions – Increase self-regulation – Have the possibility to relax and amuse **Mother:** – Relieve anxiety and stress – Decrease tiredness – Create moments for self-care **Father:** – Increase awareness of child health and developmental needs – Strengthen parenting/educational skills (focus on providing experiences of safety)	**Dalia:** – Has the number of aggressive episodes with peers decreased? – Has her focus time increased? How much and under what circumstances? – Has her vocabulary expanded? In what direction and under what conditions? – Have the number of play actions increased? – Does she seem more relaxed and laugh more? How much and in what occasions? **Mother:** – Does she practise breathing exercises regularly? – Have her reactions to noises changed, and how? – Does she feel less stressed and tired? **Father:** – Does he apply the psycho-educational skills learnt? Which ones, how often and in what contexts?	**Brother (1.5 yrs.):** – Started to have aggressive reactions, especially towards the mother. The situation was reported by the mother to the multidisciplinary team. **Father:** – Applied for a part-time employment programme outside the centre. This implies a likely additional pressure for his wife and a sudden change in Dalia's routine.

Nine weeks later, in the eleventh session, Dalia enters the room and immediately takes a sword for herself and another she gives to me, saying: "Let's go to Bah!", signalling for me to follow her. Although I do not know this character, I easily guess that he is someone to fight. In the first part of the session, Dalia repeatedly asks me to follow her to fight this character, who is very scary. We use the sword, throw objects at him and threaten him with words. At one point Dalia picks up the phone and calls the police, explaining that there is a "Bah" in the room, but the police will never arrive. She then takes a doll house, closes the doors and windows and gathers all sorts of weapons. Meanwhile "Bah" has returned, so Dalia gives me back my sword and asks me to fight with her. Later she puts on a soft cloth hat with pink ears and scares me by roaring and spreading her hands as wide as she can towards me. She takes off the hat and says smilingly: "That's me!". She repeats this sequence three times and does it again after about ten minutes. Each time I get scared, and she reassures me. The sequence reminds me of peek-a-boo led by the child. Suddenly she slips under a small table and says: "This is my house, come!" I can only stick my head inside. Dalia is not satisfied, so she looks for another solution: she empties a box and sits in it. She asks me to bring her all the weapons and to come in too. Again, I only manage to get my feet in. She comes up with another idea: taking a black cloth, sitting me next to the box and putting it on top of us. Every so often she removes the cloth and with the binoculars checks to see whether the "Bah" is still there. He is actually in the room, so we fight him together until the end of the session.

Dalia's path allowed her to express and meet different relevant needs and was characterized by a gradual openness to possibilities and alliance with the therapist. The safety cues transmitted by the playroom, me, and play as therapy made it possible for her to start expressing and exploring strong emotions, improve communication skills and self-regulation, and develop complex sequences of imaginary play. With time, aggressive episodes towards peers also decreased. In parallel, through moments of sharing, music and painting, and the practice of breathing exercises in little groups, the mother was able to start experiencing a way of getting in touch with and managing her emotions and needs. This resulted in a feeling of greater control and relaxation from which the children also benefited. The father began grasping the extent of his influence on his children's wellbeing by participating with other fathers in dedicated moments with a playful atmosphere. He started introducing more predictability into Dalia's daily life and limiting less-appropriate expectations. He had even introduced occasional brief moments of play with her, mainly using toy cars, but it was definitely a noteworthy step.

Conclusion

The destructive scope of war has no limits of space or time. This aspect should prompt us to think about interventions for children that extend in and out of the playroom, involving caregivers as much as possible. We would like to conclude the chapter by sharing some.

 Treatment Takeaways

- The avalanche metaphor supports us in understanding the destructive process triggered by war. Not only are children deeply affected by war, but so are their caregivers with the risk of intergenerational trauma.
- The Polyvagal theory supports the approach of coping with the present while building for the future (CPBF), which indicates that the starting point for children and adults is restoring a feeling of safety even in contexts where physical safety cannot be guaranteed such as war.
- In developing the safest possible environment (SaPE), the passive and active paths as illustrated by the Polyvagal theory should be considered so that the neural regulation of the social engagement system of children and caregivers can improve, promoting resilience and wellbeing.
- Play, with its therapeutic powers, is a fundamental neural exercise but, as indicated by the recovering lost play time (RLPT) approach and supported by the Polyvagal theory, it must be (re)activated and promoted as many times as possible through the involvement of trusted and relevant people in the person's life.

References

American Psychological Association. (2022). Intergenerational trauma. *APA Dictionary of Psychology*. https://dictionary.apa.org/intergenerational-trauma.

Blackmore, R., Boyle, J. A., Fazel, M., Ranasinha, S., Gray, K. M., Fitzgerald, G., Misso, M., & Gibson-Helm, M. (2020). The prevalence of mental illness in refugees and asylum seekers: A systematic review and meta-analysis. *PLOS Medicine, 17*(9).

Byers, J. (2014). Integrating play and expressive art therapy into communities: A multimodal approach. In E. J. Green & A. A. Drewes (Eds.), *Integrating expressive arts and play therapy with children and adolescents* (pp. 283–301). Wiley.

Cassina, I. (2023). Recovering lost play time. Principles and intervention modalities to address the psychosocial wellbeing of asylum seekers and refugee children. In I. Cassina, C. Mochi, & K. Stagnitti (Eds.), *Play therapy and expressive arts in a complex and dynamic world: Opportunities and challenges inside and outside the playroom* (pp. 50–68). Routledge.

Cassina, I., & Mochi, C. (2023). Applying the therapeutic power of play and expressive arts in contemporary crisis work. A process-oriented approach. In I. Cassina, C. Mochi, & K. Stagnitti (Eds.), *Play therapy and expressive arts in a complex and dynamic world: Opportunities and challenges inside and outside the playroom* (pp. 6–27). Routledge.

Castro-Vale, I., Severo, M., Carvalho, D., & Mota-Cardoso, R. (2019). Intergenerational transmission of war-related trauma assessed 40 years after exposure. *Annals of General Psychiatry, 18*(14).

Goodyear-Brown, P. (2010). *Play therapy with traumatized children: A prescriptive approach.* Wiley.

Landreth, G. L. (2002). *Play therapy: The art of the relationship* (2nd ed.). Brunner/Routledge.

Levine, P. A. (2010). *In an unspoken voice: How the body releases trauma and restores goodness.* North Atlantic Books.

Menzies, P. (2010). Intergenerational trauma from a mental health perspective. *Native Social Work Journal, 7,* 63–85.

Mochi, C. (2009). Trauma repetition: Intervention in psychological safe places. *Eastern Journal of Psychiatry, 12*(1–2), 75–80.

Mochi, C. (2022). *Beyond the clouds: An autoethnographic research exploring the good practice in crisis settings.* Loving Healing Press.

Porges, S. W. (2021). *Polyvagal safety: Attachment, communication, self-regulation* (IPNB). Norton. www.amazon.com.

Porges, S. W., & Carter, C. S. (2017). Polyvagal theory and the social engagement system. Neurophysiological bridge between connectedness and health. In P. L. Gerbarg, P. R. Muskin, & R. P. Brown (Eds.), *Complementary and integrative treatments in psychiatric practice* (pp. 221–239). American Psychiatric Association Publishing.

Sangalang, C. C., & Vang, C. (2017). Intergenerational trauma in refugee families: A systematic review. *Journal of Immigrant and Minority Health, 19,* 745–754.

Schaefer, C. E., & Drewes, A. A. (2014). *The therapeutic powers of play: 20 core agents of change* (2nd ed.). Wiley.

United Nations. (2022a, December 26). 2022 Year in review: 100 million displaced, 'a record that should never have been set'. *UN News*. https://news.un.org/en/story/2022/12/1131957.

United Nations. (2022b, June 17). A record 37 million children displaced worldwide: UNICEF. *UN News*. https://news.un.org/en/story/2022/06/1120642

van der Kolk, B. (2014). *The body keeps the score: Mind, brain and body in the transformation of trauma*. Penguin.

10

Anxiety, the Autonomic Nervous System, and Play as the Mechanism of Change

Lynn Louise Wonders

Overview

All humans experience anxiety at some point. Anxiety involves behavioral, emotional, and cognitive reactions to a perceived danger or threat (Trivedi & Gupta, 2010). It is a normal part of childhood to occasionally feel fearful, nervous, and worried (Bhatia & Goyal, 2018), but when a child's anxiety does not match the triggering events and there is impaired functioning, therapeutic treatment is in order. Anxiety disorders are the most commonly diagnosed childhood problems (Bhatia & Goyal, 2018). Since the COVID-19 pandemic began, one in five children is diagnosed with an anxiety disorder (Racine et al., 2021). The most common are generalized anxiety disorder, separation anxiety disorder, social phobias, and specific phobias. Less-common anxiety disorders include obsessive compulsive disorder, selective mutism, and body-focused repetitive behavior disorders such as trichotillomania.

Children suffering with anxiety disorders will commonly have an emotional shift along with physical symptoms rather than expressing their worries verbally, as do adults (Sharma et al., 2011). These integrated emotional and physical responses are due to connection between the autonomic nervous system and the limbic area in the brain (Mulkey & Plessis, 2019). Understanding neuroscience, and specifically Polyvagal theory, can inform the practice of play therapy in the treatment of childhood anxiety disorders (Ayling, 2019).

DOI: 10.4324/9781003352976-10

Neuroscience and Polyvagal Theory Related to Childhood Anxiety

Sharma et al. (2011) found more autonomic nervous system (ANS) activity and reactivity in children who were diagnosed with anxiety disorders than children with no anxiety disorder. The ANS is responsible for functions of the heart, lungs, blood pressure, and digestion. The limbic system is responsible for processing emotions and memories. The ANS and the limbic system, together, govern neuropsychiatric status and physical responses (Montagna & Nosarti, 2016).

As shown in Figure 10.1, the ANS has two sub-systems. The sympathetic nervous system, most often associated with hyperarousal, commonly referred to as "fight or flight", responds to a perceived threat of danger. The parasympathetic nervous system has two branches. The ventral vagal branch, often known as "rest and digest", helps one to feel safe while navigating daily challenges, engaging in positive relationships, and experiencing an embodied, grounded state (Porges, 2001). The ventral vagal branch assists in moderating sympathetic responses (Wehrwein et al., 2016). The other branch of the parasympathetic system is the dorsal vagus branch, providing a shut-down or "freeze response" in response to perceived danger, manifesting as immobility and slowing of bodily functions (Montagna & Nosarti, 2016). The intricate responsiveness of the ANS is based on interactions between these two sub-systems of the ANS (Ondicova & Mravec, 2010). When examining the effects of anxiety, it is important to understand both sub-systems and how one can affect the other (Sharma et al., 2011).

When an anxiety-evoking event occurs, the amygdala in the limbic system is activated, sending chemical and pulmonary messages to the ANS, resulting in a sympathetic arousal response. Changes in heart rate, respiratory rate, and blood pressure ensue (Montagna & Nosarti, 2016; Chokroverty & Bhat, 2021). When a child is in a sympathetic state, those physical responses will often be amplified through further physical symptoms such as stomach and digestive discomfort, shaking, sweating, or muscle tension along with emotion dysregulation (Sharma et al., 2011).

Anxiety occurs with an absence of feeling safe. Polyvagal theory provides a scientific explanation for how the nervous system perceives and reacts to safety and danger (Nicolaou, 2022; Dana & Porges, 2018). Porges (2001) explains that the physical, environmental, and social experiences humans have occur through the vagus nerve. Vagal development begins to impact social behavior, mood regulation, and behavioral states as early as six months

The Polyvagal Theory Map of the Autonomic Nervous System

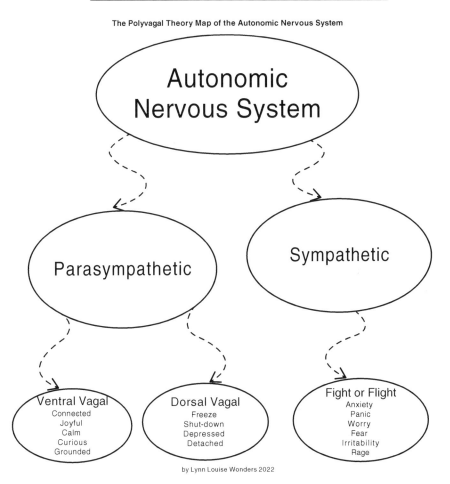

by Lynn Louise Wonders 2022

Figure 10.1 Map of the Autonomic Nervous System

of age (Porges & Furman, 2011). Anxiety disorders are impacted by low vagal tone or high levels of vagal reactivity (Beauchaine et al., 2007) typically characterized by the activation of the sympathetic system and the deactivation of the parasympathetic system (Kreibig, 2010). Polyvagal theory provides a framework for understanding how engaging the parasympathetic system can help regulate sympathetic arousal (Hastings et al., 2008), reducing anxiety symptoms and increasing positive social connections. Therapeutic interventions that focus on the vagus nerve can help to increase vagal tone and inhibit inflammatory chemicals from flaring in the brain and body (Breit et al., 2018).

With the perception of threat, the limbic center and the sympathetic nervous system are both activated, making it difficult if not impossible for a child to engage in cognitive processing (Ayling, 2019). If the child's ventral vagus branch of the parasympathetic system is activated, however, it is possible for the body and mind to experience trust, connection, and safety (Perry, 1999; Crenshaw, 2006; Van der Kolk, 2006; Siegel & Bryson, 2012; Pittman & Karle, 2015). Play therapy can provide children experiences of safety through socially engaged connection and play-based regulatory and coping activities.

Integrating Play Therapy and Polyvagal Theory

Symptom management is a significant focus of treatment planning with anxiety disorders. While literature supports cognitive behavioral therapy as the most preferred for treating anxiety (Curtiss et al., 2021), children respond best when they are engaged using their natural language of play (Landreth, 2002). Play therapy provides an opportunity for children to explore, express, and experience whatever it is they need in the emotional safety and playful environment provided by a trained mental health professional (Wonders, 2022). Integrating neurobiology with play therapy emphasizes the role of safe, connected, and therapeutic relationship, essential to nervous system regulation (Hadiprodjo, 2018; Wheeler & Dillman Taylor, 2016). Effective regulation of nervous system responses and emotions is essential for children's healthy development (Eisenberg & Sulik, 2011). As seen in Figure 10.2, if the cycle of anxiety is left unaddressed, children typically develop entrenched patterns of avoidant behaviors that ultimately perpetuate and intensify symptoms (Widdowson, 2014). If, however, a child can shift from sympathetic arousal to a ventral vagal parasympathetic response through playful engagement and practice of regulatory coping skills, anxiety symptoms will decrease (Kendall et al., 2016).

The Therapeutic Powers of Play

Figure 10.3 illustrates the powers of play as mechanisms that activate healthy changes with a child's thinking, feeling, and behaving (Schaefer & Drewes, 2014). Therapeutic play fosters emotional wellness by facilitating positive emotions, counterconditioning fears, inoculating stress, and learning to manage stress symptoms (Schaefer & Peabody, 2016). These powers of play can be facilitated prescriptively and experienced through both child-centered play therapy (CCPT) and cognitive behavioral play therapy (CBPT).

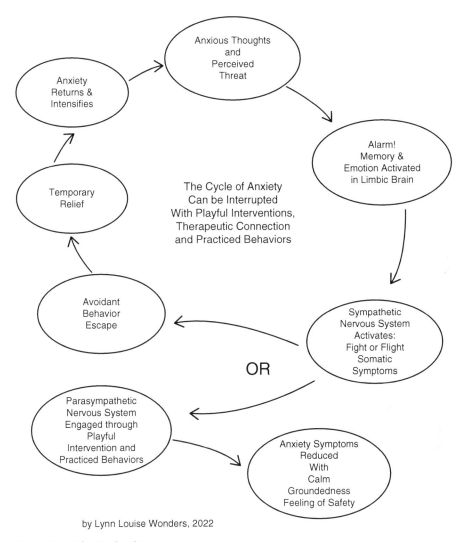

by Lynn Louise Wonders, 2022

Figure 10.2 The Cycle of Anxiety

CCPT provides interactive relationship-centered engagement, co-regulation, and expanded experiences of nervous system regulation emphasized in Polyvagal theory (Conroy & Perryman, 2022). CBPT is specifically effective in treating childhood anxiety disorders (Mohammadinia et al., 2018; Knell & Dasari, 2016). Cognitive restructuring interventions alone are ineffective in reducing a child's anxiety symptoms; rather, the use of learned coping skills through CBPT more effectively reduces symptoms (Kendall et al., 2016).

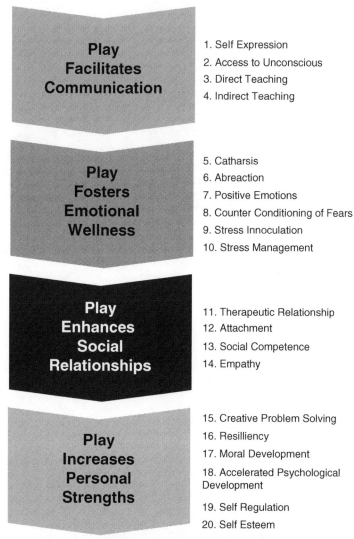

Play Facilitates Communication	1. Self Expression 2. Access to Unconscious 3. Direct Teaching 4. Indirect Teaching
Play Fosters Emotional Wellness	5. Catharsis 6. Abreaction 7. Positive Emotions 8. Counter Conditioning of Fears 9. Stress Innoculation 10. Stress Management
Play Enhances Social Relationships	11. Therapeutic Relationship 12. Attachment 13. Social Competence 14. Empathy
Play Increases Personal Strengths	15. Creative Problem Solving 16. Resilliency 17. Moral Development 18. Accelerated Psychological Development 19. Self Regulation 20. Self Esteem

Graphic Design by Lynn Louise Wonders, 2021
Content Credit Dr. Charles Schaefer and Dr. Athena Drewes
Permission Granted by Dr. Athena Drewes

Figure 10.3 Therapeutic Powers of Play

In addition to the connection and safety experienced within the therapeutic relationship, directive play-based interventions that help a child shift into the ventral vagal state can regulate sympathetic hyper-arousal symptoms. This shift can be achieved through a combination of: 1) CCPT tenets (Figure 10.4) for establishing and maintaining relational safety and

Axline's 8 Tenets of Child Centered Play Therapy

1. Develop a warm, friendly rapport with the child as soon as possible.

2. Accept the child just as they are.

3. Allow the child to express themselves freely and completely by establishing a sense of permissiveness.

4. Recognize the feelings the child expresses and reflects those them back to the client in a way that allows the client to gain insight into his/her own behavior.

5. Maintain and communicate a deep respect for the child's ability to solve problems, make choices, and institute change.

6. Allow the child to lead the way in all aspects of therapy, refraining from directing the child's play in any way.

7. Allow the therapy process to develop at its natural pace without being hurried in any way.

8. Establish limitations only when necessary to anchor the therapy to reality and with therapeutic benefit that provides insight into the child's aware of his/her responsibility in the relationship.

Axline, V.M. (1969). Play therapy. Ballantine Books.

Figure 10.4 Axline's Eight Tenets of Child-Centered Play Therapy
Source: Axline, V. M. (1969). *Play Therapy.* Ballantine Books.

connectedness in the playroom; 2) facilitative CBPT interventions for coping strategies and addressing anxious thoughts; 3) therapeutic coregulatory experiences in the playroom; and 4) caregiver involvement.

Use of Child-Centered Play Therapy with Anxiety

In CCPT, the therapeutic relationship provides a safe, consistent, and connected experience for the child. That connective relationship is the factor that contributes to meaningful and positive change (Ray, 2019). CCPT theory says that within this relationship the child will naturally move toward integration and resolution of presenting problems (Landreth, 2002). Research outcomes demonstrate that CCPT leads to reduction of symptomatic behaviors and improved functioning (Bratton, 2015; Stulmaker & Ray, 2015). The use of CCPT in the beginning of therapy allows for the essential elements of trust and connectedness to be developed.

Figure 10.4 shows Virginia Axline's Eight Tenets of CCPT (Axline, 1969). When the therapist practices these tenets, the child experiences freedom to explore and express without judgment or evaluation. This helps the child to enter a ventral vagal parasympathetic state (Conroy & Perryman, 2022). Through unencumbered play in the presence of an accepting and attentive therapist, children can express thoughts, feelings, and fantasies, and exercise their creativity for dealing with the triggers for their anxiety (Setyowati & Pandin, 2021).

Use of Cognitive Behavioral Play Therapy (CBPT) with Anxiety

CBPT is most effective when practiced on a foundation and maintenance of a connected, trusting, therapeutic relationship (Knell & Dasari, 2016). With rapport and trust, the therapist can offer facilitative play therapy interventions (Fountain, 2022). The aim of CBPT is to facilitate change in an anxious child's patterns of thoughts and behaviors to support symptom management (Knell, 2022).

Literature confirms the usefulness of therapeutic strategies and skills to reduce somatic symptoms (Alkozei et al., 2015). Through CBPT, the therapist can model and introduce methods for inducing a relaxation response. Such techniques may involve playful breathing activities, guided imagery, coloring, painting, or games for slowing down and relaxing. Once a child has shifted to a ventral vagal state, CBPT may also include puppet play, stories, bibliotherapy, and games that challenge a child's anxious thoughts and beliefs for the purpose of cognitive restructuring.

Caregiver Involvement

Children are most often part of a family system. With the recent growing prevalence and popularity of attachment theory-based models including TheraPlay®, FirstPlay®, relational models such as Child-Parent Relationship Therapy, Filial Therapy, and the emphasis on including parents in CCPT (Ray, 2021), caregiver involvement is widely supported in a child's treatment. In addition to conducting a careful intake process with caregivers, the child's therapist can provide parent-child sessions that include attachment-based games and activities to strengthen the parent-child bond and, thereby, fortify a felt sense of safety for the child. The use of nature, art, movement, and mindfulness practices in therapy with families promotes meaningful connection, safety, healing, and growth for children (Courtney, 2020).

Play therapy that includes family cooperation can minimize or reduce the child's anxiety and stress symptoms (Setyowati & Pandin, 2021). Ritblatt and Longstreth (2019) note that anxious children often feel emotionally insecure in new settings with new people. By including a child's caregiver in the first therapy session(s) the child can feel safe in the playroom with the therapist (Wonders, 2020). Bringing parents into the playroom can also provide an opportunity for the therapist to observe relationship dynamics, further informing case conceptualization (Goodyear-Brown, 2021). With CBPT, a child and the caregivers can work as a team at home between therapy sessions to track triggers, frequency, and intensity of symptoms, which will enhance treatment outcomes (Breinholst et al., 2012).

Case Example

Joanie was eight years of age. She was tearful, complaining of stomachaches and headaches before and during her school days. Joanie was unable to sleep alone at night. The pediatrician ruled out medical causes and referred Joanie for therapy. The therapist conducted a thorough intake process with Joanie's parents. Joanie had started going to school for the first time that year after having been homeschooled. She appeared panicked when her mother attempted to leave Joanie in someone else's care. When Joanie arrived at the therapist's office for the first time, she clung to her mother, staring at the floor. Knowing it was important for Joanie to feel safe and secure in the playroom, the therapist invited Joanie to bring her mom with her. Joanie appeared to relax.

The therapist had formed a working diagnosis of separation anxiety disorder. For the first five sessions Joanie's mother came into the playroom with Joanie. Joanie engaged her mother in her play, and by the third session began including the therapist. The mother and the therapist, together, planned to allow Joanie a chance to become comfortable with the therapist and the playroom and then have Joanie's mother incrementally spend less time in the playroom each week until Joanie could tolerate having her mother stay in the waiting room for the entire session. The therapist used a colorful chime-timer the child helped to set each week, and when the timer went off, the therapist, the child, and the mother recited a playful rhyme called "See Ya Later Alligator" as the mother left the playroom. This was graduated exposure, a behavioral therapy technique proven effective with separation anxiety disorder (Hagopian & Slifer, 1993; Schneider et al., 2022).

The therapist used CCPT for several weeks, tracking and reflecting Joanie's choices and action in the playroom to help Joanie feel empowered to explore while feeling seen and heard by the therapist. For several sessions in a row, Joanie went to the sand tray. She proceeded to scoop and move the sand from one end of the tray to the other, leaving an empty blue-bottomed section visible where she placed a tiny frog figure. Next, she moved all the sand back, covering the frog and left the tray to move on to another activity. Later Joanie repeated the burying of the tiny frog, but this time she plunged her hand quickly down into the sand and pulled the tiny frog out, dusted it off, and smiled triumphantly. Joanie was beginning to feel a sense of hope and empowerment related to her anxiety symptoms. The therapist introduced a specific ritual (Kenney-Noziska, 2008) at the end of each session, inviting Joanie to show the therapist how big her worries felt each week by pouring a relative quantity of dried macaroni noodles into the empty worry bowl to indicate the size and volume of her worries. Over time the number of noodles decreased more and more.

By the eighth session Joanie was separating from her mother in the waiting room with ease and feeling comfortable in the playroom. The therapist ensured Joanie was in a ventral vagal state and began including psychoeducation and CBPT facilitative techniques. Through bibliotherapy, puppet play, breathing games, and creative activities, Joanie learned about anxiety and how to manage her symptoms. Joanie and her parents were encouraged to practice together between sessions.

Parent sessions were conducted monthly. After 15 play therapy sessions with Joanie's mother staying in the waiting room, both parents reported with delight that Joanie was employing her newfound skills and was having fewer symptoms at bedtime and before school. Joanie's playfully facilitated coping skills were reinforced both in sessions and with practice at home that included her parents. When it was time for termination of therapy, Joanie and the therapist reviewed the fun experiences and all the coping skills she had learned in the playroom with a celebratory game of blowing and popping bubbles. Joanie appeared self-confident and empowered to use her skills, and she proudly reported she was experiencing fewer anxiety symptoms.

Conclusion

Through the lens of Polyvagal theory, anxiety represents an absence of perceived safety, and a resulting activation of the autonomic nervous system with a dysregulating effect impedes normal functioning. On a foundation of a trusting therapeutic alliance, play serves as the mechanism of change through which children experience a restoration to a felt sense of safety through reduction of anxiety symptoms and a sense of empowerment to manage symptoms of anxiety as they arise. Caregiver involvement can aid the child's progress through co-regulation and reinforcing at home the therapeutic progress experienced in session.

 Treatment Takeaways

- Anxiety is the experience of not feeling safe. Polyvagal theory provides a lens through which to understand the child's mental, emotional, and physical experiences of danger or threat.
- It's important to establish and maintain a therapeutic relationship grounded in play to provide the experience of safe, engaged connection.
- Directive interventions aimed at symptom reduction are best introduced after the trusted relationship between therapist and child is well-established and the child is in a ventral vagal state.
- Counterconditioning fears, inoculating stress, and employing symptom management strategies can be achieved through facilitative play therapy activities that engage the ventral vagal state and induce a relaxation response.
- Caregivers can be instrumental in the implementation of treatment strategies during, between, and after therapy sessions.

References

Alkozei, A., Creswell, C., Cooper, P. J., & Allen, J. J. B. (2015). Autonomic arousal in childhood anxiety disorders: Associations with state anxiety and social anxiety disorder. *Journal of Affective Disorders, 175*, 25–33.

Axline, V. M. (1969). *Play therapy*. Ballantine Books.

Ayling, P. (2019). Containing feelings and setting limits in play therapy: Working with aggression. In *Becoming and being a play therapist* (pp. 122–136). Routledge.

Beauchaine, T., Gatzke-Kopp, L., & Mead, H. (2007). Polyvagal theory and developmental psychopathology: Emotion dysregulation and conduct problems from preschool to adolescence. *Biological Psychology, 74*, 174–184.

Bhatia, M., & Goyal, A. (2018). Anxiety disorders in children and adolescents: Need for early detection. *Journal of Postgraduate Medicine, 64*(2), 75–76.

Bratton, S. C. (2015). The empirical support for play therapy: Strengths and limitations. *Handbook of Play Therapy*, 651–668.

Breinholst, S., Esbjorn, B. H., Reinholdt-Dunne, M., & Stallard, P. (2012). CBT for the treatment of child anxiety disorders: A review of why parental involvement has not enhanced outcomes. *Journal of Anxiety Disorders, 26*, 416–424.

Breit, S., Kupferberg, A., Rogler, G., & Hasler, G. (2018). Vagus nerve as modulator of the brain–gut axis in psychiatric and inflammatory disorders. *Frontiers in Psychiatry, 9*.

Chokroverty, S., & Bhat, S. (2021). Functional neuroanatomy of the peripheral autonomic nervous system. In *Autonomic nervous system and sleep* (pp. 19–28). Springer.

Conroy, J., & Perryman, K. (2022). Treating trauma with child-centered play therapy through the SECURE lens of Polyvagal theory. *International Journal of Play Therapy, 31*(3), 143.

Courtney, J. A. (2020). *Healing child and family trauma through expressive and play therapies: Art, nature, storytelling, body & mindfulness*. Norton.

Crenshaw, D. (2006). Neuroscience and trauma treatment. In L. Carey (Ed.), *Expressive and creative arts methods for trauma survivors* (pp. 21–38). Jessica Kingsley.

Curtiss, J. E., Levine, D. S., Ander, I., & Baker, A. W. (2021). Cognitive-behavioral treatments for anxiety and stress-related disorders. *FOCUS, 19*(2), 184–189.

Dana, D., & Porges, S. W. (2018). *The Polyvagal theory in therapy: Engaging the rhythm of regulation*. Norton et Company.

Eisenberg, N., & Sulik, M. J. (2011). Emotion-related self-regulation in children. *Teaching of Psychology, 39*(1), 77–83.

Fountain, A. (2022). *Cognitive behavioral play therapy*. Dr. Angela Fountain & Associates. Retrieved November 24, 2022, from www.drfountain.ca/cognitive-behavioural-play-therapy.com

Goodyear-Brown, P. (2021). *Parents as partners in child therapy: A Clinician's guide*. Guilford.

Hadiprodjo, N. (2018). *Clinical applications of the Polyvagal theory and attachment theory to play therapy for children with developmental trauma* [Doctoral dissertation, University of Roehampton].

Hagopian, L. P., & Slifer, K. J. (1993). Treatment of separation anxiety disorder with graduated exposure and reinforcement targeting school attendance: A controlled case study. *Journal of Anxiety Disorders*, 7(3), 271–280.

Hastings, P. D., Nuselovici, J. N., Utendale, W. T., Coutya, J., McShane, K. E., & Sullivan, C. (2008). Applying the Polyvagal theory to children's emotion regulation: Social context, socialization, and adjustment. *Biological Psychology*, 79(3), 299–306.

Kendall, P. C., Cummings, C. M., Villabø, M. A., Narayanan, M. K., Treadwell, K., Birmaher, B., Compton, S., Piacentini, J., Sherrill, J., Walkup, J., Gosch, E., Keeton, C., Ginsburg, G., Suveg, C., & Albano, A. M. (2016). Mediators of change in the child/adolescent anxiety multimodal treatment study. *Journal of Consulting and Clinical Psychology*, 84(1), 1–14.

Kenney-Noziska, S. (2008). *Techniques- techniques- techniques: Play-based activities for children, adolescents, and families.* Infinity Publishing.com.

Knell, S. M. (2022). Cognitive behavioral play therapy. In *Creative CBT with youth* (pp. 65–82). Springer.

Knell, S. M., & Dasari, M. (2016). Cognitive-behavioral play therapy for anxiety and depression. In L. A. Reddy, T. M. Files-Hall, & C. E. Schaefer (Eds.), *Empirically based play interventions for children* (pp. 77–94). American Psychological Association.

Kreibig, S. D. (2010). Autonomic nervous system activity in emotion: A review. *Biological Psychology*, 84, 394–421.

Landreth, G. (2002). Play therapy: The art of the relationship. *Brunner-Routledge. Professional Psychology: Research and Practice*, 33, 515–522.

Mohammadinia, N., Fatemi, F.-S., Nasiri, M., & Pirnia, B. (2018). The effectiveness of cognitive-behavioral play therapy on anxiety and academic achievement among children with LD. *International Journal of Applied Behavioral Sciences*, 5(1), 41–48.

Montagna, A., & Nosarti, C. (2016). Socio-emotional development following very preterm birth: Pathways to psychopathology. *Frontiers in Psychology*, 7, 80.

Mulkey, S. B., & du Plessis, A. J. (2019). Autonomic nervous system development and its impact on neuropsychiatric outcome. *Pediatric Research*, 85(2), 120–126.

Nicolaou, D. (2022). *The Polyvagal theory in our understanding of safety and danger: How our body holds on to our experiences* [Dissertation, University of Padova].

Ondicova, K., & Mravec, B. (2010). Multilevel interactions between the sympathetic and parasympathetic nervous systems: A minireview. *Endocrine Regulations*, 44, 69–75.

Perry, B. (1999). Memories of fear. In *Splintered reflections* (pp. 9–38). Basic Books.

Pittman, C. M., & Karle, E. M. (2015). *Rewire your anxious brain: How to use the neuroscience of fear to end anxiety, panic, and worry.* New Harbinger Publications.

Porges, S. (2001). The Polyvagal theory: Phylogenetic substrates of a social nervous system. *International Journal of Psychophysiology, 42,* 123–146.

Porges, S., & Furman, S. (2011). The early development of the autonomic nervous system provides a neural platform for social behavior: A polyvagal perspective. *Infant and Child Development, 20,* 106–118.

Racine, N., McArthur, B. A., Cooke, J. E., Eirich, R., Zhu, J., & Madigan, S. (2021). Global prevalence of depressive and anxiety symptoms in children and adolescents during COVID-19: A meta-analysis. *JAMA Pediatrics, 175*(11), 1142–1150.

Ray, D. (2019). The child and the counselor: Relational humanism in the playroom and beyond. *The Journal of Humanistic Counseling, 58*(1), 68–82.

Ray, D. C. (2021). *Advanced play therapy essential conditions, knowledge, and skills for child practice.* Routledge.

Ritblatt, S. N., & Longstreth, S. (2019). Understanding young children's play. *National Association for the Education of Young Children, 74*(2). 78–85.

Schaefer, C., & Peabody, M. (2016). Glossary of play therapy terms. *Play Therapy,* 20–24.

Schaefer, C. E., & Drewes, A. A. (2014). *The therapeutic powers of play: 20 core agents of change.* Wiley.

Schneider, S., Pflug, V., & Lavallee, K. L. (2022). Applying exposure therapy with children. In *Clinical guide to exposure therapy* (pp. 221–237). Springer International Publishing. https://doi.org/10.1007/978-3-031-04927-9_12

Setyowati, W. E., & Pandin, M. G. (2021). *Play therapy to reduce anxiety in children.* https://doi.org/10.20944/preprints202104.0148.v1

Sharma, R. K., Sagar, R., Deepak, K. K., Mehta, M., & Balhara, Y. P. (2011, May–June). Clinical and autonomic functions: A study of childhood anxiety disorders. *Annals of Saudi Medicine, 31*(3), 250–257.

Siegel, D. J., & Bryson, P. H. D. T. P. (2012). *The whole-brain child.* Random House.

Stulmaker, H. L., & Ray, D. C. (2015). Child-centered play therapy with young children who are anxious: A controlled trial. *Children and Youth Services Review, 57,* 127–133.

Trivedi, J. K., & Gupta, P. K. (2010). An overview of Indian research in anxiety disorders. *Indian Journal of Psychiatry, 52*(7), 210.

Van der Kolk, B. A. (2006). Clinical implications of neuroscience research in PTSD. *Annals of the New York Academy of Sciences, 1071*(1), 277–293.

Wehrwein, E. A., Orer, H. S., & Barman, S. M. (2016). Overview of the anatomy, physiology, and pharmacology of the autonomic nervous system. *Comprehensive Physiology*, 1239–1278.

Wheeler, N., & Dillman Taylor, D. (2016). Integrating interpersonal neurobiology with play therapy. *International Journal of Play Therapy*, 25(1), 24.

Widdowson, M. (2014). Avoidance, vicious cycles, and experiential disconfirmation of script. *Transactional Analysis Journal*, 44(3), 194–207.

Wonders, L. L. (2020). Play therapy for children with selective mutism. In H. G. Kaduson, D. Cangelosi, & C. E. Schaefer (Eds.), *Prescriptive play therapy: Tailoring interventions for specific childhood problems* (pp. 92–104). The Guilford Press.

Wonders, L. L. (2022). https://wonderscounseling.com/helping-parents-understand-how-and-why-play-therapy-works/

11

Polyvagal Theory and Play Therapy with Children Who Exhibit Aggression

Lisa Dion and David Crenshaw

Overview

Although aggression is a common part of play in a play therapy session, as well as behaviors exhibited in children, many play therapists are unsure of what to do or how to work with the aggression when it enters the playroom. As a result, therapists may unintentionally increase aggression and dysregulation resulting in both the child and the therapist not feeling safe. It can also leave the therapist feeling beat up, weary, and hyper-aroused, which can influence their ability to be attentive and present to the child, as well as leaving a long-term impact on their longevity in the play therapy profession.

This chapter aims to help the play therapist reframe aggression, as well as understand how to work with aggression from a Polyvagal theory perspective. At its heart, Polyvagal theory is about safety (Porges, 2011, 2021). It provides an understanding that feeling safe is dependent on autonomic states and that our cognitive evaluations of risk in the environment, including identifying potentially dangerous relationships, play a secondary role to our visceral reactions to people and places. Learning how to establish safety within the child's body, the therapist's body, and in the therapeutic relationship in order to enable the social engagement system and support integration is key to successful therapy, especially with youth exhibiting aggressive behavior signaling underlying trauma and lack of safety.

DOI: 10.4324/9781003352976-11

A New Lens

Children at times exhibit aggression, but Jerome Kagan (1998) made it clear that there are no aggressive children. Kagan insisted that no child is aggressive all the time. Some are aggressive in school under certain conditions but not at home. Some are aggressive at home but not at school. Some are aggressive when teased by older siblings but not when teased by others. Kagan reminded us that our choice of words is extremely important. When mental health professionals use shortcuts and refer to an "aggressive child," they are committing an error that would not be acceptable in any other discipline in science. They are categorizing without any specification of descriptors. The more scientific approach would be to describe a child who shows aggression at times under certain conditions such as when his older brother teases him about missing his two front teeth or when he doesn't play well in sports. He spends plenty of time with his older brother when no aggressive behavior is observed at all. Without the specifiers, our labeling children as "aggressive" would not be helpful from the perspective of scientific study.

Just as there are many contributing factors when children and youth exhibit aggression, there are many contributing factors to a successful course of treatment. Badenoch and Kestly (2015) discussed the relational foundations of healing play as one of them. "For we humans, safety is supported when we can connect with someone who is present without judgments or expectations, someone who can receive us just as we are" (Badenoch & Kestly, 2015, p. 525). This is even more important when working with children exhibiting aggression, as these children likely already receive messages that their aggression is not okay, and thus they are not okay. Being with a therapist who is able and willing to view aggression as an adaptive strategy and not view the child as a "bad child" is fundamental in beginning to create a felt sense of safety in the therapeutic relationship and thus increasing the success of treatment.

Aggression and Polyvagal Mechanisms

What makes working with aggression so different from working with other types of play and symptoms is that aggression in and of itself challenges the therapist's own internal sense of safety. It is thus crucial that play therapists learn the Polyvagal mechanisms that influence aggressive behaviors, so that they understand what is happening inside the child and also within themselves. Without this knowledge, play therapists are at greater risk for labeling the child, mis-attuning to the child, and/or attempting to shut down the child's aggression out of fear and their own increased experience of vicarious trauma.

As described in the chapter introducing Polyvagal theory and the nervous system, it is understood that when children perceive a challenge, threat, or don't feel safe, they will either rev up in a fight or flight sympathetic response or they will engage in a dorsal response by shutting down or withdrawing. These are normal and healthy protective responses designed to help the child manage the challenge, threat, or feelings of lack of safety. As this chapter focuses specifically on aggressive behaviors, we will explore what happens when a child revs up into a fight or flight sympathetic response.

One thing to understand is that it is the child's perception about whether or not the child has the ability to do something about the challenge, threat, or lack of safety that initiates the activation of a particular response. With aggression, the child is perceiving that they can do something, which begins to mobilize the child. This deserves to be acknowledged as the aggressive child is a child who still has some hope and still believes that they have the ability to influence a situation. As the sympathetic nervous system is activated, energy will become concentrated in the child's extremities, as well as in their face. This energy concentration sets the stage for the child to be able to run, hit, yell, or whatever else the child perceives is needed in the moment (Dion, 2018). The most important thing to understand is that this is the child's attempt to protect. It isn't because the child is mean, bad-mannered, evil, or any other label that might be placed upon the child. As this protective response is a normal response of the autonomic nervous system, the question then becomes, "How does the play therapist work with the aggression in such a way that it becomes therapeutic while enhancing feelings of safety within the child?"

In order to answer this question, understanding the ventral vagal response in the context of aggression is important, as it is the ventral vagal response that allows a feeling of safety to emerge. The ventral vagal response is able to act as a brake of sorts on the expression of aggression by supporting the sympathetic system to slow down, ultimately allowing the individual to register a neuroception of safety as well as feel safe enough to socially engage with others (Porges, 2011). The term *regulation* is another way to describe this process, as the ventral vagal response has the ability to help modulate the activation of the sympathetically (fight/flight) aroused system supporting its arousal or changing it, if needed.

There is a common misconception in the understanding of this process that can impair a play therapist's capacity to help a client's integration of aggression that occurs in sessions. The mistaken idea is that regulation equals calm. *Regulated* means *connected*, not *calm*. From a Synergetic Play Therapy perspective, the concept is expanded to encompass mindfulness and self-awareness (Dion, 2018). As an example, as the child becomes aware of the aggressive urge in their body, the child takes a deep breath. In this moment of mindful awareness, the child is now connected to themselves as they simultaneously activate their ventral vagal system in the midst of their sympathetic activation. This means that in the moment the child is both regulated and dysregulated at the same time. It is this dual attention experience that allows the child to feel the aggression in their body while simultaneously knowing they are safe. As this neuroception of safety begins to emerge in the body, the child is now able to move towards the activation, go into it, even feel it more. Why is this necessary? Because integration requires moving towards, not moving away from (Badenoch, 2017). The therapeutic goal from a Polyvagal lens is to enhance the ability for the child to mindfully be with themselves (access their ventral state) during their play and stories as they recall the challenging thoughts, feelings, and bodily sensations that are giving rise to the aggression. This allows the client to continue to move towards the intensity for integration.

Amplified Integration

The most vexing therapeutic task and the one that requires emotional strength and stamina is the ability to listen, really listen in a fully receptive, present, and nonjudgmental way when aggression is expressed. This is a challenging task especially for therapists where the expression of aggression activates their own unresolved trauma, thereby activating their own protective patterns. When caseloads are full of aggressive play and stories, even well-trained and experienced therapists can experience "compassion fatigue" (Figley, 2002) or even secondary or vicarious trauma. The challenge is intensified because as the child shares their challenging thoughts, feelings, and sensations through their play and stories, both the child and therapist relive the pain of the original events *together*. It is here that applying Polyvagal theory becomes paramount.

When therapists are unable to acknowledge the changes taking place inside of them as they listen to and witness the child's play or aggressive behaviors, they are likely to start avoiding those specific bodily sensations and feelings, denying their existence, trying to shut them down in some manner, or emotionally flooding. Therapists must experience what is happening in their bodies while simultaneously accessing their own ventral vagal response to create their own neuroception of safety in order to take on the role of the external psychobiological regulator, a concept introduced by Allan Schore (2003), for co-regulation during aggression. Teresa Kestly (2014) defined it as the ability to track the felt sense (right hemisphere) while maintaining conscious awareness (left hemisphere) at the same time. The capacity to hold both or to be regulated and dysregulated in the same moment helps the therapist to retain a neuroception of safety through ventral vagal activation, allowing the therapist to attune, regulate, and be present as the intensity arises.

In her book *The Heart of Trauma* (2017), Bonnie Badenoch describes the process as a client's window of tolerance meeting the therapist's window of tolerance to form a combined window of tolerance. The therapist energetically wraps their arms around the child. Co-regulation then happens inside this window as the child is allowed to explore their sympathetic arousal and aggressive urges while being regulated by the therapist.

When a therapist allows themselves to become aware of their own uncomfortable internal states and mindfully move towards them, it opens up a new possibility for the child as the child is able to borrow the therapist's regulatory capacity to move towards their own difficult thoughts, feelings, and bodily sensations that are arising through their play and stories. Children are then able to make new neural connections and rewire the activation of their sympathetically aroused system, which can eventually lead to new neural organization and a new relationship with the aggressive urges inside of them (Edelman, 1987; Tyson, 2002; Dion & Gray, 2014).

As the therapist creates their own neuroception of safety by connecting to themselves and accessing their own ventral state, they are able to attune more accurately and hold the energy of the aggression in a more conscious way, creating more opportunity for conscious choice regarding what would be most therapeutic in the moment instead of defaulting to needing to calm the child down out of fear and lack of tolerance. Without this level of attunement, the therapist is not able to externally regulate the child (Schore, 1994). In other words, the therapist is able to now respond to the situation, instead of reacting to the situation.

Part of attuning also means understanding when it is necessary to set limits as the aggression threatens to spin out of control. In doing so, the therapist is not only facilitating self-regulation but also establishing safety as a non-negotiable pillar of play therapy. A child with out-of-control anger is often frightened about the extent of their own aggression and may shut down or engage in fight/flight because they have lost confidence in the therapist to maintain safety in the therapy space. The therapist's ability to stay connected to themselves and the child while "holding" the intensity of the aggression as it is worked through therapeutically will not only increase safety in the therapeutic endeavor but in the child's own internal sense of security.

As already mentioned, aggression impacts both the child and therapist in session, and inevitably, emotional flooding by either is a possibility. Emotional flooding can be understood as whatever is being experienced is registering as "too much," and it is challenging to access the ventral system for regulation and connection. For example, the child lashes out verbally or physically at the therapist, throws or breaks something, or the therapist scolds the child. When these moments occur, the only task at hand is to help create a neuroception of safety and if there is a rupture in the relationship to come back and do the repair.

Case Example

Timmy, eight years old, was brought to play therapy to help with anger outbursts and aggression that continuously got him in trouble at school and at home. He would often yell at his teachers and pick fights with his classmates, as well as his younger siblings at home. In sessions, Timmy was often drawn to a table tennis game in the office. Being extremely competitive, his window of tolerance for losing was low, and on the occasion that he would begin to lose, would become incredibly upset, insist that the game ended, and sometimes even throw the paddle. During one particular session, after already winning the first three games, during the 4th game he began to lose. He immediately slammed the paddle down and screamed, "This game is so stupid" and then ran out of the room smashing and breaking the therapist's answering machine on his way out.

As this interaction took place, Timmy's sympathetic arousal escalated quickly. The feelings emerging inside him felt overwhelming, and he was not able to stay connected to himself. At the same time, while observing and listening to Timmy's escalation, the therapist simultaneously began to feel the sympathetic arousal inside their own body. This mindful awareness was the clue to the therapist that it was time to access their own ventral state through mindful breathing, so that a neuroception of safety could be brought to the moment and Timmy could begin to borrow the therapist's own regulatory capacity. At this particular moment; however, Timmy had already emotionally flooded and was on the run, and the highest priority now was to make sure he was safe.

The therapist went looking for Timmy, who was running full speed down the hallway towards the front entrance, which was near a busy road. The therapist, now also in a full speed run to make sure he did not get injured, ran out the front door and found him kicking pebbles in the parking lot. The therapist continued to work to stay connected to self during this intensity, so that Timmy could feel the therapist's presence and empathy. The therapist did not view Timmy as a bad kid or a kid with bad behavior, but rather a hurting child overwhelmed by the challenging feelings and thoughts being held inside. The therapist's acceptance of his anger was pivotal for helping Timmy feel seen and safe, and for allowing the healing to proceed. The therapist gently brought attention to the kicking of the pebbles by beginning to kick them alongside. In a short time, Timmy's movements began to slow down, and he walked over to a grassy area, laid down, and began to sob.

The therapist supported Timmy to begin to connect with himself and move towards his overwhelming feelings by offering gentle touch (putting an arm around his shoulder), talking with him in a soft and soothing voice, and telling him it was going to be okay. The result was that as Timmy's sobs subsided and his breathing slowed down; he was able to disclose the sudden death of his grandfather and his feeling responsible. He said, "My grandmother says it was my fault that my grandpa died." She told me lots of times that my grandfather had a heart condition, and he gets really stressed when my brothers and I come over and run around and make a lot of noise, and that is why he died. I killed my grandfather!"

Timmy had been carrying a huge burden and was made to feel responsible for his grandfather's death, someone he loved deeply. His aggressive outbursts were masking the painful guilt he was feeling, while also attempting to offer some sense of empowerment since he felt hopeless to change the situation. Timmy asked the therapist if they were mad that he broke the answering machine. The therapist understood this to be a crucial moment to help him re-pattern his experience of guilt and shame. Once again, accessing their ventral state, the therapist became present, sharing that although they weren't thrilled about what happened, it helped get to the bottom of the pain and understand the burden Timmy was carrying. The therapist shared that in their opinion, it was the most important thing that happened. Timmy responded with, "Worth more than the broken answering machine?" The therapist replied with a soft smile, "Worth more than a thousand answering machines!"

Caregiver Involvement

A close partnership between the therapist and the family is essential to positive outcomes, and this conclusion is data-driven (Ray, 2015). During a consultation with the Astor Home for Children in 1994, Salvador Minuchin stated, "It is not enough to let the parents know that it would be nice to have them involved in treatment; we need to convince them that their collaboration with us is essential and without it, we will surely fail" (Crenshaw & Mordock, 2005). Minuchin also explained, "If we are very competent, we don't really need the parents. We are the experts and can take care of everything. In that case the parents will not feel comfortable setting foot on our turf. They will simply leave their child in the care of the 'medical experts,' expecting the child to be 'fixed' and their only role is to take the child home, when the treatment ends."

In the work with Timothy, a central and crucial part of the therapy was involving the family, as his aggression was the byproduct to his belief that he "killed his grandfather." It took a number of sessions to work through the guilt that was unrealistically placed on him and a lot of family work to reinforce the idea that Timmy's grandfather's heart disease was caused by many factors. A tearful reunification with his grandmother in a family session was a key event in resolving the painful rift in the family and to resolving the aggressive outbursts that he had been displaying.

In addition to addressing family dynamics that could be contributing to the aggression, teaching the caregivers how to connect to themselves and to co-regulate with their child is also important, as likely their own dysregulation and feelings of lack of safety impact their ability to be present with their child when their child is exhibiting aggression.

Conclusion

While it is important in play therapy to help children gain access to the wide range of feelings they would otherwise need to grapple with on their own and that may be contributing to why they are exhibiting aggression, an important take-home message from this chapter is that this goal can only be achieved in a climate of safety co-created by therapist and child. Play therapy strives to be a safe space to explore feelings, conflicts, interpersonal effectiveness, self-understanding, and self-regulation, and to achieve greater attachment security. Aggression is no exception to this exploration. Children must be allowed to explore their aggressive thoughts, urges, and behaviors while in relationship with an attuned therapist who is able to hold the intensity for integration and healing to be achieved. Understanding Polyvagal theory and learning how to access their own ventral vagal response in the midst of the activation allows the play therapist to feel safe enough inside, so that they can co-regulate the child towards their own internal experience of safety.

Treatment Takeaways

- There is no such thing as an aggressive child. There are only children who exhibit aggressive behaviors under specified conditions.
- Working with aggression is different from working with other types of play and symptoms because aggression in and of itself challenges the therapist's own internal sense of safety.
- In order to support children who exhibit aggression, it is necessary for therapists to create a felt sense of safety within the child and also within themselves.
- Children must be allowed to explore their aggression in the playroom for integration and healing to be achieved.
- Addressing family dynamics and teaching caregivers how to co-regulate with their child is important, as likely their own dysregulation and feelings of lack of safety impact their ability to be present with their child when their child is exhibiting aggression.

References

Badenoch, B. (2017). *The heart of trauma*. Norton.

Badenoch, B., & Kestly, T. (2015). Exploring the neuroscience of healing play at every age. In D. A. Crenshaw & A. L. Stewart (Eds,), *Play therapy: A comprehensive guide to theory and practice* (pp.524–538). Guilford.

Crenshaw, D. A., & Mordock, J. M. (2005). *Understanding and treating the aggression and violence of children: Fawns in gorilla suits*. Jason Aronson.

Dion, L. (2018). *Aggression in play therapy: A neurobiological approach for integrating intensity*. Norton.

Dion, L., & Gray, K. (2014). Impact of therapist authentic expression on emotional tolerance in synergetic play therapy. *International Journal of Play Therapy, 23*, 55–67.

Edelman, G. M. (1987). *Neural Darwinism*. Basic Books.

Figley, C. (2002). Compassion fatigue: Psychotherapists chronic lack of self-care. *Journal of Clinical Psychology/In Session*, 58(11), 1433–1441.

Kagan, J. (1998). *How we become who we are* [Paper presentation]. A presentation at the Family Therapy Networker Symposium, Washington, DC.

Kestly, T. (2014). *The interpersonal neurobiology of play: Brain-building interventions for emotional well-being.* Norton.

Porges, S. W. (2011). *The Polyvagal theory: Neurophysiological foundations of emotions, attachment, communication, self-regulation.* Norton.

Porges, S. W. (2021). *Polyvagal safety: Attachment, communication, self-regulation.* Norton.

Ray, D. C. (2015). Research in play therapy: Empirical support for practice. In D. A. Crenshaw & A. L. Stewart (Eds.), *A comprehensive guide to theory and practice* (pp. 467–482).

Schore, A. N. (1994). *Affect regulation and the origins of self: The neurobiology of emotional development.* L. Eribaum Associates.

Schore, A. N. (2003). *Affect regulation and the repair of the self.* Norton.

Schore, A. N. (2015). *Affect regulation and the origin of the self: The neurobiology of emotional development.* Routledge.

Tyson, P. (2002). The challenges of psychoanalytic developmental theory. *Journal of the American Psychoanalytic Association*, 50(1), 19–52.

12

Helping Depressed, Dissociative, and Withdrawn Children

Integrating Holistic Expressive Play Therapy and Polyvagal Theory

Marie José Dhaese and Richard L. Gaskill

Overview

Neuroscientific knowledge has grown exponentially since the 1990s, providing support for many play therapy methodologies (Dhaese & Gaskill, 2013; Gaskill, 2019; Lilly & Gaskill, 2021). This chapter reviews current neuroscientific evidence and assumptions supporting the use of Holistic Expressive Play Therapy (HEPT) (Dhaese, 1986) with a Polyvagal lens (Porges, 2011), particularly when working with depressed and dorsal vagal shutdown responses.

Maltreated children possess little self-value, their basic needs having been ignored. They have been misused or attacked emotionally, physically, and/or sexually. Commonly, this occurred at the hands of caretakers, who created chaos by being unavailable, unpredictable, or out of control. These repugnant conditions impair normal sequences of development, resulting in depression, dissociation, withdrawal, and other maladies. In fact, over 50 years of research links child maltreatment to virtually all DSM disorders (De Bellis et al., 1999; Gaskill & Perry, 2011, 2017). Porges (2017) observed that while initial reactions to a traumatic event may be adaptive, it becomes maladaptive when repeated in less-threatening situations. Mercifully, maltreated children can recover, develop, and heal when provided healthy relational experiences. Their resilience and innate potential to recover and grow within a protective relational environment are embedded in Holistic Expressive Play Therapy (HEPT) core concepts (Dhaese, 2011):

DOI: 10.4324/9781003352976-12

1. All human beings have within themselves an innate wisdom guiding their development.
2. Innate wisdom holds the potential and drive to "grow towards the light."
3. The capacity for self-healing is likened to an internal "immune system" guiding us physically, emotionally, cognitively, and spiritually, each level influencing, interacting, and interconnecting.
4. Just as a seed needs earth, light, and water to develop into a healthy plant, a child's Self needs someone with whom they can form a secure and nurturing attachment.

Many Polyvagal concepts validate these premises, providing a sound theoretical basis for understanding and treating symptoms of withdrawal, dissociation, and depression characteristic of traumatized children. The first is neuroplasticity, the ability of neural structures to modify, change, and adapt both structurally and functionally throughout life in response to experience (Porges, 2017). Second, our nervous system elicits responses prior to conscious awareness. These urges or impulses to act arise from lower brain regions, being unconscious, nonverbal, and independent of cognition, prompting Porges to observe that "wisdom lies in the body." Porges (2017) labeled this process *neuroception*, observing that Western society places greater emphasis on thinking than on foundational experiences of feeling or sensing. This emphasis produced a long history of corticocentric perspectives emphasizing cognition in education, parenting, and treatment modalities while minimalizing bottom-up healing methods that emanate from our bodies. Call it the spirit world, ancestral voices, a gut feeling, or neuroception, low-brain processes are essential to healing (Dhaese, 2011; Dhaese & Gaskill, 2013; Gaskill & Perry, 2011, 2017; Porges, 2017). Considering children's limited cognitive capacity, "bottom-up" methods offer the most viable approach to help children struggling with depression, dissociation, withdrawal, or other trauma. To facilitate transformational healing with severely maltreated children, HEPT utilizes a variety of attachment-based, body-centered, and expressive methods encouraging strengthening, nurturing, and safe expression. The methods include sensory experiences as well as creative activities including crafts, sewing, knitting, music, movement, dress-up, dollhouse play, storytelling, nature walks, gardening, and playing outdoors. Companion animals are also welcome in the therapeutic process if they aid the child's ability to calm, sooth, and engage socially. Such activities offer safe expression and transformation of emotional blocks or what neuroscience calls "memory states"(Perry, 1999; Perry et al., 1991; Van der Kolk, 2002).

Such activities produce images, expressions, and stories that evolve as the child feels safe enough to connect with and express their inner world. Body-centered, expressive methods are also used to create and strengthen nurturing experiences, promoting safe expression of the child's unique transformational healing (Dhaese, 1986). Polyvagal theory advocates similar modalities intended to strengthen and create new pathways using repeated multisensory input, including music, movement, play, breathing, meditation, and language (Porges, 2022). Porges continued, explaining, that embodiment techniques can help move the children from dissociative or shutdown responses toward an active fight or flight response, leading to a safe sense of social engagement.

HEPT also views a safe, protected, nurturing, and relational environment as essential for healthy child development and healing, not dissimilar to Polyvagal theory. Dhaese (2011) stated that attachment begins with the mother lending her physical body to the embryo, providing nurturance and protection so the infant can grow and be born. During pregnancy, mother and child are viewed as one, growth and development dependent on this fusion. Once born, this dependency continues through the close physical and emotional relationship between mother and child (Patton & Benedict, 2015;

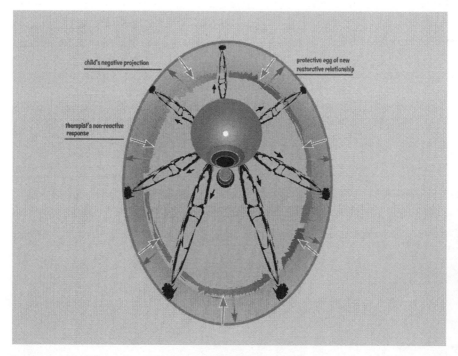

Figure 12.1 Beginning stage of therapy: Providing a safe space to connect to Self

Booth & Winstead, 2015). This intimate connection has been referred to as the *second womb* or the *emotional womb* (Dhaese, 2011; Sanders & Thompson, 2022). The emotional womb might be viewed as a protective egg or container, affording the child novel interactions and creative play within safe boundaries and the restorative relationship with the mother.

Ideally, safe containment provided by the mother allows the child's developing Self to grow, forming an intact, functional, "emotional body" of its own. The child's Self is compelled to attach to the mother for protection, emotional warmth, unconditional love, and safety, facilitating the child's potential for growth, development, and individuation as a separate being (Dhaese, 2011; Sanders &Thompson, 2022). In this process, the mother unfailingly reflects the true nature of the child within consistent limits, providing containment. The mother becomes the protective filter, exposing the child to appropriate social, emotional, and physical experiences in manageable doses. These interactions create a secure attachment encouraging the growth of the child's true nature. This relational web is steadfastly consistent no matter the experience. The Self is always reflected, and the child is guided to handle powerful feelings with consistent age-appropriate limits, allowing sufficient freedom to connect with the innate wisdom of the Self. "What the child sees reflected in mother's eyes, becomes the child's self-image" (Dhaese & Gaskill, 2013). Over time, the child develops the capacity to manage powerful experiences by themselves.

HEPT replicates this healthy, secure attachment process between mother and child (Dhaese, 2011; Sanders & Thompson, 2022). Through this process, the child forms a secure attachment with another, encouraging their true nature to be reflected, nurtured, and protected. Polyvagal theory addresses this process through the concept of prosody, the intonations in one's voice conveying emotional meaning (Porges, 2017). Parent-child interactions are laden with emotional interchanges as they experience the social and emotional world, parental intonations facilitating containment and regulation. Looking, listening, and feeling the other exemplifies social engagement, while somatic responses inform us of our mood and emotional states as they activate the child's social engagement system (Porges, 2017). Porges clearly viewed play as possessing co-regulatory properties, especially when patterned and repetitive.

Many children experience trauma in their life. Trauma occurs when untoward experiences cannot be processed and integrated. The better the ability to play, the greater the capacity to think, feel, and do, thereby enhancing the child's capacity to play out traumatic experiences (Crenshaw & Tillman, 2015; Dhaese, 2011; Goodyear-Brown, 2019; Lilly, 2015). Creative play allows the child to safely process, integrate, learn, and grow from traumatic experiences. This necessitates staying connected to one's body as well as being connected and guided by the wisdom of the Self. The facilitative caregiver re-establishes stasis (regulation) for the child through somatosensory activities, creating healthy implicit and explicit memories that will be used for a lifetime (Saeri et al., 2018; Sori & Schnur, 2013; Whelan & Stewart, 2014). The Pyramid of Activities in the Safe and Sound Protocol also addresses the use of play in involving trauma (Porges, 2022).

Maltreated children have encountered traumatic experiences beyond their ability to express, transform, and integrate these experiences themselves. The emotional blocks created are too large and require expert help, lest they continue to grow, becoming a driving force, triggering compulsive reenactment of the trauma both internally and externally (Perry, 1999Malchiodi, 2020; van der Kolk, 2014). Unless the traumatic experiences are assimilated by the ego, the blocks continue to build layer upon layer resulting in repression, denial, or other defenses preventing connection to their innate wisdom. Untreated, such symptoms may result in clinical symptomatology such as anxiety, withdrawal, depression, somatization, or dissociation among other symptoms of chronic fight/flight or "shut down response" of the nervous system (Porges, 2017). Such children lose their ability to play creatively. If they play at all, it is compensatory play or repetitive reenactment of traumatic experiences in defense of their sense

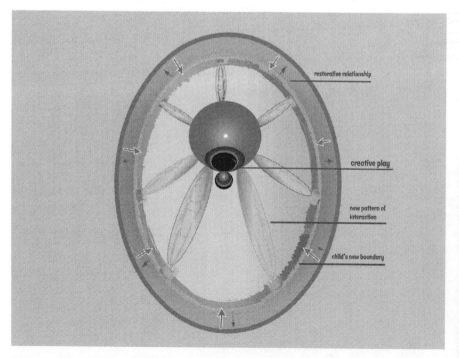

Figure 12.2 Later Stage of Treatment: New Boundary and Repair of Attachment Trauma

of helplessness. No relief, empowerment, or learning is gained. In severe cases, such children may erupt into frantic but ineffective attempts to process their trauma. The profound disconnection from their true nature impedes healthy, appropriate development. The child is left with multiple negative, traumatic projections and blockages, hindering the development of restorative relationships. In the end, the child has no sense of self, little personal worth, little impulse control, and limited self-regulation or personal boundaries.

Relational Attachment

Healing requires relational attachment, providing a safe and protected space for positive experiences and memories promoting hope. This space provides opportunities for play, encouraging integration of developmental experiences, stimulating development of ego strength, and the capacity for self-regulation. Healthy ego development generates the capacity for self-regulation, self-esteem, self-value, self-confidence, and self-discipline. Attachment is integral to our survival, growth, development, and healing (Stewart & Echterling, 2014; Gaskill, 2014; Whelan & Stewart, 2014).

HEPT incorporates layers of safety while the child is involved in a transformational experience with a relationally attuned therapist. The therapist follows, guides, and offers appropriate amounts of freedom and containment at each step, typically through safe social engagement with the child. The child desires this relationship, but historically this has been fraught with danger. Due to past negative associations, the child may initially resist forming the relationship. Repairing damaged relational patterns requires the therapist to consistently mirror the child's Self while providing unconditional acceptance and consistent limits. The therapist creates the healthy container the child needs to develop their own boundaries, which become clearer, stronger, and more flexible over time.

The therapist's primary tool is the Self. The therapist must bring a sense of being real, accepting, understanding, and present. Such "psychological holding" or social engagement is necessary for self-healing. The sense of "felt safety" is paramount for connecting to the Self. Accordingly, the playroom must be a safe, protected space where the child is given the opportunity to connect to their innate wisdom. This therapeutic attitude produces four rubrics, communicated verbally and nonverbally through words, attitudes, and behaviors while responding to the child's play.

- Physically: No one gets hurt here.
- Emotionally: All feelings expressed here are accepted. No matter what you do, say, or play, you will not be attacked or rejected.

- Cognitively: I will help you find, make sense of, understand, and speak the truth of your situation.
- Spiritually: I remember and see who you are. I see the power and sacredness of your true nature.

Positive Memories

Positive memories are created through nurturing, grounding, pleasurable, and ego-enhancing activities. Once the child feels safe enough to let themselves and the therapist know they have needs, the therapist responds in a warm, unconditional, and accepting manner. Nurturing acts such as feeding the hungry child healthy, tasty food; providing experiences of the wonder of the natural world; finding a safe and secluded nook to play or read; or being the center of the therapist's benevolent, attuned attention builds positive memories of what the world can be (Dhaese & Gaskill, 2013; Porges, 2017)). The positive memories become a source of strength and support when the child begins to process traumatic experiences. The child is introduced to a wide variety of expressive therapies providing the opportunity to develop imagination and creativity while building an internal safe place to go as needed.

Ego Enhancement

As the shoot grows out of the seed, the ego is born out of the Self (Edinger, 1972). The full potential and unity of the personality resides within the Self. Since the Ego manages the expression of the Self, a healthy Ego-Self Axis is desirable. If the Ego defenses are too strong, the Self can't influence the Ego, and there is no sense of inner direction or wisdom. If defenses are too weak, there is no control or modulation of impulses. Healthy Ego-Self expression and modulation are accomplished through the language of symbols, as the child recovers imaginative and creative play (Lilly, 2015). As the child plays out their experiences, the Self enrobes the experience in language of symbols. Through the protection of the image and the richness, strength, and wisdom of the Self (the source of possible solutions) the child is more able to transform traumatic blocks into manageable experiences and integrate them into the Ego, growing larger, stronger, and more capable. As the blocks are addressed, they are transformed into past memories, a smaller part of the child's history book, becoming more comfortable than current traumatic memory experiences. The safety provided becomes the flexible, protective filter allowing tolerable amounts of the outer world to be taken in and integrated into the Ego.

The encompassing, reparative experience of safety allows the child to utilize expressive therapies to transform their trauma. Flexibility is required when exposing a child to expressive methods and materials conducive to facilitating expression, always allowing the right amount of containment and safety at each step. The therapist's words and intonation must reflect what the child is playing out. In so doing, the child becomes more cognizant, verbal, and aware of their whole body image of their experience. The initial traumatic play becomes satisfying, empowering, and creative play, allowing the child to discover what he thinks and feels, eventually exploring solutions counteracting the overwhelming sense of helplessness of the sympathetic nervous system response.

Such healing must take place at all experiential levels, as each influences the other. The physical level, being body-centered, provides healing of the senses. The emotional level repairs attachment and the entire array of feelings so they can be expressed creatively. Cognitively, erroneous views and faulty understanding are clarified, promoting the healing process. The child is then able to make sense of their experiences. On the spiritual level, the child can access their true nature for wisdom and guidance, providing a magical and powerful sense of Self. The transformation of painful images (blocks) releases energy that the psyche must be ready to integrate, irrigating versus flooding the child's inner world. In this way, the energy is available to the child in daily life. Diminishment and removal of the trauma blocks increasingly connects the child to their innate wisdom, expressed through healing images. The Ego grows stronger and larger, embodying the interconnected experiences physically, emotionally, cognitively, and spiritually creating an inner guidance that can be used in the future. Play is the natural method used to learn, grow, heal, and integrate experiences.

Polyvagal theory describes this as an integrative process of mind and body, being mediated through the vagal nerve. The vagal nerve processes internal and external signals, determining how to respond, feel safe, seek social connectedness, and understand our world. Polyvagal theory calls the parasympathetic nervous system our "centered or true self state," where social interaction, connection, and cognition occur. The sympathetic nervous system is called the "center of feeling threat or danger," evoking the need for safety through fight, flight, or freeze. The vagal nerve serves the parasympathetic nervous system as a calming aspect, balancing the activation of the sympathetic part of the autonomic nervous system. The dorsal branch of the vagal nerve mediates the "freeze, faint, or shut down state," being most active when we feel neurocept life threat, resulting in immobilization and the slowing of our responses, even to the point of death feigning or collapse. Life-threatening neuroception usually results when there is no time to select a more sympathetically active response. The ventral branch of the vagal nerve serves the social engagement system. It works to dampen the body's regularly active state, allowing for a more nuanced quality of sympathetic activation. It is able to make quicker adjustments of activation and calming than the dorsal branch. Looking, listening, and feeling are critical parts of bidirectional communication during social interactions. Cues varying in intonation and prosody convey safety within the social engagement system, supporting co-regulation with others. This circular regulatory process between child and adult defines our physical and mental health, laying the foundation for bottom-up expressive therapies to change and improve how we feel, think, and connect with others (Porges, 2017).

Imaginative/Creative Play

Fostering self-awareness necessitates the child experiencing being seen and valued throughout the healing process. Language enables the use of imagination to give voice to experiences and to heal. Play and relational safety help the child remain connected to their bodies, aware of their feelings, and avoid dissociation as they use imaginative play to experiment, find solutions, resolutions, and regain value, strength, and purpose. This creative expression encourages transformational healing. No patent formulas or protocols exist for this process. It is an organic, therapeutic dance between guiding and following. This process is directed by the therapist's awareness of the child's needs in the moment, but at such a physical and emotional distance that the child feels neither invaded nor abandoned. The child explores the playroom, discovering what they like, forming boundaries, and inventing symbolic and creative play to resolve trauma as they go. As this child-centered process unfolds, expression, transformation, and integration evolve as the child progresses. This approach requires being attuned to both the child's needs and the therapist's wisdom, creating the appropriate method at any given moment.

Playroom Milieu

The playroom offers a variety of materials for expression: art, sand, doll house, puppets, music, movement, and storytelling to aid transformation of feelings. The materials are used for soothing and to create imagery. Through the use of multi-sensory experiences the child learns to be in their own body rather than to dissociate, as they express and share painful experiences previously avoided. They learn to recognize and exercise their own strength, growing new boundaries. The therapist helps them withstand the pain without withdrawing, dissociating, numbing, distracting, or acting out at their own or another's expense. They are now able to use symbolic play to express and transform trauma (Lilly, 2015). Van der Kolk (2003, p. 310) supported this observation when he said, "Children must learn to know what they feel, put those feelings into words, or find some other symbolic expression that can allow them to gain distance from the traumatic events and help them imagine alternative outcomes."

The playroom's purpose is to create a safe, protected, and sacred space facilitative of self-healing. It must provide a soothing, harmonious, and calming atmosphere, in contrast to the chaotic, harsh, and punitive environment to which the child was exposed. The healing atmosphere is created through walls painted white with a warm rosy tint. The room is well-lit with windows looking upon natural surroundings providing an extension of the playroom, including water features, flowers, trees, grass, shrubs, and bird feeders. The playroom requires flexibility, allowing a range of self-expression through a variety of materials, appealing to as many senses as possible. The scent of lavender or lemon, the sound of rain on the skylights, or light filtering through filmy curtains over the windows creates lovely, cozy, safe refuge in the world. It becomes a safe place to explore, learn about oneself, and see the world in ways unimagined, including the beauty of nature, whether outdoors or indoors through a display of natural objects. The natural world affords healing experiences: soothing, comforting, organizing the senses, and connecting the physical body to the inner spiritual world.

Though touch is essential to soothing, comforting, and calming physically and spiritually, it has also been associated with pain. Consequently, nonthreatening repair of sensory modalities is critical to the child's recovery and future development. This may involve the use of therapy dogs, a wonderful source of soothing and healing as they quickly react and respond appropriately to the child (Dhaese & Gaskill, 2013; Signal et al., 2017). For those uncomfortable with dogs or with whom a dog would not be safe, a warm water bottle inside a stuffed animal may be another solution. Blankets, pillows, or stuffed animals made of soft, natural materials also assist regaining a healthy sense of touch. It is also important to consider the layout of large/small spaces facilitating movement, imagination, and creativity: offering opportunities for a "cozy corner" for reading; curling up with the dogs; a place for dress up; building a fortress for protection; a stage to sing, dance, or perform a puppet show.

To avoid overstimulation, materials may be kept behind curtains, in containers, in drawers, or inside cupboards that can be opened and closed as needed. The therapist must also possess familiarity with the therapeutic materials, understanding when and how to use them. The choice to use any expressive modality always involves starting from where the child is and the child's essential needs at every moment. The therapist must also determine the pace of release, the capability for expression, and capacity for integration unique to each child. Art, doll house, sand play, or puppets assist the child's expression of an array of feelings and is called healing from the inside-out. Modalities used for soothing, while grounding, are referred to as healing from the outside-in. These approaches are woven together as the therapist follows the child's expression, using the mode they favor, at a comfortable pace for the child. Typically, this process follows a ratio of one inside-out intervention to three outside-in interventions (Dhaese, 1986). Play sessions intentionally offer many body-centered opportunities. Often the most effective are rhythmic activities involving both hands and feet in an expressive mode, helping ground the child to stay in their body whether they tend to dissociate, shut down, or act out of control. A person-centered orientation is maintained to keep the focus on the child's needs, according to their physical and emotional age, history, strengths, wounds, and present circumstances. The intent of HEPT to heal without overwhelming is similar to the Pyramid of Learning concept of a developmentally staged treatment protocol (bottom-up), including the basic tenet of helping the child feel safe so they are not retriggered by the traumatic experiences from the past (Porges, 2022).

How the play session ends is as important as how it began or what was done during the session (Dhaese & Gaskill, 2013; Gil & Crenshaw, 2016; Goodyear-Brown, 2010). Closing rituals are an outward symbol of the relationship with the child, representing the meaningful time spent together. It becomes the final layer for the therapy experience, preparing the child to go back into their world. The ritual evolves from the experiences child and therapist had together and helps the child feel comfortable. This is vital for children living in chaotic circumstances where events may transpire, preventing the therapist from seeing them again. The ritual may take the form of reading a story, lighting a candle and making a wish, or having a healthy tasty snack and glass of juice, providing closure to the session. During this time they may reflect on what they did during the session, providing some final sense of grounding to the experience. Children exposed to unstable, chaotic environments need to close the session in a healing way, providing images of a beautiful and secure place. These images are utilized to create faith that a better future is possible.

Case Study

A psychiatrist referred Bobby, an eight-year-old male, to play therapy. Bobby consistently refused to get out of bed and persistently wore a hoody and cap to hide his face, trying to shut out the world. Bobby lived with his mother after she left his father because of his violent behavior. Bobby was exposed to wild parties thrown by his mother, who struggled with addictions. Bobby also exhibited sexualized behaviors resulting from his own abuse. Initially, he was withdrawn and depressed, making little eye contact, virtually devoid of any interaction with others. He was unresponsive for weeks in therapy, until Yannick, a therapy puppy in training, pulled his shoe laces wanting to play. Bobby's laughter was his first positive relational response in therapy, and he began to play on the floor with Yannick.

The following session, he took off his jacket and hoody. A few sessions later, Bobby took off his hat. In time, he played with the doll house, reenacting traumatic party scenes as Bijou (adult therapy dog) and Yannick curled up at his side and against his back. His therapist sat close by, reflecting with words and intonation the horrors he witnessed, always mindful of his tendency to dissociate and become lost in his traumatic play. When he became dissociative, she invited him to stand, move, or walk to another part of the play room. They also went to the garden, picked flowers, or smelled herbs. Breathing deeply helped Bobby stay grounded. Sessions began with Bijou and Yannick welcoming Bobby before engaging in play, and they ended with snack, juice, making a wish, lighting a candle, and pretending it was his birthday. Frequently, when in the garden, Bobby cut dead flowers, making room for new ones to grow or spread seeds, hoping new flowers would grow. Later, Bobby engaged in the sand, standing and feeling the texture of sand. Its healing properties helped him stay grounded and in his body.

As the play therapy process progressed, Bobby engaged his therapist in war play in the sand tray. His images suggested chaos, poor organization, and catastrophic destruction, illustrative of his hopelessness in coping with the disorganized, aggressive, and destructive world he knew. He was delighted when his therapist agreed to play war with him without hesitation. He also reveled in being messy, dumping baskets of rocks, chestnuts, and acorns, but readily accepted the limit of doing so only in the sand tray. He began to consider females as supportive, capable, strong, and effective.

Finally, Bobby asked his therapist to choose her men and he would choose his for an impending war. As they set up the sand tray, Bobby asked why she placed rocks in front of her men. She explained that if her soldiers were to be at risk, she wanted them protected as best she could. Bobby responded, "Me too" and built barriers protecting his men. Bobby had accepted a healthier conception of protection, rather than his traditional nihilistic narrative. This was a major step for Bobby, he was learning and changing through play, abandoning his ritualized, despondent trauma play. Later, when one of the therapist's men was wounded, she moved him from the battlefield to a hospital constructed of seashells. Bobby again questioned her. She responded, "I'm not going leave him on the battlefield without attempting to help him with his wound." Bobby said, "Me too," constructing his own hospital for his wounded characters. His therapist had illustrated the notion of aiding injured people needing to heal, without imposing change or taking over his play. She said, "People get hurt, but when they do, they need to be looked after so they can recover."

As she continued following, guiding, and responding to his play, Bobby gradually explored his images, progressively creating new images on his own. In a later session, Bobby constructed a castle with layers of seashells. Marbles on each layer represented bombs for protection of the people in the castle. Previously, they were weapons of aggression and destruction. At the top of his castle, he placed a king, queen, and their nurse to care for the others. The nurse was present in all subsequent healing images. Eventually, his images displayed nurturing themes with nests of small birds, Snow White, the dwarfs, and the cabin he built for her.

Bobby was admitted to a residential facility after exhibiting sexualized behavior toward his sisters, his mother being unable to protect them. Bobby confided to his therapist that he believed he was becoming bad like the person who abused him. He reported at night in the residential facility the sound of other children breathing compelled him to want to get up and touch them. He pleaded with his therapist to help him avoid this behavior. Clearly, Bobby's conscience had developed enough that his compulsions troubled him greatly. This illustrates significant growth in self-awareness, a sense of morality, problem-solving, and the ability to use verbal narrative to resolve his problems. Development of these skills afforded Bobby greater capacity to manage his life in the future.

In a later session, Bobby pulled out the large box full of blankets of different colors and textures, and he climbed into it. He instructed his therapist to put the gold-colored blanket over him and to give him a baby bottle, a toy, and some healthy chips (his favorite snack). He called this his "Golden Room." The therapist and her dog companions sat by the box, read stories, had wonderful conversations, or sometimes just hummed. Bobby continued his migration from traumatic play to creative, soothing, nurturing play that felt healing to him. He had internalized a helping, nurturing figure (nurse), making it his own.

Toward the end of treatment. Bobby engaged in drawing, sometimes what he wanted to draw, other times asking for ideas. On one occasion, his therapist asked him to draw a picture of what he loved best during his time in the playroom. His picture was of the time she let him climb the cherry tree in the garden. He said, "You let me climb, but not so high that I would hurt myself." He understood the freedom he enjoyed to explore and grow, but within the safe containment she supplied. This wisdom is now his to use in the future.

 Treatment Takeaways

- Human beings have within themselves an innate wisdom guiding their development.
- Innate wisdom drives therapeutic growth.
- Self-healing is possible, guiding us physically, emotionally, cognitively, and spiritually "towards the light."
- The Self needs someone with whom to form a safe, secure, and nurturing attachment.
- Work with dissociative children requires grounding and knowledge of movement and nature play.

References

Booth, P. B., & Winstead, M. L. R. (2015). Theraplay repairing relationships: Helping families heal. In D. A. Crenshaw & A. L. Stewart (Eds.), *Play therapy: A comprehensive guide to theory and practice.* Guilford.

Crenshaw, D. A., & Tillman, K. S. (2015). Trauma narratives of children in foster care: Individual and group play therapy. In D. A. Crenshaw & A. L. Stewart (Eds.), *Play therapy: A comprehensive guide to theory and practice.* Guilford.

De Bellis, M. D., Baum, A. S., Birmaher, B., Keshavan, M. S., Eccard, C. H., Boring, A. M., Jenkins, F. J., & Ryan, N. D. (1999). Developmental traumatology part I: Biological stress systems. *Biological Psychiatry, 45*(10), 1259–1270.

Dhaese, M. J. (1986). *Counteracting the effects of media and technology through art and play therapy* [Paper presentation]. International Mental Health Conference, University of British Columbia, Vancouver, British Columbia.

Dhaese, M. J. (2011). Holistic expressive play therapy: An integrative approach to helping maltreated children. In A. Drews, S. C. Bratton, & C. E. Schaefer (Eds.), *Integrative play therapy*. Wiley.

Dhaese, M. J., & Gaskill, R. L. (2013). *Neurobiology of holistic play therapy* [Paper presentation]. 30th Annual International Play Therapy Conference, Palm Springs, CA.

Edinger, E. F. (1972). *Ego and archetype*. Shambhala Publishing Inc.

Gaskill, R. (2014). Empathy. In C. E. Schaefer & A. A. Drewes (Eds.), *The therapeutic power of play: 20 core agents of change*. John Wiley & Sons.

Gaskill, R. I. C. K. (2019). Neuroscience helps play therapists go low so children can aim high. *International Journal of Play Therapy, 25*(1), 8–10.

Gaskill, R. L., & Perry, B. D. (2011). Child sexual abuse, traumatic experiences, and their impact on the developing brain. In P. Goodyear-Brown (Ed.), *Handbook of child sexual abuse: Identification, assessment, and treatment* (pp. 29–47). Wiley.

Gaskill, R. L., & Perry, B. D. (2017). A neurosequential therapeutic approach to guide play, play therapy, and activities for children who won't talk. In C. Malchiodi & D. Crenshaw (Eds.), *What to do when children clam up in therapy*. Guildford.

Gil, E., & Crenshaw, D. A. (2016). *Termination challenges in child psychotherapy*. Guilford.

Goodyear-Brown, P. (2010). *Play therapy with traumatized children: A prescriptive approach*. Wiley.

Goodyear-Brown, P. (2019). *Trauma and play therapy: Helping children heal*. Routledge.

Lilly, J. P. (2015). Jungian analytical play therapy. In D. A. Crenshaw & A. L. Stewart (Eds.), *Play therapy: A comprehensive guide to theory and practice*.

Lilly, J. P., & Gaskill, R. L. (2021). *Unifying Jungian theory and neuroscience to build healing pathways with play therapy* [Paper presentation]. 38th Annual International Play Therapy Conference, Little Rock, Arkansas.

Malchiodi, C. (2020). *Trauma and expressive arts therapy: Brain, body, and imagination in the healing process*. Guilford.

Patton, S. C., & Benedict, H. E. (2015). Object relations and attachment based play therapy. In D. A. Crenshaw & A. L. Stewart (Eds.), *Play therapy: A comprehensive guide to theory and practice*. Guilford.

Perry, B. (1999). Memories of fear: How the brain stores and retrieves physiological states, feelings, behaviors, and thoughts from traumatic events. In J. Goodwin & R. Attias (Eds.), *Splintered reflections: Images of the body in trauma*. Basic Books.

Perry, B. D., Conroy, L., & Ravitz, A. (1991). Persisting psychophysiological effects of traumatic stress: The memory of "states". *Violence Update*, *1*(8), 1–11.

Porges, S. W. (2011). *The Polyvagal theory: Neurophysiological foundations of emotions, attachment, communications, and self-regulation*. Norton.

Porges, S. W. (2017). *The pocket guide to the Polyvagal theory: The transformative power of feeling safe*. Norton.

Porges, S. W. (2022, May 10). Polyvagal theory: A science of safety. *Frontiers in Integrative Neuroscience*. Retrieved March 14, 2022, from www.frontiersin.org/articles/10.3389/fnint.2022.871227/full

Saeri, A. K., Cruwys, T., Barlow, F. K., Stronge, S., & Sibley, C. G. (2018). Social connectedness improves public mental health: Investigating bidirectional relationships in the New Zealand attitudes and values survey. *New Zealand Journal of Psychiatry*, *52*(4), 365–374.

Sanders, M. R., & Thompson, G. S. (2022). *Polyvagal theory and the developing child: Systems of care for strengthening kids and families*. Norton.

Signal, T., Taylor, N., Prentice, K., McDade, M., & Burke, K. J. (2017). Going to the dogs: A quasi-experimental assessment of animal assisted therapy for children who have experienced abuse. *Applied Developmental Science*, *21*(2), 81–93.

Sori, C. F., & Schnur, S. (2013, December 6). Integrating a neurosequential approach to the treatment of traumatized children: An interview with Eliana Gil. Part II. *The Family Journal*, *22*(2).

Stewart, A. L., & Echterling, L. G. (2014). Therapeutic relationship. In C. E. Schaefer & A. A. Drewes (Eds.), *The therapeutic power of play: 20 core agents of change*. John Wiley & Sons.

van der Kolk, B. (2014). *The body keeps the score: Brain, mind, and body in the healing of trauma*. Penguin.

van der Kolk, B. A. (2002, January 4). Trauma and memory. *Psychiatry and clinical neurosciences*. Wiley Online Library. https://doi.org/10.1046/j.1440-1819.1998.0520s5S97.x

Van der Kolk, B. A. (2003). The neurobiology of childhood trauma and abuse. *Child and Adolescent Psychiatric Clinics*, *12*(2), 293–317.

Whelan, W. F., & Stewart, A. L. (2014). Attachment. In C. E. Schaefer & A. A. Drewes (Eds.), *The therapeutic power of play: 20 core agents of change*. Wiley.

13
Nature and Play as Polyvagal Partners in Play Therapy

Maggie Fearn and Janet A. Courtney

Overview

This chapter highlights how Nature can enhance the therapeutic powers of play to support communication, connection and co-regulation in play therapy with a dysregulated parent/child relationship. We underline how closely human physiology resonates with natural materials and familiar natural locations, providing a sense of 'self in relationship' with that which supports us in our environment. This is underpinned by Porges' theory of a neuroception of safety, which links implicit memories of safety and containment with current environmental sensory feedback (Porges, 2004). This is mediated by the therapist's understanding of the importance of connection and prosocial engagement in co-regulating a child's hyperaroused state.

The Connecting Power of Nature

The process of collaboration between the authors that led to this chapter happened online in a series of easily flowing conversations. We discovered a mutual fascination with rocks as we marveled at the Gorlech Stones from the Cothi valley bedrock in west Wales, which echo the contours of ancient hill and field boundary systems still farmed here, and contrasted them with the equally beautiful crystalline formations from the deserts and mountains of North America. Janet was in her house near the ocean in south Florida, surrounded by her amazing collection of rocks, waiting for a hurricane. Maggie was in her office amongst the Welsh oaks amid the constant sound of rushing water from the waterfall nearby. We shared moments of insight and

DOI: 10.4324/9781003352976-13

Figure 13.1 A Gorlech Stone, Found in the Cothi River, Carmarthenshire
Source: Photo by Maggie Fearn

amazement, the elementals symbolizing for us our mutual respect and deeply honored connections with the more-than-human world.

Maggie Remembers

On a coach journey long ago, my friend and I stopped at a church in a Medieval French town near the German border. We were told there was a vast meteor crater in the valley and that chunks of the asteroid were kept in the village. When we arrived, I saw a meteorite shard in the entrance to the church in front of a beautiful stained-glass window: shafts of colored light illuminating the billion-year-old carbon. In my mind's eye, I saw it travelling across the universe at unimaginable speed. I imagined the earth's juddering quake as it came to ground, and I sensed deep in my cellular being the beginnings of life on earth. Many years later, I read that Professor Furukawa and his team conducted experiments that simulated an asteroid impact into the ocean and demonstrated that the ensuing chemical reaction induced the

Figure 13.2 Meteorite Example from the Collection of Janet A. Courtney
Source: Photo by Janet A. Courtney

formation of amino acids such as glycine and alamine, the building blocks of protein molecules essential for life on earth (Takeuchi et al., 2020).

Janet Remembers

I have long been connected to stones of varied species. Growing up in New Jersey, my father had a rock garden where he collected stones from every US state he visited. I remember on vacation he would stop the car when we drove over the border of a new state to search for a special stone to bring home for our rock garden. When we later moved from New Jersey to Florida, I would return there over the years to visit. During one visit, when I was going through a deep time of transition in life, I hiked a trail alone in a wooded forest. At one point, I felt pulled to look down at the ground, and at my feet was a palm-sized, perfectly shaped, purplish heart stone. It was a treasure indeed—a magical moment of earth attunement and somehow a divine message from the universe that all is well, and I am loved. In Josie Iselin's book, *Heart Stones*, she contemplates:

> The heart stone is a lovely vessel. When you take it home and set it on your windowsill or dresser, its presence buoys you up. When you give it to a friend or lover, you give what you have filled it with: strength, love, and confidence.
>
> (Iselin, 2007, p. 1)

Figure 13.3 Purplish Palm-sized Heart Stone Found on a Hiking Trail in Butler, New Jersey
Source: Photo by Janet A. Courtney

Both Janet and I are child therapists, exploring how to bring nature into our therapeutic work. This chapter was written for all therapists who are interested in exploring and expressing embodied awareness of our profound connectedness with wild nature even as we work in the human-controlled environment with our young clients. Humans are nature; we are not separate. We are made up of the same atoms and molecules that give life to all natural organisms. In this microbiological universe we constantly and deeply unconsciously exchange matter that is profoundly interactive, emotionally responsive and, sometimes, defensively reactive to our environment. "Matter" in the psychotherapeutic field comprises of that which is exchanged in relationship, inducing the felt sense of being seen and being honored, to which all sentient beings respond.

The fast paced, human-controlled environment, in which all natural things are subject to functionality, has lost the subtle dynamic interactions that tell us that, as a species, we also belong in balanced relationship with the more-than-human world. We can rediscover this profound connection through play (Fearn, 2022), and the following composite case study from Janet's practice shows how we can call on nature to support our therapeutic work through the medium of play, establishing multiple channels of communication that offer the child a consistent felt sense of being safe and being seen in the presence of older, wiser, regulatory witness to her self-actualizing process

(Courtney, 2020; Kestly, 2014; Fearn & Troccoli, 2017). Exploring the case study from an interpersonal neurobiological perspective has given us insight into the relational healing inherent in application of the Polyvagal theory to case conceptualization.

Case Vignette: "The Touch of the Sand Helps Me to Feel Better"

Katy was a ten-year-old girl who lived with her parents and, until recently, her sister Marta, 18 years old, who had left home for college. During the first intake session, Katy's mother shared: "Katy has always been an anxious child—even when she was a baby she was slow to warm up to people or to take risks to engage in new situations. But come to think of it, I was much the same way when I was a child." The intake meeting with the child's mother gave Janet valuable information about the child's lived world. Neurobiology tells us that the human nervous system develops in response to experience (Perry & Szalavitz, 2006). The unconscious autonomic nervous system that regulates breathing, heartbeat, circulation, temperature regulation, digestive system, sensory and emotional systems is fully formed in utero in profound relationship with the mother's nervous system (Stern, 1985). Fearn (2022) reminds us that our very first experience of relationship is environmental and that it is "through movement and touch that we experience 'being here' within the living body of our mother, who in turn exists and responds to the world through her senses in environmental relationship" (p. 3). On a deeply unconscious level we are acutely responsive to our environment, a process of continuous unconscious scanning that Porges (2004) defines as 'neuroception'.

During the intake meeting, Katy's mother told Janet that she recognized Katy's anxiety as her own. It is something they share, and her growing consciousness of this was an important indicator for the therapeutic journey that began in this first meeting. We cannot work with children in isolation. The child is woven into an intricate lacework of relationships, and the more we can learn about the family environment, the more effective we can be.

The mother advised that recently Katy was refusing to go to school and was experiencing migraines, stomach aches, and sometimes breaking out in a rash, which was a relatively new phenomenon. Katy's physical symptoms were an expression of her distress through autonomic arousal. With the demands of the new school term, her anxiety increased. This was an unconscious defensive state, engendering resistance and immobilization in response to an unpredictable future and an environment that threatened to overwhelm her. Porges (2017) advises that "the physiological states that support defense are incompatible with those that support creativity and expansive theories" (p. 43). When children are stressed, their nervous system perceives the environment as threatening, and their curiosity and ability to learn shuts down (Porges, 2004; Panksepp & Biven, 2012). We know that Katy shared this defensive pattern with her mother. It was possible that their attachment relationship may have established a status quo that managed anxiety by limiting their range of environmental experiences, a patterned coping strategy that established a shared environment they could both tolerate, but one that lacked resilience and engendered low tolerance of additional stressors, risk and change.

When Janet explored whether any new situations had emerged recently, she was advised that Katy's older sister had just left for college and that they had a close relationship. Katy's mother felt that Katy had adjusted well to the change but realized that it was possible that some of her new behaviors could be related to her loss and her inability to adapt quickly to a different relationship with her sister. The mother tried to help Katy by giving her something for her migraine and stomachache, and then if she was feeling better, she encouraged her to go to school. She felt that her husband was more impatient with Katy and dismissive of her feelings, as he believed Katy was missing out on her schoolwork. She said he did not seem to understand what Katy was going through. This family was accustomed to behavioral and medical models that traditionally govern parenting in their culture. However, her mother admitted that neither her treatment of the symptoms nor her husband's dismissiveness and insistence that Katy attend school made any significant difference for Katy.

If we look again at the referral information from the perspective of interpersonal neurobiology and Polyvagal theory, we discover that the child's physical symptoms may be linked to her inability to manage her own fear when she is out of her narrow comfort zone. She needs a regulatory relationship that can re-pattern her autonomic reactive defensiveness and give her the confidence that she can manage the challenges she faces. As Katy's mother intuited, the traditional prioritization of cognitive learning tends to ignore the vital grounding of regulation, a felt sense of safety that a child needs from their environment and key people within it (Porges, 1995).

When Janet asked what Katy enjoys in life, her mother said that Katy loved the beach. This family lived about a 10-minute drive to the ocean, where Katy has lived all her life. Her mother advised in a half-laughing way, "If school was held at the ocean every day, I don't think we would have any problems getting Katy to go!" Janet asked if she could share with Katy that she knew about how much she loves the beach. Janet was drawing on her knowledge of the importance of the child feeling seen, understood and safe in therapeutic relationship, and she called on Nature as her therapeutic ally right from the start in developing her relationship with Katy. From a polyvagal perspective, creating a sense of safety activates the social engagement regulatory response, which calms a defensive autonomic arousal and supports the child's curiosity and playfulness (Porges, 2004; Perry, 2001; Panksepp & Biven, 2012).

The beach provides an immersive, sensory and playful environment. Salt water and constant wave motion resonate with our first in-utero environment. The rhythmic sound of the ocean provides a background frequency that is calming and regulating and that combines with the spaciousness of far horizons and expanses of muted colors and textures, calming and soothing the ocular/auditory/vestibular systems. On a microbiological level, we rely on otoliths to tell us where we are in relation to gravity. These are tiny grains of calcium crystal (like minute grains of sand) embedded in a gelatinous layer that holds the neural networks that inform proprioception in the semi-circular canals deep within the ear. Our first question is not "Who am I?"; it is "Where am I?" (Straus, 1966); and perceiving *where* I am provides the ground for discovering *who* I am (Fearn, 2022).

For the first session, Katy entered the waiting room with her mother, and Janet observed her as shy as she sat close to her mother in the chair with her head hiding behind her mother's back. However, to Janet's surprise, she was willing to enter the playroom without her mother coming with her.

> "Hi. I am Miss Janet, and your Mom shared with me that you love going to the beach."
> Katy nodded her head and said, "yes."

Janet: "Awesome! I have some different kinds of sand in my office that you might be interested in seeing."

> Janet introduced the sand invitation straight away because she wanted Katy to connect being with Janet in her office to her familiar and beloved beach. Janet had four different types of sand in her office—some pink-hued sand from Bermuda, crushed coquina sand from Ormond Beach, Florida (see Figure 13.3), red "quicksand" from Utah and garnet "ruby red" crushed sand. Each type of sand created a unique sensory experience when touched. She also had a large

container of collected smooth sea glass that made a soothing sound when moved around in the container. Through the touch of the sand and sea glass, Janet wanted Katy to have a bodily *felt* sense of familiar sensory experiences that would support co-regulation in the early stages of their therapeutic relationship. Janet lifted the tops off the varied sand containers for her to view, and Katy immediately got down on the floor and started to touch each of the different sands, and Janet joined her. Katy especially liked the coarser coquina sand. "I like this one the best."

Janet: "Yes, I like the coquina sand too."

Playing close attention to Katy, giving empathic responses and naming the sand, Janet was warmly responding to Katy's actions and words. She was using social engagement at the child's pace in a gentle and non-threatening exchange that communicates to the child: "I see you; I hear you; I care about you; you are safe with me" (Landreth, 2012).

Figure 13.4 Coquina Crushed Sand from Ormond Beach, Florida, Along with the Colorful Whole Coquina Shells

Source: Photo by Janet A. Courtney

Katy's impulse was to touch the sand. The skin is the largest organ of the body. It mediates the threshold between inner and outer worlds and is a vital medium for self-expression. The sense of touch brings the body into relationship: to touch is also to be touched, and when experienced with care and love, it is a profoundly meaningful conduit that regulates the central nervous system and supports regulation, healthy development and curiosity. Movement and touch are inextricably linked and inform the vitality of the organism (Courtney & Nolan, 2017; Fearn & Troccoli, 2017).

Katy responded by moving her hands around the large container and soon began to engage her whole body. She moved her body forward to gather the sand in her arms and then pulled the sand to the back of the container towards her body. Then she quickly pushed the sand away from her body and back towards the end of the container. She did this back-and-forth whole-body movement several times until she was almost in a rhythmic trance. Janet stayed quiet, paying careful attention. As Katy pulsed through the sand, Janet started to breathe out a long exhale when the child pushed her body forward, and then Janet took a breath inward when the child drew her arms and body back towards herself, relaxing more deeply into the rhythm.

Janet activated Katy's parasympathetic nervous system through the synchronous regulation of their breathing coupled with the child's kinesthetic embodied movement. Rhythmic breath and movement activated the long winding vagus nerve, which exits the skull and branches out to create a two-way interface between the brain and the heart, lungs and digestive system. The highly responsive myelinated ventral vagus nerve that enervates the face, jaw and major organs helps to stimulate the rest and recovery system to slow down the pulse and blood pressure (Porges, 1995). The constant repetitive hand and body movements connect to the somatosensory part of the brain that supports the creation of empathetic resonance between child and therapist. Janet's empathic response through breath and movement put her in touch with the child's inner world, encouraging interoception (awareness of internal states) and co-regulation.

Katy's mother came into this session for the last 15 minutes. Katy continued to keep her hands in the sand, then moved to the sea glass container that made a soothing "shhhh" sound as she moved the smooth glass all around. Janet quietly observed out loud that Katy enjoyed touching the sea glass with its varied muted colors. Modulating her voice to match the gentle sound, Janet was able to maintain co-regulation of the parent/child/therapist relationship when Katy's mother joined them. She brought Katy's mother into the regulatory relationship by tracking and empathically responding to the child's actions and allowing the mother to witness her child in a regulated state. Building trust in the therapeutic process and giving her the opportunity to witness her child's embodied regulatory experience was an important step in expanding the mother's own window of tolerance and beginning the process of differentiating her own anxiety patterns from those of her daughter.

During the next session, Katy entered the room and immediately opened the sea glass box. Her nervous system was seeking out the regulatory experience begun in the previous session. She had begun the process of repatterning her ability to self-regulate in a more healthy and effective manner. In therapy she was accumulating sensory and relational memories that embed themselves in the right-brain implicit memory, expanding her repertoire of response in moments of autonomic arousal (Schore, 2019). Her mother shared that she had done well during the past week with going to school without too many issues. Over the next two sessions, Katy started to open up about her sister going away to college, and she expressed how much she was missing her.

Perry and Hambrick (2008) highlight the benefits of finding language for experience, 'moving' undifferentiated emotional arousal from the brainstem (autonomic reactivity) via the mid brain (relational connection) into the corticol realm of symbolic thought and abstraction. The Polyvagal theory tracks the role of the vagus nerves in supporting the regulatory power of social engagement with a mature and regulated "other", such as Katy experiences with her therapist (Prengel, 2011; Porges, 2017) and with Nature's elementals (Courtney et al., 2022; Fearn, 2022).

About a month later, Janet received an early morning call from Katy's mother. She sounded very frustrated, "Katy is really digging in and is refusing to get out of bed and go to school!" It was clear to Janet that the two of them were locked into resistance, a state of alarm on the adaptive continuum of hyperarousal (Perry et al., 1995). It took an experienced third eye to notice this entrenched pattern re-emerging in the attachment dynamic between the two. In the moment, Janet was inspired to ask the mother if she was willing to take Katy to the beach and then to call once they got there. The mother agreed.

It took a lot of trust on the part of the mother to follow Janet's guidance to take Katy to the beach so early in the morning and to do something so out of pattern from their normal impasse of emotional struggle when Katy was not wanting to go to school. It was not an option for Janet to meet with Katy at the beach, as she lived about a 45-minute drive from the location and she had set appointments, but these challenges presented an opportunity for therapeutic growth by offering the mother support in co-regulating her daughter. When the call came, Janet asked to speak to Katy, and she let Katy know that she had asked her mother to bring her to the beach.

Katy: "Yes, I know she told me."

Janet: "How are you feeling now."

Katy: "Better."

Janet: "You know how you enjoy playing in the sand in the office? I was wondering if you could do the same now on the beach to take your hands and arms to move and play in the sand. While you are doing that, see if you can breathe out a long exhale through your mouth. When you do that, imagine that any of your worry feelings are leaving your body on the exhale. And, when you breathe in, you can breathe in a calming and relaxing feeling. Can you do that now with me? Just see your worries leaving your body on the exhale while breathing a calm warm feeling. How does that sound to you? Your mom can sit with you as you do that."

Janet recognized that the sand could act as an external regulator of the child's inner state, as she experienced feelings of safety and familiarity within the beach environment and connected with Nature and her therapist via sand play, which had become a significant element in her therapy. Janet utilized a very tender and caring voice over the phone, as she knew Katy was not able to see her to pick up on nonverbal cues, so the prosodic sound of Janet's voice needed to be enough to create a felt sense of safety and containment. Janet then spoke with Katy's mother. She asked her to just to sit quietly with Katy while she played with the sand. A little later that morning, they were on the way to school and Janet received a call. Katy's mother said that Katy was able to play in the sand for a while and then they went for a walk together on the beach. Katy tells Janet she is feeling better. Janet reminded her that they have another appointment coming up and they could share more at that time.

Case Concluding Summary

Over time the sand became a central co-regulating ally to support Katy's healing. New interventions were introduced to engage in the sand tray, including the utilization of other nature objects—such as stones, shells and ocean driftwood. Through sensitivity and knowledge of the child's lived world, Janet was able to bring Nature into the playroom as a therapeutic ally and to make the connection beyond the playroom into the child's lived world to extend the mother/child relationship to include Nature as a regulatory resource, thus increasing their resource base and expanding their resilience.

The triadic relationship between Katy, Janet and nature objects in the play-room created a bridge to an oasis for Katy, where she experienced permission to explore her own anxiety as separate from her mother's.

It became clear that Katy's older sister was one of her close attachment figures, and it was very upsetting for her to lose that support system when her sister went to college. As her mother was a working mom and prone to anxiety herself, Katy would turn to her older sister as a stabilizing emotional force if for some reason her mother was not available. Once the sister left for college, she lost that significant emotional support. The therapeutic relationship in play therapy with Janet provided Katy with interim stability, expanding her ability to tolerate stress whilst she adapted to a different relationship with her sister and her mother.

Drawing on Nature as her ally, Janet was able to provide Katy with a regu-lating and nurturing relationship that allowed Katy to separate her anxiety from her mother's and begin to manage her own autonomic arousal, expand-ing her tolerance of risk and change. Janet also provided Katy's mother with alternative strategies and a felt sense of effective parenting, developing her confidence and lessening her anxiety and helplessness. The opposite of trauma is pleasure and belonging (Van der Kolk, 2016), and through play therapy that incorporates the natural world, Katy was able to build up her internal resources and recognize a profoundly healing connection with her local environment.

Treatment Takeaways

Applying the principles of Polyvagal theory to a nature-based play ther-apy intervention, this case study demonstrates the positive effect of the therapist's ability to:

1. Understand the child's lived world and the importance of her con-nection with nature. This was vital in tailoring therapeutic support to meet the underlying neurophysiological needs that drove her dys-regulated behaviours. Identifying the connections that the child had already established with the natural world informed provision of a regulating environment for establishing the therapeutic relationship and provided a continuum between the play therapy room and the child's lived world.

2. Calm and regulate the child's nervous system by synchronizing shared connections with nature through sensory experience and key prosocial engagement behaviors, such as using a gentle tone of voice, meeting the child with curiosity and attention, maintaining a regulating presence and consciously reaching out for connection with her.
3. Build a trusting and supportive relationship with a caregiver and involve them in the process of therapy, which encourages a therapeutic alliance between parent and therapist that supports the child's healing.

References

Courtney, J. A. (2020). *Healing child and family trauma through expressive and play therapies: Art, nature, storytelling, body and mindfulness.* W. W. Norton & Co.

Courtney, J. A., Langley, J., Wonders, L., Heiko, R., & LaPiere, R. (2022). *Nature-based play & expressive therapies: Interventions for children, teens, and families.* Routledge.

Courtney, J. A., & Nolan, R. D. (2017). *Touch in child counseling and play therapy: An ethical and clinical guide.* Routledge.

Fearn, M. (2022). Nature-based play therapy interventions in the digital age. In I. Cassina, C. Mochi, & K. Stagnitti (Eds.), *Play therapy and expressive arts in a complex and dynamic world: Opportunities and challenges inside and outside the playroom.* Routledge.

Fearn, M., & Troccoli, P. (2017). Being, becoming and healing through movement and touch. In E. Prendiville & J. Howard (Eds.), *Creative psychotherapy: Applying the principles of neurobiology to play and expressive arts based practices.* Routledge.

Iselin, J. (2007). *Heart stones.* Abrams.

Kestly, T. A. (2014). *The interpersonal neurobiology of play.* W. W. Norton & Company.

Landreth, G. L. (2012). *Play therapy: The art of relationship* (3rd ed.). Routledge.

Panksepp, J., & Biven, L. (2012). *The archaeology of mind.* Norton.

Perry, B. D. (2001). The neuroarcheology of childhood maltreatment: The neurodevelopmental costs of adverse childhood events. In B. Geffner (Ed.), *The cost of child maltreatment: Who pays? We all do* (pp. 21–43). Family Violence and Sexual Assault Institute.

Perry, B. D., & Hambrick, E. (2008). The neurosequential model of therapeutics. *Reclaiming Children and Youth, 17*(3), 38–43.

Perry, B. D., Pollard, R. A., Blakley, T. L., Baker, W. L., & Vigilante, D. (1995). Childhood trauma, the neurobiology of adaptation, and "use-dependent" development of the brain: How "states" become "traits". *Infant Mental Health Journal*, 16(4), 271–291.

Perry, B. D., & Szalavitz, M. (2006). *The boy who was raised as a dog and other stories from a child psychiatrist's notebook: What traumatized children can teach us about loss, love, and healing*. Basic Books.

Porges, S. W. (1995). Orienting in a defensive world: Mammalian modifications of our evolutionary heritage. A Polyvagal theory. *Psychophysiology*, 32, 301–318.

Porges, S. W. (2004, May). Neuroception: A subconscious system for detecting threats and safety. *Zero to Three*, 24(5), 19–24.

Porges, S. W. (2017). *The pocket guide to the Polyvagal theory: The transformative power of feeling safe*. W. W. Norton & Co.

Prengel, S. (2011). *Somatic perspectives on psychotherapy: Interview with Stephen Porges*. Retrived from http://www. somaticperspectives. com

Schore, A. N. (2019). *Right brain psychotherapy*. Norton.

Stern, D. N. (1985). *The interpersonal world of the infant. A view from psychoanalysis and developmental psychology*. Basic Books.

Straus, E. (1966). *Phenomenological psychology*. Tavistock Publications.

Takeuchi, Y., Furukawa, Y., Kobayashi, T., Sekine, T., Terada, N., & Kakegawa, T. (2020). Impact-induced amino acid formation on Hadean Earth and Noachian Mars. *Scientific Reports*, 10(1), 9220.

Van der kolk, B. (2016). Commentary: The devastating effects of ignoring child maltreatment in psychiatry—a commentary on Teicher and Samson 2016. *The Journal of Child Psychology and Psychiatry*, 57(3), 267–270.

14
Child-Centered Play Therapy

Person of the Therapist Presence, Neuroception of Safety, and Co-Regulation

Sue Bratton and Alyssa Swan

Overview

Child-centered play therapy (CCPT) is a developmentally appropriate and culturally responsive approach to play therapy (Landreth, 2023). Decades of research demonstrate the beneficial effects of CCPT across presenting issues including trauma (Bratton et al., 2015). CCPT is grounded in person-centered philosophy and in the foundational belief that children possess an innate capacity for resiliency, growth, and healing. In CCPT, the therapist is fully present without agenda and verbally and nonverbally communicates their genuine, unconditional, positive regard and acceptance of the child.

In this chapter, we highlight the Polyvagal theory concepts of neuroception of safety, therapeutic presence, and co-regulation (Porges, 2017) as well as Therapeutic Powers of Play most salient to the philosophy and practice of CCPT. In the case example, you will read how Alex became increasingly receptive to a therapeutic relationship with Sue in CCPT. A felt sense of safety in the therapeutic relationship is developed over time, reliant on the intentions and sincerity of the child-centered play therapist to be consistently accepting, authentic, and present with the child.

Polyvagal Mechanisms

Three concepts in Polyvagal theory are particularly relevant to CCPT: neuroception of safety, therapeutic presence, and co-regulation. Neuroception is a subconscious neural process during which humans distinguish whether

DOI: 10.4324/9781003352976-14

environmental stimuli are safe, dangerous, or life-threatening (Porges, 2021b). Children initially develop their neuroception of safety in relationship with their primary caregivers. In Polyvagal theory, the nervous system is classified into three components. The parasympathetic nervous system responds to threatening stimuli by immobilizing the body (e.g., freezing). The sympathetic nervous system responds to potentially dangerous stimuli by mobilizing the body (e.g., fight or flee). The social engagement system is active when an individual feels safe to engage their environment and be in relationships with others. These responses are not dependent on prosocial expectations. For example, if a child perceives someone to be threatening, their adaptive physiological response may be to mobilize, regardless of the truthfulness of whether the person is an actual threat to the child. Children are constantly working to maintain physiological homeostasis, e.g., regulation of their nervous systems. This ongoing process relates to the foundational belief in CCPT that children possess an innate potential for growth and resiliency, referred to as the *self-actualizing tendency*.

The therapeutic presence facilitated by the child-centered play therapist in CCPT is a communication of social engagement (Geller & Porges, 2021). The play therapist is fully present with the child in the moment and remains open and receptive to the totality of the child's experiences. During CCPT, the child is constantly interpreting the play therapist's cues, including body movements, facial expressions, posture, and vocal tones, as communicators of either safety or threat. As the child experiences consistent and authentic cues of safety from the play therapist across CCPT sessions, the neuroception of this familiar person can be coded as a positive social interaction, which promotes the child's sense of safety. These non-verbal cues of safety "invite an individual's nervous system into ventral vagal safety and co-regulation" (Dana, 2018, p. 112). The consistent therapeutic presence of the play therapist provides the necessary relational conditions for the child to play and engage with the play therapist with increased spontaneity and reciprocity. In other words, when safety is experienced by the child, their social engagement system can operate without being unnecessarily shielded by sympathetic and parasympathetic nervous system responses.

Children who have experienced trauma or abuse may rely on their defense systems to withstand danger and life-threatening experiences, remaining in sympathetic or parasympathetic neural states of alarm for prolonged periods of time (Porges, 2017). When a child engages in new relational experiences, they may unconsciously and readily disengage their social engagement system, even when no threat is present. Children can more freely reengage with their social engagement system when they can experience co-regulation and neuroception of safety in consistent and safe relationships. The face-heart connection is an essential component of the social engagement system. The child-centered play therapist listens with their heart and whole body, genuinely hearing both the nonverbal and verbal intentions and observations of the child. Landreth (2023) proposed, "If you aren't listening with your heart, you aren't really listening." In Polyvagal theory, this type of genuine deep listening regulates the child's nervous system. The play therapist verbally and nonverbally communicates their genuine acceptance, unconditional positive regard, and delight of the child during CCPT. Because the child uses the play therapist to co-regulate their nervous system during play therapy, it is imperative that the play therapist engages in ongoing and honest self-reflection of their own regulatory states and processes during and between play sessions.

Therapeutic Power of Play

In CCPT, play affords children developmentally appropriate communication and relational opportunities that foster regulation and enhance capacities for meaningful social engagement. Play facilitates the development of the therapeutic relationship, considered the primary healing agent in CCPT (Landreth, 2023). The therapeutic relationship provides context in which the child can experience more genuine ways of being in relationship with others. This type of consistent therapeutic relationship in the context of play provides the safe milieu needed to help children attain a sense of safety and activate their innate drive toward healing, social connection, and resiliency.

Self-regulation, an important factor in resiliency, develops from experiences of co-regulation. Much like an infant relies on the mother's nervous system to co-regulate and develop emotional regulation, a child in CCPT can rely on the attuned play therapist to co-regulate. In CCPT, child-led play in the context of a safe therapeutic relationship allows children who have experienced difficult and traumatizing relationships to play out those experiences and associated feelings at their own pace within their windows of tolerance. The CCPT therapist is actively present and sensitively attuned to the child's autonomic state and nonverbally and verbally communicates in a manner that the child feels safe, understood, and accepted. If the child becomes dysregulated, the child can use the nervous system of the attuned and regulating therapist to return to a calm state. Over time and within the safety of a consistent therapeutic relationship, the child can engage in playing out distressing experiences at increasingly deeper levels, gradually expand their window of tolerance of stress, and expand their capacity for self-regulation.

Integration Effect

In CCPT, the core conditions of genuineness, unconditional positive regard, and congruence on part of the play therapist are essential. As the child experiences the play therapist as someone whose nonverbal communication (e.g., facial expressions, body posture, and head tilts) matches their verbalizations (including prosody, timbre, and emotionality in voice) and as someone who is honest and authentic, the child can begin to perceive that this individual is safe. When the child feels safe, they can engage their social engagement system and focus less emotional and physical energy on unconsciously protecting themselves; consequently, the child can more freely play, using toys and materials in the play therapy room to communicate and process their lived experiences and emotions. Over time, the child becomes increasingly free to express themselves genuinely in their play and in the play therapy relationship. In this process, the child is gradually freed to access their innate drive toward growth and resiliency.

The child's nervous system constantly engages its neuroception of safety (Porges, 2017): 'Am I safe enough to be myself and be genuinely connected, or do I need to protect myself from this environment or person?' In the beginning of CCPT, despite the play therapist's efforts to provide a safe space and a genuine and authentic relationship, the child may initially make an unconscious effort to protect themself, their natural and adaptive reaction to relational closeness in past relationships and experiences. The child may present to play therapy in a state of incongruence. In other words, their behavior or presenting concerns do not accurately characterize their true capacities for regulation and connection. When a child does not feel safe and has unconsciously employed their defense systems in response to a potential interpersonal threat, they may present a façade, which can externalize in the play therapy relationship as a child being rejecting, pleasing, or ambivalent in relationship with the play therapist. A child does not choose how their nervous system will react to environmental stimuli.

Trust develops over time and in the context of consistent, repetitive, safe relational experiences. The play therapist cannot make the child trust the play therapist. The play therapist structures the play therapy room and the play therapy relationship at the onset and throughout the CCPT process by establishing safety as priority (Landreth, 2023). The therapist presents a consistent way of being in relationship with the child, which the child can come to count on and anticipate from session to session. The play therapist is genuinely accepting, warm, interested, and intentional in sending cues of safety. For a child who has not known spaces or people to be consistent and reliable, the predictability of the play therapy room and therapeutic relationship nurtures the development of their neuroception of safety.

In CCPT, the child has reliable opportunities to increasingly experience safety in relationship with the play therapist. As the child experiences the core conditions from the play therapist, the child can come to trust the play therapist's unconditional acceptance of them (Landreth, 2023). During the process of CCPT, the child learns about themselves through their play and from the therapist's nonverbal cues and verbal observations of them and their play. When the child is guided by the social engagement system, they can more readily remain in the present moment during play and in relational connection with the play therapist. Over time in CCPT, the child can develop a more accurate felt sense of safety and can remain mobilized rather than shut down in defense when they have difficult emotions. The child's sense of safety in relationship with a play therapist is not a one-time achieved experience. The CCPT therapist understands that the child is constantly and unconsciously assessing and reassessing the trustworthiness and authenticity of the play therapist.

The CCPT therapist allows the child to make a genuine, authentic relational contact with the play therapist through play, trusting in the child's self-actualizing tendency and respecting the child's process of establishing a felt sense of safety in play therapy. The CCPT therapist does not try to speed up the child's process of making relational contact with the play therapist and accepts that the child will have their own unique ways of connecting with the therapist, as the child increasingly perceives that the therapist and the therapeutic relationship are safe (Landreth, 2023). The play therapist actively attunes to the emotional world of the child, observing moments when the child is authentically receptive to relational connection with the therapist. These receptive moments are opportunities for relational closeness, typically initiated by the child through play. Receptive moments in CCPT vary from child to child; for example, the child may make eye contact, touch the play therapist's hand with a paint brush, or lean onto the play therapist as they build a tower.

In CCPT, limits are set on behaviors that are unsafe or might interfere with therapist acceptance and stated in a way that offers the child an opportunity for co-regulation. Children's behaviors are adaptive, not bad. This perspective aligns with CCPT core condition of unconditional positive regard; the child is acceptable regardless of their behavior. The child can experience limits in a way that is non-threatening and continues to convey understanding and acceptance of the child. Perhaps in contrast to other experiences of discipline outside of CCPT, the child and child-centered play therapist remain in relational contact and authentically connected, even when the child exhibits behavior that requires limits.

Caregiver Involvement

Empowering parents to see themselves as essential partners in their child's healing process is a major objective for CCPT therapists and is supported by research. A meta-analysis of CCPT-controlled outcome studies indicates that involving caregivers in children's treatment, particularly through Child-Parent Relationship Therapy (CPRT) when clinically dictated, optimizes treatment outcomes (Lin & Bratton, 2015). Caregiver involvement is especially crucial for children who have experienced attachment disruptions and other interpersonal traumas that resulted in unavailability of a safe, attuned primary caregiver. These children have difficulty regulating their nervous system, resulting in intense emotions and behaviors that can be confusing to parents. Helping caregivers understand their child's behavior through the lens of Polyvagal theory (Porges, 2017) and interpersonal neurobiology (IPNB; Siegel & Bryson, 2021) can help caregivers become more sensitive to their role as their child's main source of a felt sense of safety and security and co-regulator of distress. Although the principles of Polyvagal theory and IPNB can be infused into CCPT parent consultations to educate and support parents, for the purpose of this chapter, we focus on engaging caregivers in CPRT (Landreth & Bratton, 2020) to become therapeutic agents for their child as the optimal course of action.

CPRT is an evidence-based therapeutic parenting model grounded in CCPT that incorporates didactic and supportive components. Consistent with Polyvagal theory (Porges, 2017) and IPNB (Siegel & Bryson, 2021), CPRT focuses on the importance of a secure parent-child relationship for the development of the child's regulatory capacity and sense of safety in their world. Controlled outcome studies support the efficacy of CPRT for children exhibiting a range of relational and behavioral issues including attachment and trauma-related concerns (Bratton et al., 2015). In CPRT, caregivers share their struggles and receive emotional support while they learn to apply the basic principles, attitudes, and skills of CCPT in weekly play sessions under the direct supervision of a CCPT- and CPRT-trained therapist. Whereas most parenting approaches rely on teaching parents verbal discipline strategies to respond to behavioral challenges, CPRT uses play and the principles of CCPT to foster safety, connection, and healing. When a child is engaged in play, their social engagement system is activated and the child is more able to connect and engage relationally (Porges, 2021a), especially important for parent-child dyads with relational difficulties.

CPRT emphasizes that parents prepare for the required weekly play sessions by choosing a consistent time when they can be intentionally emotionally present and in a state of calm. Polyvagal theory emphasizes the importance of the face-heart connection and sending intentional cues of safety. Similarly, in CPRT, parents learn the skill of reflective responding to children's emotions, which includes attuning to the child's needs and understanding the importance of verbal and non-verbal congruence including facial expressions, voice intonation, and emotionality and eye contact to convey safety, unconditional acceptance, empathy, and understanding. Parents focus on being fully present and attuned through the "Be-With" attitudes: I'm here; I hear you/see you; I understand; I care; I delight in you (Bratton & Landreth, 2020). When children experience this kind of parental presence and acceptance, they are more able to use their parent's nervous system to regulate and their capacity for neuroception for safety is increased (Geller & Porges, 2021). Additionally, parents learn to set limits on undesirable behavior in a way that is non-punitive, conveys verbal and nonverbal acceptance and understanding of the child's feelings, and fosters self-regulation. These repeated experiences of a felt sense of safety, connection, and regulation support the child's development of their internal regulatory system, fostering resiliency as the child can more quickly recover from experiences that were previously encoded as a threat (Porges, 2017).

Clinical Case Example

The following case provides a glimpse into six-year-old Alexander's journey toward felt safety, genuine connection, and self-regulation in child-centered play therapy with the first author. Alexander's adoptive parents brought him to play therapy after he was diagnosed with Reactive Attachment Disorder. His parents adopted Alex from a Russian orphanage at four years of age and brought him to the United States. Alex had experienced multiple disruptions in his attachment relationships beginning before the age of one year. Presenting concerns included hypervigilance, violent outbursts that often resulted in physical restraint, refusal to leave his mother, eating and sleeping difficulties, and limited language expression.

Alex came to play therapy in a state of incongruence with many conditions of worth regarding how he needed to be in order to be accepted and loved. Alex's sympathetic nervous system was easily activated at home and school, resulting in intense emotions and fight or flight behaviors. Alex lived in fear of abandonment, scanning his environment for potential threats of rejection. His drive to be in relationship with others was evident in Alex's numerous strategies for connecting, including seeking indiscriminate affection. When others, particularly Alex's caregivers, got too close, he responded with defensive (adaptive) behaviors to push them away.

Although not described in this case example, involving Alex's parents in regular consultations and eventually Child-Parent Relationship Therapy (CPRT) were critical components of treatment. The first priority was to help them understand Alex's behavior through the lens of Polyvagal theory and IPNB, including their important role in helping Alex develop a felt sense of safety and security that was lacking in his pre-adoption experiences. Alex's experience with his parents in CPRT in the last half of his treatment process was a significant factor in expanding his capacity to be in safe and regulated relationships with others.

My objective upon meeting Alex was to begin to establish a safe therapeutic relationship through my therapeutic presence (Geller & Porges, 2021) and a welcoming play space. As a CCPT therapist, I conveyed cues of safety by my full presence and my genuine and congruent communication of unconditional positive regard and delight in Alex expressed though my facial expressions, vocalizations, and entire being. I trusted that over time, in the context of a consistently safe, regulating therapeutic relationship, Alex's neuroception of safety and capacity for social engagement and co-regulation would increase, allowing him to express himself and his worries more authentically through play. During our time together, Alex initiated three significant play scenarios ("I see you; you see me," "hide and find," and "the "spinning game") that fostered his sense of safety and genuine engagement in the therapeutic relationship, prerequisites for healing to occur.

Alex's first four sessions were characterized by incongruent/anxious attempts to connect with me by pleasing, impressing, and being overtly affectionate, strategies he had used with some success with strangers in the past. It was clear that despite my genuine acceptance and delight in him, I could not make Alex feel safe and ready to engage in relationship in genuine ways. I could only reflect my acceptance and understanding. The first instance of authentic connection and reciprocal play occurred during session five. Alex turned off the light in the room and came close, shining a flashlight between us so that we could see each other's faces. He looked into my face and stated in his limited vocabulary, "You, me." I leaned in slightly and responded with a smile, "I see you; you see me" in a soft rhythmic voice. He responded by looking at me intently and smiling as he tilted the flashlight towards him and then towards me. I repeated the phrase two times as I rocked forward and back in rhythm with the flashlight. When he suddenly stopped and turned on the light, I understood that a moment of connection was all he could tolerate for today. Over the next several weeks, Alex delighted—and the feeling was mutual—in repeating the flashlight game, gradually expanding his window of tolerance for being in genuine connection. Alex had found his own way to connect in a way that felt safe.

An enduring play theme of trust in the context of our relationship emerged around session 12 with Alex introducing "Hide-and-Find," a game we played for the next 7 weeks and from time to time throughout our time together. It was important to Alex that I ask each time, "Are you going to be easy or hard to find?" He was emphatic in his answer, communicating to me that he trusted me to find him in the way he needed. It was important during the searching that I communicated through my vocalizations my determination to find him. He delighted most in moments of "finding" when I exclaimed, "There you are!" Times when I took too long to find him, he would send me obvious signals that I needed to find him immediately. He had reached the edges of his window of tolerance of the stress in not being found. My immediate presence and delight in finding him provided the co-regulation he needed to calm and return to a state of playfulness and social engagement.

From sessions 20–22, Alex was less relational, and his play was less focused and, at times, chaotic. Alex expressed a significant increase in negative affect and became more easily dysregulated than in previous sessions. My ability to provide a calm, accepting, and regulating presence was important to help Alex regulate through discomfort and return to a state of calm (vagal safety). It seemed that as our relationship deepened, his sense of safety vacillated. It made sense in the context of understanding that Alex's early traumatic experiences occurred in important relationships. He seemed to be trying to make sense of early implicit memories of abandonment and feeling unworthy of being loved. His play was often destructive, and I felt that he was testing our relationship to see whether I would reject him as others had. It seemed as though he was asking me over and over, "Am I really safe with you?" "Can I count on you to still accept me/love me if I'm bad/do bad things?" No words could convince Alex that my acceptance and delight in him never wavered. I relied on consistent relationship and unconditional warmth to communicate this to him. I am not implying that there were never times when I misread Alex's cues or misattuned to his feelings causing a disruption in our relationship, but I was intentional in immediately repairing the relationship. Alex needed repeated experiences of my full acceptance and unconditional positive regard before he began to trust that there was nothing that he could do or say that would cause me to reject him.

In session 23, there was a notable shift in Alex's affect. His play this week was more spontaneous and joyful. Alex introduced the "spinning game" in which he directed me to sit very close and spin him around and around in a swivel chair while he told me exactly what to do. He directed me to touch and count his fingers and toes and give creative high-fives, all the while giggling and playing tricks on me, e.g., "not counting right," "those not my toes." Over the next several weeks, the "spinning game" became increasingly more intimate. He would often lie in the chair and suck juice from the bottle, gazing in my eyes as he had me gently rock him back and forth. Other times he exhibited pure joy, giggling while he made up new and increasingly complicated variations of the spinning game that often involved touch. Alex had chosen yet another playful and safe way to deepen our relationship and work through his early experiences of what I guessed, at best, included inconsistent responses to his attachment and nurturing needs.

At this point in play therapy, I believed that Alex genuinely experienced the safety of our relationship and had expanded his capacity for self-regulation. He was now ready to begin to explore his early distressing relationships at a deeper level, knowing that he could rely on my consistent presence to support his internal regulation process. Alex's play was also clearly communicating readiness for attachment work with his parents, indicating that it was time to move from weekly consults to involving his parents fully in Alex's play therapy process through CPRT/filial therapy. I continued to see Alex weekly over the next 20 weeks while he also participated in weekly play sessions with his parents under my supervision.

Summary

Applying the principles of Polyvagal theory to CCPT provides a unique lens through which to conceptualize what children need to feel safe and the process by which the CCPT therapist establishes a safe therapeutic relationship and increased opportunities for neuroception of safety and co-regulation. Through self-initiated play, in the context of a secure relationship, children can spontaneously and genuinely express themselves including difficult feelings and experiences, confront and make sense of those experiences, and expand their window of tolerance in ways that are manageable. CCPT provides safety, therapeutic presence, relational acceptance, and experiences of co-regulation to activate a child's social engagement system and capacity to engage in the therapeutic relationship. The therapeutic relationship is the mechanism for change and nurtures the child's natural propensity for resilience and drive for self-actualization.

Treatment Takeaways

- The CCPT therapist authentically conveys cues of safety through an internalized way of being with the child. The therapist is fully present and congruent in communicating unconditional positive regard and delight in the child through facial expressions, eye contact, prosody, voice intonation, and emotionality in the context of an attuned therapeutic relationship.
- The CCPT therapist trusts in the child's self-actualizing tendency and respects the child's unique pace and process of establishing a felt sense of safety by allowing space for the child to initiate relational contact and engage in reciprocal play as the child increasingly perceives the therapist and the therapeutic relationship as safe.
- The CCPT therapist appreciates the importance of use of self and seeks opportunities for consultation/supervision and engages in ongoing and honest self-reflection of their own regulatory states and processes during and between play sessions.
- The CCPT therapist involves caregivers as partners in their children's therapy, to the degree clinically determined, to help caregivers become more sensitive to their children's needs and their role as their children's main source of felt safety, co-regulation, and attachment.

References

Bratton, S. C., Dafoe, E., Swan, A., Opiola, K., McClintock, D., & Barcenas, G. (2015). *Evidence-based child therapy: Play therapy outcome research database*. http://evidencebasedchildtherapy.com/research/

Bratton, S. C., & Landreth, G. (2020). *Child-parent relationship therapy (CPRT) treatment manual*. Routledge.

Dana, D. (2018). *The Polyvagal theory in therapy: Engaging the rhythm of regulation*. Norton.

Geller, S., & Porges, S. (2021). Therapeutic presence: Neurophysiological mechanisms mediating feeling safe in therapeutic relationships. In S. Porges (Ed.), *Polyvagal safety: Attachment, communication, and self-regulation*. Norton.

Landreth, G. (2023). *Play therapy: Art of the relationship* (4th ed.). Routledge.

Landreth, G., & Bratton, S. (2020). *Child-parent relationship therapy (CPRT: An evidence-based 10-session filial therapy model*. Routledge.

Lin, Y., & Bratton, S. (2015). A meta-analytic review of child-centered play therapy approaches. *Journal of Counseling and Development*, 93(1), 45–58.

Porges, S. (2017). *Pocket guide to the Polyvagal theory*. Norton.

Porges, S. (2021a). Play as a neural exercise. In S. Porges (Ed.), *Polyvagal safety: Attachment, communication, and self-regulation*. Norton.

Porges, S. (2021b). *Polyvagal safety: Attachment, communication, self-regulation*. Norton.

Siegel, D. J., & Bryson, T. P. (2021). *The power of showing up: How parental presence shapes who our kids become and how their brains get wired*. Ballantine Books.

15
Safety in Sand and Symbols

Polyvagal Shifts in the Sand Tray

Marshall Lyles and Linda E. Homeyer

Overview

When Polyvagal theory was shared with the scientific community in the 1990s (Porges & Dana, 2018), Stephen Porges was yet unaware of the enthusiastic response that would soon be shown by mental health practitioners. This theory captured the felt sense, inner wisdom, and client-inspired learning of therapists who had been waiting for neuroscientific validation that safety in relationship offers more hope for healing than the most sophisticated interventions. Polyvagal theory articulated the beautifully complex internal workings of the autonomic nervous system's orientation to survival and gently offered a protective context to a variety of clinical presentations, especially for trauma survivors. Reaching even further, it presented the case for meeting complexity with safety because Porges asserts that "safety is the treatment" (Badenoch, 2018, p. 73).

Sandtray therapists have long believed that the experience of working in the sand tray provides a nonverbal place of safety for the client. The tray itself provides a physical container to hold the child's emotional and psychological expression of their journey as a relational being. This tray is a concretely defined somatosensory space within which to share through miniature figures and metaphoric ideas. The sand provides a tactile, soothing experience. Miniature figures provide the nonverbal words and symbols through which safe expression may occur.

Polyvagal Mechanisms

Children are born with varying levels of sensitivity to their environments, as illustrated by studies on heart rate variability (HRV) that inform major

DOI: 10.4324/9781003352976-15

constructs within Polyvagal theory (Badenoch, 2017). Whether born with low HRV or high HRV, children have shown that they make use of their inherited and relationally influenced neurobiological tendencies in order to adapt to the stressors in their environments. These self-protective strategies, often seen as "problem" behaviors, are illustrations of foundational resilience. However, no one deserves to rely solely on their own self-protective strategies for extended periods of time, as multiple consequences may develop. Therapeutic safety provides an opportunity for a reconfiguration of resilience that moves beyond self-protection to a more wholly integrated connection to security and strength. Polyvagal theory advocates that this is accomplished through gratefully meeting protective nervous states and gradually welcoming them into safe relationship. These protectors often become concrete and visual in a sandtray world, allowing for both therapist and client to notice these representations and honor them.

As the sandtray therapist and the child co-regulate and resonate throughout the session, the therapeutic work in the sand tray is facilitated and continues to flow. Touching sand and the holding and placing of the miniature figures enhance the regulation moment by moment, soothing the brainstem as well as acknowledging the presence of the whole autonomic nervous system (ANS) (Badenoch, 2008; Homeyer & Lyles, 2022; Homeyer & Sweeney, 2022). To bridge from a guarded nervous system state to one that allows for more flexibility and openness, the play client must neuroceive safety externally and internally. This takes practice over time. Play clients who begin to experience relational felt safety can experiment with tolerating *intertwined* nervous system states, or "complex interactions of more than one autonomic state" (Dana, 2018, p. 178). With play in the sand tray as mediator, therapist and client enter moments of resonance where the ventral state of the therapist co-regulates the client, and the client holds their sympathetic arousal or dorsal collapse *with* their own emerging ventral state. Kestly speaks of this phenomenon further,

> Play, in the absence of danger, helps us to broaden our repertoires of possible thought–action tendencies. The high-arousal thought–action tendencies overlap two branches of the autonomic nervous system, the social engagement and the sympathetic. Normally the sympathetic system is associated with fight/flight/freeze as a result of the neuroception of danger, but in the case of play, face-to-face interactions allowed the players to co-opt the sympathetic branch for purposes of play. We learn to manage pleasurable high-arousal states (sympathetic) for positive purposes, thus building resilience. Play therapy is instrumental in widening the window of tolerance.
>
> (2016, p. 21)

Therapeutic play also allows for experimentation of ventral meeting dorsal, where clients can experience the healing potential of stillness, which is immobilization without fear (Dana, 2018). The natural rhythms of play dance from arousal to stillness and back again. When experienced within a safe, healing relationship where ventral states can be repeatedly offered (and repaired when falling out of sync), a client's capacity for resilience blossoms. The process of creating sand worlds and processing their narratives offers many moments of both playful arousal and healing stillness.

In order to welcome more than one state online at a time, clients need their therapists to hold co-regulating space while modulation is practiced (Lohrasbe & Ogden, 2017). Sometimes discussed as "working the edges" of a client's window of tolerance (Siegel, 1999), clients will often pendulate and titrate into a capacity to hold these parts of self together. Sandtray therapy offers multiple avenues for engaging this ability (Homeyer & Lyles, 2022). Though it may seem paradoxical, clients who come from trauma backgrounds may struggle to tolerate the positive emotions offered by therapeutic safety as they sense a stepping away from their familiar, and often necessary, self-protective states. If the sandtray therapist can remain steadfast in co-regulation during these moments of intolerance by the client, states of arousal can become moderated, allowing the beneficial power of neural plasticity to grow toward embodied resilience (Cozolino, 2017). As Rita Grayson states that during the sandtray session, the client's "nervous system could lean on mine as I remained in the ventral state" (2022a, p. 47). The presence of therapeutic and sustained intertwined states allows clients to update their narratives to include a sense of capability and strength. In polyvagal terms, "Neuroception precedes perception" and "Story follows state" (Dana, 2018, p. 6).

Activated Therapeutic Powers of Play

Charles Schaefer, with Athena Drewes (Schaefer & Drewes, 2014; Drewes & Schaefer, 2015) and Mary Ann Peabody (Peabody & Schaefer, 2019), identified the therapeutic powers of play (TPOP), which are now considered a foundational element of the discipline of play therapy. They organized the TPOP into four categories: facilitates communication; fosters emotional wellness; enhances social relationships; and increases personal strengths. This original organization was based on perceived similarities among the function of the various TPOP.

We suggest an alternative organization for the TPOP that corresponds to hierarchical brain functioning (Figure 15.1). Some of the TPOP appear in more than one area to emphasize the different purposes a single therapeutic

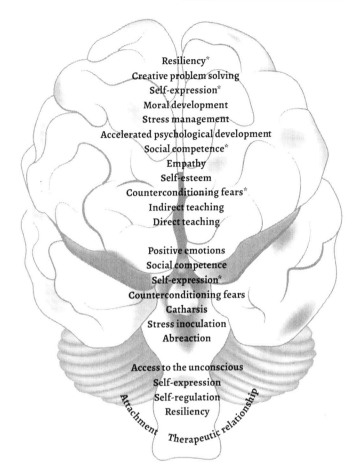

Resiliency*
Creative problem solving
Self-expression*
Moral development
Stress management
Accelerated psychological development
Social competence*
Empathy
Self-esteem
Counterconditioning fears*
Indirect teaching
Direct teaching

Positive emotions
Social competence
Self-expression*
Counterconditioning fears
Catharsis
Stress inoculation
Abreaction

Access to the unconscious
Self-expression
Self-regulation
Resiliency

Attachment

Therapeutic relationship

Figure 15.1 Therapeutic Powers of Play with Brain Functions

power of play may serve within therapeutic work. (These are identified with an asterisk.) With the emphasis on relationship and safety brought forward by the relational neurosciences, including Polyvagal theory, the proposed reorganization features the necessity to view *Therapeutic Relationship* and *Attachment* as the holding container in which all other TPOP exist. These two elements are what allow the remaining TPOP to be experienced as safe and therapeutic. Porges writes, "Before a social bond can occur, both individuals have to perceive each other as safe" (Porges, 2011, p. 193). Without the social bond, a sandtray (or play) client cannot make new safe state meanings about self and others, which is supported through pendulating in and out of intertwined states. Without experienced safety, mindful and expressive pursuits will only reinforce old survival patterns (Cozolino, 2021) and will not permit self-protective emotions to integrate. While observing the child's play in the sand, the therapist can see clues of, and develop a working assessment of, their inner attachment world. Miniature figures may display relational (Attachment) information through placement in the sand tray: Are the figures in close relational stances, separated and distant, isolated and alone? The child may also speak through a miniature figure, using the TPOP of Catharsis. Abreactive play between figures may reflect Attachment data and use Counterconditioning Fears to resolve the distressing implicit memory. Humans are born with a fully functioning brainstem. The brainstem also communicates most directly with the rest of the body through the autonomic nervous system. The limbic system is alive with neurons at birth, but it is waiting on developing relationships to direct the connecting of these neurons into patterns (Badenoch, 2008). The critical roles played by these lower regions of the skull brain, including housing the upper end of the vagus nerve (Porges, 2011), highlight the reason why *Therapeutic Relationship* and *Attachment* present as holding all other TPOP. Furthering this thinking, the TPOP labeled as *Self-regulation* might be more consistent with relational neuroscience concepts if thought of as *internalized co-regulation*. Memories with safe others whose ventral states support moments of regulation during stressful moments can create neural nets of regulation to be accessed in later moments. However, this Regulation could not be internalized without the co-regulation of others. Regulation is also repeated in higher brain functioning. This is potentially reflected in the Direct or Indirect Teaching to further develop Regulation. The play therapist receives these cues and clues through playful Self-expression, which is a creative outlet informed by the same neurobiology as reciprocal relational enjoyment and love (Schore, 2019).

When these primary TPOP are consistently experienced in a relationship between play therapist and client, the lower regions of the brain grant access to incorporating other parts of the developing mind. These attempts at practicing neural integration will present in such TPOP as Abreaction, Stress Inoculation, Access to the Unconscious, and others. If a safe Therapeutic Relationship continues to be a felt experience for the client, other TPOP will be welcomed such as Counterconditioning Fears, Empathy, and ultimately, Resilience. Along the way, "Sandtray therapy, which taps bodily held pathways, offers a way to bring these influences into awareness and into the therapeutic process" (Grayson, 2022b, p. 28).

Integration

Historically, discussions of the TPOP have focused on the client. However, as previously emphasized, Polyvagal theory insists on a relational conceptualization. For the sandtray therapist to welcome both Polyvagal theory and the TPOP into an integrated, consolidated framework, consideration of the self of the therapist within the relationship will be necessary (see Figure 15.2).

In order to maintain healing potential, the person of the sandtray therapist (POST; Homeyer & Lyles, 2022) deserves attention and care. In tending to the POST, the therapist also increases and maintains capacity for remaining in ventral while offering care and co-regulation during distressing client sessions. One of the most critical responsibilities of competent and ethical work tasks the sandtray therapist to regularly create their own worlds in the sand (Badenoch, 2022; Homeyer & Lyles, 2022). This reassures the POST's body and mind of the sand tray's trustworthiness and keeps the POST connected to the TPOP.

Additionally, the POST must be at ease with uncertainty (Grayson, 2022b) in order to remain relationally available to clients during extended moments of ambiguity. It serves the sandtray therapist well to repeatedly study emerging details about the human nervous system. Being more secure in their understanding of the embodied brain, the sandtray therapist can relax into the ambiguity of nonverbal and metaphor-based communication (Badenoch, 2022). As sandtray is a metaphor-rich expressive play approach, the TPOP are

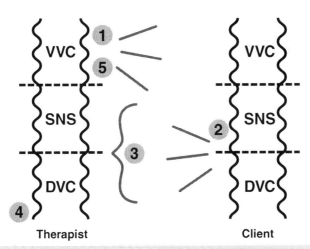

Terms: VVC-ventral vagal complex; SNS - slympathetic nervous system; DVC - dorsal vagal complex

Process: 1. Therapist's initial offering of relationship 2. Client's learned protective response 3. Therapist receives and attunes to client's protective states 4. Therapist brings VVC online to hold with attuned distress 5. Therapist re-offers safety with more awarencess of client's needs

Figure 15.2 Polyvagal Therapeutic Resonance Process

often alive through externalization. This is particularly evident in sandtray work through the use of figures and creative arrangements in the sand tray. Awareness of the child's subtle (or not so subtle) shifts in the sand creations, and their approach to doing so, is part of the ever-evolving metaphor.

Looking at the Neural Theory of Metaphor (Lakoff, 2014), current understanding of metaphorical meaning making emphasizes that the mind needs to make abstract ideas concrete. In so doing, abstract and concrete processing fall into rhythm and welcome many aspects of the nervous system into these integration attempts. Interpretation is not necessary for shared understanding as sandtray metaphors primarily allow access to implicitly held, unprocessed states (De Little, 2019). "Knowing" the meanings of figures and worlds is not the goal; the goal is for the sandtray client to feel known and safe; reaching for certainty can compromise this beautiful relational dynamic. The POST most honors the healing nature of sandtray therapy and most welcomes the TPOP by embracing "the centrality of embodiment as the mechanism of meaningfulness" (Lakoff, 2014, np).

The Polyvagal therapeutic process in the sand tray is outlined in Figure 15.2. An embodied sandtray therapist trusts both the sandtray process and the client. This sends cues of safety into the Therapeutic Relationship, offering disconfirming moments (Badenoch, 2008) for the client's internalized attachment wounds that may complicate their participation in a secure relationship. The sandtray therapist begins the process by offering a safe therapeutic relationship (Figure 15.2, #1). The resonance held within this space allows the sandtray therapist to heighten awareness of the client's shifting ANS states during sandtray work. These shifts can occur at any point of the sandtray process (Homeyer & Sweeney, 2022). A client may drop into an SNS state (Figure 15.2, #2) during the creation phase of the sand world, possibly shown through verbal disclosures of "I'm not sure how to do this" or "This feels like you're analyzing me." It could also manifest as rapid speech during an often-quiet part of the process. Nonverbally, a sandtray client might express SNS state change by moving quickly, placing the figures in the tray with force, or unintentionally spilling sand.

SNS state change can also appear during processing of a completed world. The client's narrative might feature tension that begins to parallel their somatic presentation. A child client might become agitated in the sand work or even experience a play disruption and leave the sand tray altogether. When the sandtray therapist notices the client's SNS becoming activated, they will feel it in their own body (Figure 15.2, #3) and have the opportunity to regulate that energy by bringing VVC online with SNS activation (Figure 15.2, #4). Returning this regulated energy to the sandtray client (Figure 15.2, #5) allows the TPOP to be experienced as truly therapeutic. An Abreaction is welcomed and treated as important. Self-expression is honored. As the client experiences their own VVC come online with their SNS, other TPOP become neurobiologically possible such as Indirect Teaching through metaphor processing. The hopeful and anticipated outcome is that this occurs, *over time*. However, a word of caution noted here is that this should not become the agenda of the therapist; agenda compromises the ability to maintain the felt safety in the therapeutic relationship (Badenoch, 2008).

This same process can occur with child sandtray clients dropping into DVC during sandtray therapy world creation or processing. If helplessness, shutdown, humiliation, or confusion become prominent, the secure base therapist will work to maintain attuned awareness that this collapse has come from the client and did not necessarily originate in the therapist (preventing some of the common resulting imposter self-judgments that can result from unacknowledged attuned dissociative states). Bringing VVC online and offering this co-regulation to the client may look like holding a container for the client as they select figures (especially if seeing frozen states or loss of some motor functioning while interacting with figures on the shelves) or inviting the client into a sensory, regulating experience of touching the sand again before asking for the figures to be placed in the tray. DVC state clues may also present in the child client's incoherent narrative about the sand world or hiding/burying figures in the sand (Kestly, 2016). Our proposed conceptualization of the TPOP highlights the priority to honor the needs of the enlivened nervous system state with an appropriate welcome instead of trying to bypass or control the importance of the moment.

Kestly writes about Fredrickson's use of

> the term *positivity resonance* to describe moments of relational connection, those moments that I believe bring us into the heart of play therapy relationships. She [Frederickson] said it involves three tightly interwoven events: (a) positive emotions, (b) biobehavioral synchrony, and (c) mutual care. She invited us into an image of what happens in these special moments of connection when we experience ourselves with another, having the sense of being in sync. She said, "For just a moment, you each become something larger than yourself. This is no ordinary moment. Within this mirrored reflection and extension of your own state, you see far more. A powerful back-and-forth union of energy springs up between the two of you, like an electric charge."
>
> (Kestly, 2016, p. 18)

Recognizing state shifts in the sandtray process (Dana, 2018) requires relational awareness and allows for those emerging states to honored. The sandtray materials and the process are extensions of the POST. They join in the offering of co-regulation and inviting modulated practice for intertwining states. "All this takes place within the safe boundaries of the physical space as it is held by our ventral presence" (Grayson, 2022b, p. 40). The full benefits of the TPOP will unfold over time, building capacity for holding Positive Emotions and integrating neural networks of resilience (Kestly, 2016).

> When autonomic patterns begin to change, your clients find themselves in the unfamiliar experience of being between-not held in old patterns and not yet predictably in new ones. They may feel untethered, ungrounded, unsure of how to engage with others or how to move through daily living experiences. Attending to the beginnings of change and wiring in new neural expectations is an essential part of the integration process. The integration process takes the small shifts that are the essence of autonomic shaping, brings implicit experiences into explicit awareness, and utilizes the emergent properties of the new patterns to create a new story.
>
> (Dana, 2020, p. 147)

A sandtray client will often communicate Attachment needs through Self-expression, sometimes in a regulated manner and sometimes through dysregulation. The dysregulation may originate in sympathetic arousal or in dorsal collapse (or both). The client's attachment history is whispering an expected outcome from the relational exchange. A safe, regulated sandtray therapist will have worked with their own attachment system in order to welcome all parts of the client into the sand tray and will offer secure Therapeutic Relationship as an attempt to meet the need (or repair the rupture of misattunement) without an agenda that imposes meaning or deadlines (Badenoch, 2008).

Figure 15.3 shows the container of the sand tray metaphorically demonstrating the holding nature of the POST. This includes Therapeutic Relationship, Empathy, Social Competence, and Attachment. These, we believe, are crucial to the POST's ability to hold the client's work. The client accesses and uses these TPOP through therapist-client interactions and attunement.

The client is shown in the center of the tray as it is *in* the tray the client creates their world and has therapeutic experiences. The client, in turn, is held by the Therapeutic Relationship (Kosanke, 2013; Homeyer & Lyles, 2022) and Attachment. The client easily connects to their Resilience and Access

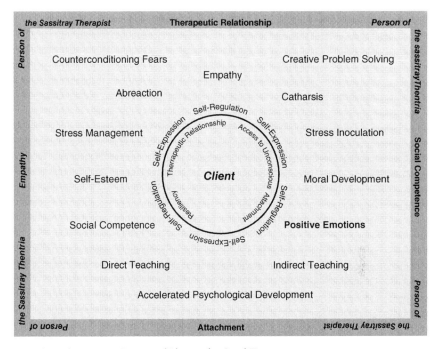

Figure 15.3 Therapeutic Powers of Play in the Sand Tray

to the Unconscious. The client employs Self-expression and Self-regulation to use the other TPOP within the tray, their metaphoric world, and their narrative. These TPOP may be child- or therapist-initiated, depending on the therapist's clinical theory and approach to therapeutic work.

Caregiver Involvement

Meta-analytic research in play therapy has revealed the importance of involving caregivers in the therapeutic process (LeBlanc & Ritchie, 2001). This has been the factor most shown to positively influence clinical outcomes. Since Polyvagal theory underscores the need for maintaining relational safety, caregivers deserve to feel secure about their own roles in their child's healing, and they need to be prepared for contributing to the atmosphere of safety during sandtray sessions, whether the therapeutic work will occur with caregivers in the sandtray room or not. This ensures that the TPOP maintains an aliveness during the work.

In a first parent consultation appointment, the sandtray therapist must hear caregiver concerns with sincere attunement while beginning to introduce a treatment plan that privileges process over agenda. Being prepared to describe how sandtray therapy works, including thoroughly discussing the benefit of staying in metaphor and avoiding interpreting/personalizing, is a critical step (Lyles & Homeyer, 2015). Table 15.1 shows a worksheet that can be used to facilitate caregiver understanding of how to be therapeutically supportive while witnessing a child's sandtray world. (This chart has been slightly adapted from its original publication, see Lyles, 2020.)

Following the flow of the worksheet, the sandtray therapist discusses with a caregiver what it means to focus on *creator* over *creation*. It can be helpful to predict for caregivers the strong pull to assign meanings to their child's work. The Polyvagal theory-aware sandtray therapist emphasizes that the child develops and heals most thoroughly when they are provided with relational scaffolding toward building secure meaning making infrastructure for themselves instead of having meaning given to them. This honors the TPOP and increases capacity for resilience, which is the ultimate goal for most caregivers even if they cannot articulate it. The worksheet then provides the opportunity for sandtray therapists to discuss with caregivers about the need to reflect on their own inner worlds while trying to hold curious space for their child. This preview for the importance of parental reflective functioning accomplishes informed consent regarding the type and feel of the sandtray work to come. Whether caregivers are involved in the sandtray sessions or not, subsequent parent consultations are necessary in order to maintain therapeutic alliance, answer caregiver questions about the sandtray treatment process, and provide feedback and practice for caregivers to meet the unfolding needs of their children. If proper consents are in place and safety allows, sandtray sessions can be recorded, and then a caregiver can fill in the worksheet while reviewing session videos with the therapist. This process can naturally highlight opportunities for improving a reflective stance and knowing how to repair relational ruptures.

Parent consultations also provide space for caregivers to create their own worlds in the sand. As previously advocated, sandtray therapists benefit from using their materials for monitoring and nurturing self. This is true for caregivers as well. As caregivers experience the risk and courage and power involved in processing worlds, they will be more prepared to hold space for trusting the unfolding nature of metaphor-based work.

Table 15.1 Structuring Attunement

Structuring Attunement:
Knowing What to Notice During Sandtray Sessions

Since attunement requires noticing your child's inner world while monitoring your own internal states, many things can get in the way of privileging relational safety and curiosity above all else. This sheet will aid you in organizing your observations in a manner that encourages attunement. Remember to focus on developing curiosity and not reaching for interpretations. Sandtray best offers healing when you structure your observations into what you see in the creator *and* what you hear in how the narrative is told while reflectively monitoring self.

Observations about the sandtray creator (child) and their metaphors
Body language
Facial expression
Voice
Needs expressed
Emotions
Beliefs about self
Beliefs about world
Problem solving
Humor/playfulness
Interactions
Response flexibility

Observations about self (parent)—What is occurring in me as I witness this tray?
Body language
Facial expression
Voice
Needs
Emotions
Thoughts about self
Thoughts about child

Am I communicating (through presence) . . . ?
Regulation
Interest/responsiveness
Playfulness/delight
Flexibility
Care
Acceptance
Curiosity
Empathy

Case Example

Ten-year-old Renee, an only child, was brought to therapy by their single father. Renee had begun to show symptoms of intense anxiety following the loss of their mother to COVID-19. After an initial parent consultation that provided informed consent about the processes involved in relational sandtray therapy, the therapist then met with Renee in the sandtray room for five sessions.

Renee seemed interested in the sand materials from the beginning but struggled with selecting figures and creating narratives during the first few sessions. They alternated between showing anxiety through both SNS and DVC presentations (Abreaction, Counterconditioning Fear, Self-expression). The sandtray therapist increased support and scaffolded Renee toward full sandtray processing by co-creating worlds (Therapeutic Relationship, Resilience, Self-regulation; Social Competence). After three sessions, Renee was capable of initiating the creation of worlds and was able to sustain slightly longer verbal processing of the narratives (Stress Management, Social Competence, Counterconditioning Fears, Stress Inoculation). Renee's sand themes focused on loss (Attachment—loss of mother, Self-expression).

The sandtray therapist met with Renee's father to debrief treatment progress and to prepare him for a joint sandtray session. They reviewed the *Structuring Attunement* worksheet as a means of discussing how he could therapeutically engage with Renee in the work. The therapist shared photos of Renee's trays so that the concepts from the worksheet could be applied. Renee's father initially struggled to allow ambiguity to remain present; he frequently asked what something meant in the tray. This allowed the therapist to discuss how he could notice his own internal cues of anxiety that paired with uncertainty, connecting this to how Renee might be feeling. The therapist strived to remain in VVC and allowed the attunement experience to be modeled and internalized. When Renee and their father met together in the sandtray room for the first time, there was slight discomfort apparent in their bodies, and both seemed less talkative than they had been individually. Renee created a world, and their father was hesitant and distant. When the therapist invited him into the process, he became overly intellectual with his asking questions and teaching about the nature of some of the symbols. While no crises occurred, the shared experience was a bit flat.

The therapist later met with the father for subsequent parent consultation. He was invited to do his own tray, which released some emotion, and he allowed comfort from the therapist. Next, they reviewed a section of the recording from the joint session, using the worksheet to discuss successes and struggles. The felt experience allowed him to increase his understanding of how to remain in VVC (while honoring SNS and DVC moments as they arose) while honoring metaphor-based exploration. This became a pivotal moment for the family treatment plan, and father and child were able to move to more synchronized healing in future sandtray sessions.

Conclusion

As shown in this chapter, the therapeutic powers of play (TPOP) play well with Polyvagal theory. A view of the TPOP aligned with the nervous system provides a new way of looking at brain and whole body engagement while play occurs. Then, the TPOP in the sand tray provides a way to conceptualize how they are activated within the sandtray therapist and the client. The understanding of the intertwined states of the autonomic nervous system provides the opportunity for the play to become therapeutically empowered. Finally, a form is provided to assist the sand therapist with guidelines on what to notice in a sand therapy session.

Treatment Takeaways

- The therapeutic powers of play (TPOP) are activating (change) agents in the sand tray (Figures 15.3).
- When identified, the TPOP can be used to conceptualize the client's work in progress notes.
- The attuned sandtray therapist identifies the flow of the Polyvagal Therapeutic Resonance Process (Figure 15.2) to maintain the connection with the client.
- Parents can be taught skills to be attuned to their child during a family sandtray therapy session (Table 15.1).

References

Badenoch, B. (2008). *Being a brain-wise therapist: A practical guide to interpersonal neurobiology*. Norton.

Badenoch, B. (2017). *The heart of trauma: Healing the embodied brain in the context of relationships*. Norton.

Badenoch, B. (2018). Safety is the treatment. In S. W. Porges & D. Dana (Eds.), *Clinical applications of the Polyvagal theory: The emergence of polyvagal-informed therapies* (pp. 73–88). Norton.

Badenoch, B. (2022). Sandtray with a mind of its own: Developing trust in the wisdom of the process. In R. Grayson & T. Fraser (Eds.), *The embodied brain and sandtray therapy: Stories of healing and transformation.* (pp. 28–53). Routledge.

Cozolino, L. (2017). *The neuroscience of psychotherapy: Healing the social brain.* Norton.

Cozolino, L. (2021). *The development of a therapist: Healing others-healing self.* Norton.

Dana, D. (2018). *The Polyvagal theory in therapy: Engaging the rhythm of regulation.* Norton.

Dana, D. (2020). *Polyvagal exercises for safety and connection: 50 client-centered practices.* Norton.

De Little, M. M. (2019). *Where words can't reach: Neuroscience and the Satir Model in the sand tray.* Friesens.

Drewes, A. A., & Schaefer, C. E. (2015). The therapeutic powers of play. In K. J. O'Connor, C. E. Schaefer, & L. D. Braverman (Eds.), *Handbook of play therapy* (2nd ed., pp. 356–362). Wiley.

Grayson, R. (2022a). Healing the embodied brain. In R. Grayson & T. Fraser (Eds.), *The embodied brain and sandtray therapy: Stories of haling and transformation* (pp. 28–53). Routledge.

Grayson, R. (2022b). The heart of the matter: Common experiences of the sandtray therapist. In R. Grayson & T. Fraser (Eds.), *The embodied brain and sandtray therapy: Stories of haling and transformation* (pp. 28–53). Routledge.

Homeyer, L., & Lyles, M. (2022). *Advanced sandtray therapy: Digging deeper into clinical practice.* Routledge.

Homeyer, L., & Sweeney, D. (2022). *Sandtray therapy: A practical manual* (4th ed.). Routledge.

Kestly, T. A. (2016). Presence and play: Why mindfulness matters. *International Journal of Play Therapy, 25*(1), 14–23.

Kosanke, G. C. (2013). *The use of sandtray approaches in psycho-therapeutic work with adult trauma survivors: A thematic analysis* [Master's dissertation, Auckland University of Technology]. http://aut.researchgateway.ac.nz/handle/10292/5592.

Lakoff, G. (2014). Mapping the brain's metaphor circuitry: Metaphorical thought in everyday reason. *Frontiers in Human Neuroscience, (8)*958.

LeBlanc, M., & Ritchie, M. (2001). A meta-analysis of play therapy outcomes. *Counselling Psychology Quarterly*, *14*(2), 149–163.

Lohrasbe, R. S., & Ogden, P. (2017). Somatic resources: Sensorimotor psychotherapy approach to stabilising arousal in child and family treatment. *Australian and New Zealand Journal of Family Therapy*, *38*(4), 573–581.

Lyles, M. (2020). Room for everyone: EMDR and family-based play therapy in the sand tray. In A. Beckley-Forest & A. Monaco (Eds.), *EMDR with children in the play therapy room: An integrated approach* (pp. 75–108). Springer.

Lyles, M., & Homeyer, L. E. (2015). The use of sandtray therapy with adoptive families. *Adoption Quarterly*, *18*(1), 67–80.

Peabody, M. A., & Schaefer, C. E. (2019). *The therapeutic powers of play. Play Therapy*. Association for Play Therapy.

Porges, S. (2011). *The Polyvagal theory: Neurophysiological foundations of emotions, attachment, communication, self-regulation*. Norton.

Porges, S. W., & Dana, D. (Eds.). (2018). *Clinical applications of the Polyvagal theory: The emergence of polyvagal-informed therapies*. Norton.

Schaefer, C. E., & Drewes, A. A. (2014). *The therapeutic powers of play: 20 core agents of change* (2nd ed.). Wiley.

Schore, A. N. (2019). *Right brain psychotherapy*. Norton.

Siegel, D. J. (1999). *The developing mind: Toward a neurobiology of interpersonal experience*. Guilford.

16
Expressive Arts Therapy as Polyvagal Play

Shifting States Towards Safety

Carmen Richardson

Overview

Expressive arts therapists utilize diverse creative modalities for self and inter-active expressions. Art modalities invite clients to fully engage body, mind and soul in the expression of suffering through moving, creating, sounding, all forms of expression, thus entering into possibilities for the transmutation of life's hurts. Levine (1997) states, "The task of therapy is not to eliminate suffering but to give a voice to it, to find a form in which it can be expressed. Expression is itself transformation; this is the message that art brings" (p. 15). Thus, therapists search for the most meaningful portal allowing the client to enter their body and mind safely, from their unique neurological perspective, and be transformed. Expressive arts therapy (EXAT) serves as a vehicle to move from a place of danger to an oasis of safety.

EXAT can be viewed and understood through the lens of Polyvagal theory (PVT) (Porges, 2011, 2017), providing a neurobiologically informed per-spective to choices made when working with children and the arts. PVT is the foundation the therapeutic process is built upon, with safety being the primary ingredient to developing and maintaining a strong and resilient nervous system required to navigate life's challenges. Sanders and Thompson (2022) identify that regulating experiences begins within the intrauterine womb, being the first womb, and continue within the caregiving environ-ment, identified as the second womb:

> The intrauterine womb provides regulation of nutrition, hydration, tem-perature, and moderation of stress for the fetus. From the moment of

DOI: 10.4324/9781003352976-16

birth through early childhood, the parental caregiving environment is the second womb taking over these regulatory activities to promote early health and well-being.

(p. 23)

When disruptions happen within the second womb, families may seek the support of a therapeutic relationship. EXAT provides an opportunity to co-create a safe environment, a "third womb" for children and caregivers. The therapeutic relationship and the art studio become a healing space, a surrogate womb, providing restoration to self and co-regulatory states, using a variety of art modalities. EXAT help children shift from dysregulation into social engagement, experiencing restoration, safety and aliveness. First, three principal features of PVT most relevant to the work of EXAT with children will be explored, followed by a review of four powers of expressive arts most prominent in "Polyvagal play." Understanding how the arts deepen healing experiences for families, utilizing the metaphor of the third womb will be considered through the lens of PVT.

Polyvagal Theory: Shining the Light Within the Third Womb

Dr. Stephen Porges (2011, 2017) gifted the world with PVT, considered "the science of safety." PVT explains and illuminates how the body and brain work together to send information in a bidirectional fashion to keep one safe, protected and alive. His decades of scientific study shine the light on why the therapeutic relationship can be considered the third womb. To be experienced as a safe enough relationship with regulatory capacities, therapists must offer families interventions tailored and designed to their unique autonomic nervous system (ANS).

Neuroception, co-regulation and social engagement provide a foundation to the work of EXAT with children and assist with shaping the Polyvagal-informed therapist. These three mechanisms inform the *why* of what is done in therapy and highlight the *healing qualities* of the therapeutic relationship most effective, transformative and meaningful. Dana (2018) states, "Clients most often come to therapy with nervous systems that are shaped away from connection toward protection. For many clients, co-regulation is unfamiliar, frightening, and something to be avoided" (p. 191). Understanding how children move from patterns of protection to patterns of connection is central to understanding their ANS and how it perceives self, others and the world around them (Porges, 2011, 2017).

Neuroception: The Internal Sentry

Porges' concept, neuroception, is the unconscious way the ANS is automatically and continually scanning within, around and between self and others for cues of safety and cues of danger (Dana, 2018; Porges, 2011). Like *an internal sentry*, continually on alert to ensure survival, it asks essential questions such as, "Am I safe in this space? Am I safe with you? Am I safe within my own body?" Neuroception invites one to examine how this relates to the third womb and to consider the implications of the therapist's ANS, the dynamic between therapist and child, and the space of the expressive arts studio.

Therapists' authentic connection to what they offer is essential. Engaging with the arts can be experienced as rejuvenating, replenishing and restorative for the body, mind and soul. This genuine relationship aligns within, moves the therapist into a ventral vagal state and extends energetically to how the therapist is experienced by the child. The therapist holds awareness about how they show up, what their face portrays, what their tone of voice implies (Dana, 2018) and how clients experience their energetic presence. Therapists also become triggered, have neuroceptive experiences of danger *and* have the weight of responsibility to know what to do when this happens. The therapist's internal sentry highlights what is being triggered within themselves and within the therapy relationship.

Van der Kolk (2014) states, "For our physiology to calm down, heal, and grow we need a visceral feeling of safety" (p. 79). Accordingly, in sessions, therapists track their own and the child's nervous system activation. The "befriending" (Dana, 2018) process begins by receiving children in the state they are in, offering non-verbal cues suggesting, "You are welcome here." Not always knowing what children will neurocept as cues of danger, therapists do their best to navigate this potential minefield. It's an ongoing journey to co-create and shape the third womb experience. The goal is to ensure there is sufficient safety experienced to access parts within the child who is longing to be seen, held, welcomed and known.

Neuroception also relates to the space of the art studio, the materials and invitations the therapist offers. The intention is to create an atmosphere that will be neurocepted as safe, playful and inviting. As co-creators, children will communicate what is experienced as "safe" enough. It's not simply an enjoyable experience for children to feel safe in therapy; it is an imperative and an opening of the gateway for healing. Approaching the space, materials and invitations in this light allows this "knowing" to shape the most optimal therapeutic experience.

Co-Regulation: The Gift of the Compassionate Compass

Co-regulation is the process of one ANS reading and connecting with another ANS. Dana (2018) asserts that co-regulation is "a need that must be met to sustain life. It is through reciprocal regulation of our autonomic states that we feel safe to move into connection and create trusting relationships" (p. 4). Within the third womb, it is necessary for the therapist to offer their regulated nervous system. When soundly situated in their own ventral vagal state, the therapist brings a sense of regulation and has access to their internal compass to help orient to and navigate the needs of the therapeutic relationship. The therapist's compass has the capacity to act as guide. The information accessed by the compass provides the therapist with the ability to detect the child's autonomic patterns moving through states of connection and disconnection.

Expressive arts are inherently relational and, when used intentionally, offer co-regulatory experiences through interactive creativity and specific art materials. In the art studio, there is a wide range of mediums offering diverse sensory, kinesthetic, perceptual and cognitive experiences (Hinz, 2009) that invite restoration. These mediums assist with intentional regulation and toning of the autonomic state of the child, having their own inherently regulatory qualities of calming, restoring and reconnecting the creator of the art back to themselves. The bilateral movements of hands and arms while painting, the rhythmic experience of drumming, the full-body play with dramatic enactment all provide a vehicle to explore the ANS. Therapists become curious about what experiences regulate or activate the child's ANS. Children's autonomic story is played out within the arts as the therapist witnesses the experience, using their internal compass to guide and direct the art processes.

Social Engagement: Optimal Grounds for Healing

The social engagement system (SES) is a powerful communication network between humans, providing infants and caregivers a pathway to develop secure attachments and bonds. Sanders and Thompson (2022) note that the SES "provides resources for collaboration, cooperation, creativity, and play" (p. 183). This keenly developing neural circuitry is strengthened by welcoming facial expressions, warm tone of voice and safe gestures (Sanders & Thompson, 2022). The SES is the same portal therapists utilize to create the most optimal grounds for healing. The primary goal of therapy is to help shift states of dysregulation to social engagement. Four features of the third womb serve to meet this goal, including co-collaboration, reparative experiences, caregiver involvement and the therapist's ventral vagal energy.

First, therapists enlist the child's ANS as co-collaborator to stay in or return to social engagement. They do this by tracking the child's autonomic state and shaping the expressive arts experience in response to their moment-to-moment needs within the session. Therapists also invite co-collaboration through teaching about autonomic states, creating opportunities to interrupt autonomic patterns as they happen in real time, inviting the child to create, identify and become aware of their own autonomic experiences. Second, therapists utilize the natural relational experiences of rupture and repair to support returning to social engagement. There will be moments of disconnection, repair and reconnection. Reparative experiences provide a blueprint or repatterning for life outside the third womb.

Third, caregivers are vital to the therapy process for resetting movement towards social engagement behaviours. Caregivers are the bridge for the child as they develop safety within the therapeutic relationship. Further, valuable information is gathered as therapists witness larger relational patterns between caregiver and child. Within the second and third wombs, caregivers are the child's most important ally as both learn pathways back to a ventral vagal state.

Finally, the physical, sensory and energetic manner in which the therapist shows up matters. Qualities of playfulness, reliability, creativity and kindness create an environment rich with cues of safety, manifesting through voice, eyes and posture, all non-verbal cues saying, "I am interested in your well-being. You matter to me." Therapists are inviting the child's SES to open, increasing their likelihood of accepting invitations to play, thus becoming engaged in reparative art-making processes.

Supporting Neuroceptive Experiences of Safety Through Expressive Arts Processes

How does therapy help children work with natural vigilance that has served them well, helped them survive and cope with hurtful environments and relationships, and move them from neuroceptions of danger to "safe enough"? Expressive arts therapists have resources for play, and they utilize art materials with an abundance of medicinal qualities, all in service of healing. The following highlights the unique healing alchemy of four expressive arts processes activated through the PVT lens of shifting states from danger to safety.

The Reality of the Imaginal Realm

Imagination is an ally for healing experiences. So powerful, if one thinks they are biting a sliced lemon, salivation can happen automatically. The body is responding as though the experience is real. Harnessing imaginal power creates opportunities to envision new stories where symbols and metaphors come to life. Children bravely enter into "alternate worlds" where possibilities exist, moving beyond self-limiting beliefs and visualizing different ways of being. If a child becomes activated, imagining resources (people, places, pets) calms the nervous system, restoring a sense of safety and power. Children call on the power of imaginal characters, heroes and mythical creatures to come to their aid.

Children are invited to embody the ways of their heroes, finding gifts of inner power, accessed through imagination, brought to life through creative expression. They practice novel ways by pretending, acting, drawing, offering fresh empowering sensory experiences to learn from. The therapist acts as witness to the child's developing imaginal skills and reflects the child's creative expressions back to them. Imagination opens the child to empowering possibilities, thereby effecting change in the body's physiology.

Seven-year-old Joey testified in court on several occasions then learned his abuser (his uncle) was found not guilty. In therapy, Joey created and directed a court scenario where he, his mother and the therapist played various characters, using specific hats for judge, uncle and mother. The theme of the play was putting his uncle in prison. Joey directed the scenario three times, allowing him to play each character. Each time the uncle was "locked" away, he would shout out cheers and jump for joy. Acting out this scenario changed nothing about the circumstances but changed everything about his autonomic state. His mother and therapist witnessed Joey move from feeling sad and confused to feeling empowered and alive, becoming the hero of his own story.

Poiesis: The Act of Creative Embodiment

Poiesis is a creative work, the process of making art, bringing into the world something new that has not before existed (Levine, 1997). Poiesis is a creative "process" and a "product" created. As chief collaborators, children are highly involved in the expressive arts therapy process, whether playfully engaged or working with immobilized states. They actively re-story and rework raw feelings and sensations through creative means where restored expressions find form and perhaps a home within the child's world. The painting, song and story are tangible artifacts taking on significance in the child's life story. This is the heart of poiesis, one's ability to reshape their suffering.

Creative reshaping generates autonomic shifts, moving along the autonomic map from dorsal vagal, sympathetic, to finding one's way home to ventral vagal. The creative process guides the child through various states by giving form to the hurts, having it witnessed by caregiver and therapist, followed by re-creating and re-doing their experience with a preferred outcome. The evidence of its medicinal power is experienced in the nervous system. The medicine of the product created may be tangible as the poem, sculpture, song, or intangible, as sound, movement, story told. Whatever form, this embodiment of suffering, or resource created, becomes an artifact or experience now witnessed, responded to and held safely in the third womb. The therapist's way of being with the newly formed art, when approached with curiosity and compassion, opens doors for something innovative to emerge. In this emergence, the child may be experiencing what Levine (2010) calls an "island of safety" (p. 79) or what Dana (2018) refers to as "glimmers" (p. 67) of ventral vagal state. When experienced, these glimmers are expanded within the child's body and their art.

Nine-year-old Renee painted in response to sharing her trauma. When asked what she was aware of in her body, she reported she felt good to have painted, open and less heavy and sad. She naturally made small hand movements in front of her, acknowledging it helped her feel more open. Renee and her therapist experimented with different movements including a playful round of dance. She returned to her image and identified orange aspects that were pleasing to her. Expanding this color, she noted, "Orange is bright and beautiful. That's how I feel." Renee cut out the orange parts and created a sunflower on canvas to take with her.

Expressive Art Modalities and Materials as Natural Autonomic Regulators

Symbolic expression using art modalities and materials provides a natural distancing mechanism between the child and their distress. Van der Kolk (2003) writes, "Children must learn to know what they feel, put those feelings into words, or find some other symbolic expression (drawing, play acting) that can allow them to gain distance from the traumatic events and help them imagine alternative outcomes" (p. 310). The words of a song or poem, the movement within the dance, the roles one acts out, the boundary of the "stage" or the physical clay image offer space from, or container for, intense feelings. A different perspective emerges as feelings, memories or images of trauma become tangible, external, where they are worked with, becoming something the child now has agency over. With sufficient distancing and containment, the child increases access to their SES, allowing easier engagement in therapy versus being hijacked by dysregulated states. There is additional bandwidth to manage daily stresses. Like a safety valve, children come and go from the distressing events held safely in the arms of the art.

There is observable relief and calming in the nervous system when children put their pain into their artwork. After drawing an image of a traumatic event, ten-year-old Addy began shaking, crying and couldn't speak. When asked if there was something she wanted to do to (or with) the image, she took paper and covered the upsetting part. Once completed, she appeared regulated and grounded. Engaging with her art helped Addy return to social engagement behaviours and modulated her therapeutic process.

The expressive arts act as natural autonomic state shifters by providing playful interventions. Having fun with the arts buffers stress related to emotionally challenging therapy work. Levine (2010) states, "Curious exploration, pleasure and trauma cannot coexist in the nervous system; neurologically, they contradict one another" (p. 175). Therapists model human capacity to engage in moments of playfulness while still addressing suffering. The message to the child is, "You are enjoyable and fun to be with, *and* we will work on the hard stuff together." Playfulness is the regulatory medicine.

Aesthetic Response: An Act of Attuned Witnessing

In the third womb, one of the primary roles of the therapist and caregiver is to witness the child and their expressive arts processes. Witnesses may viscerally experience the anguish through the artwork as the child's autonomic story unfolds through creative expression. Therapists are fully present and actively attentive to the child through "ear of the heart listening" (Richardson, 2016, p. 53), curiously observing their artistic process and at times offering an aesthetic response (AR). ARs describe ways "of being in the presence of an art-making process, ritual play or work of art—ways that touch the depth of soul, evoke imagination, and engage emotions and serene thought" (Knill et al., 2005, p. 136). An AR is a three-part act: witnessing the child's art; art-making by caregiver and therapist; and sharing the art with the child. Offering regulating messages of "I see you; you matter," it is a deeply attuned process summoning heartfelt compassion for the child's experience.

The AR holds the power of something newly forming, slowing down the typical patterns of communication, taking one out of the ordinary pace of life into an alternate realm where something novel is occurring. Caregivers and therapist listen within, then in symbolic form create their offering, often in the child's preferred artistic language. This vulnerability calls forth the adult's courage, modelling how to be vulnerable *and* stay in the blended sympathetic and ventral vagal states.

The AR is an artifact of the offering. The arts are both an embodied experience and a creation of artifacts holding strong energetic medicines offered to the child as reminders of what was witnessed, of their significance in the adult's life and of their power as potential resources. Children experience this process of embodied co-regulation as highly restorative, strengthening their sense of wellbeing both within self and in relationship with caregiver and therapist. This act of attunement conveys, "I am listening. I see your suffering."

Eleven-year-old Madi came to therapy to process her feelings of grief. In one session she chose to paint her "big sad," sharing how the dark colors reflected her grief and the yellow circle represented hope. Madi placed the painting in the sunlight, sharing how the sunlight was changing her painting as she noticed fresh images emerging. Noting a calming sound in her voice and knowing she loved poetry, the therapist wrote her words as she spoke:

> *Light Changes Everything*
> *As I shift and move the light changes my art.*
> *I begin to see a glimpse of happy in all this sadness.*
> *The happy feels good, I feel more space inside.*
> *My feet feel like dancing.*
> *I dance with the happy and with the hope.*
> *Light changes everything.*

Reading her words back to her, Madi was invited to find gestures for the words. Smiling as she moved, Madi remarked how surprised she was to hear her words, like they were someone else's. Offering the written words on paper, she tucked her poem into her poem journal. Leaving the session, Madi remarked, "The light really can help my sad. I feel good inside."

Conclusion

Building upon the concepts of the first and second womb (Sanders & Thompson, 2022), creating safe spaces for children and families is at the heart of the third-womb experience, the therapeutic space and relationship. Polyvagal theory forms the foundation of the third-womb experience as understood through neuroception, co-regulation and social engagement. Expressive arts play provides natural co-regulatory healing experiences through witnessing, aesthetic responses, intentional use of imagination and poiesis, reshaping distress through creative embodiment. These natural healing processes support children with shifting from states of dysregulation to states of safety. The world looks very different when a child feels safe; they begin to see, feel and sense how the light changes everything.

 Treatment Takeaways

- The therapeutic third womb offers children and families safe, creative and playful opportunities for co-regulation.
- Imaginative play and engaging with the arts opens children to empowering healing experiences, thereby affecting change in the body's physiology.
- Designing expressive art invitations is guided and shaped by the child's unique neuroceptive experiences.

References

Dana, D. (2018). *The Polyvagal theory in therapy: Engaging the rhythm of regulation.* Norton.

Hinz, L. (2009). *Expressive therapies continuum: A framework for using art in therapy.* Routledge.

Knill, P. J., Levine, E. G., & Levine, S. K. (2005). *Principles and practice of expressive arts therapy: Toward a therapeutic aesthetics.* Jessica Kingsley Publishers.

Levine, P. A. (2010). *In an unspoken voice: How the body releases trauma and restores goodness.* North Atlantic Books.

Levine, S. K. (1997). *Poiesis: The language of psychology and the speech of the soul.* Jessica Kingsley Publishers.

Porges, S. W. (2011). *The Polyvagal theory: Neurophysiological foundations of emotions, attachment, communication and self-regulation.* Norton.

Porges, S. W. (2017). *The pocket guide to the Polyvagal theory.* Norton.

Richardson, C. (2016). *Expressive arts therapy for traumatized children and adolescents: A four-phase model.* Routledge.

Sanders, M. R., & Thompson, G. S. (2022). *Polyvagal theory and the developing child: Systems of care for strengthening kids, families, and communities.* Norton.

Van der Kolk, B. A. (2003). The neurobiology of childhood trauma and abuse. *Child and Adolescent Psychiatric Clinics of North America, 12*(2), 293–317.

Van der Kolk, B. A. (2014). *The body keeps the score: Brain, mind and body in the healing of trauma.* Viking.

17
Animal Assisted Play Therapy™ as a Polyvagal Process

Mary Rottier and Rebecca Dickinson

Topic Overview

Research has shown that animals play a significant role in the overall development of children. Children learn about social interactions, boundaries, emotional reciprocity, and responsibility through animal relationships. Studies have shown that children who own pets have more empathy for others, higher self-esteem, and better social skills than other children (Jalongo et al., 2004). One specific approach involving animals as part of the therapeutic intervention is Animal Assisted Play Therapy™ (AAPT). VanFleet and Faa-Thompson (2017a) define AAPT as:

> The integrated involvement of animals in the context of play therapy, in which appropriately trained therapists and animals engage with clients primarily through systematic playful interventions, with the goal of improving clients' developmental and psychosocial health, while simultaneously ensuring the animal's well-being and voluntary engagement. Play and playfulness are essential ingredients of the interactions and the relationship.
>
> (p. 17)

There are many different approaches to involving animals in mental health therapy, in visitation programs (such as in hospitals), as support systems (e.g., for children testifying in court, school reading buddies, etc.), and as part of therapeutic residential facilities (e.g., Green Chimneys in New York). AAPT refers to a specific treatment modality developed by Risë VanFleet and Tracie Faa-Thompson. In AAPT, the animal is not equivalent to a toy in the playroom. The animal is an active, independent, and self-determining participant, with the play therapist facilitating interactions between the client and the animal through various interventions.

DOI: 10.4324/9781003352976-17

One misconception of AAPT is that it involves only petting the animal. Other interventions are wide-ranging and depend heavily on the animal's species, what the individual animal enjoys, and what suits the client's therapeutic goals. Other examples of interventions in AAPT include: (1) interactive puzzles that can stimulate and challenge both the child and the animal to learn problem-solving skills, frustration tolerance, and coping skills; (2) games, such as fetch and tug, to allow opportunities for modeling regulation skills, mental stimulation, and providing an opportunity for cooperative play, which often leads to mutual enjoyment and enhances the therapeutic relationship; (3) teaching a head tilt in response to verbal communication from a child or training a look cue to stimulate eye contact between a child and animal, which can communicate signals of safety. This can especially be helpful during elevated arousal states such as during a tantrum or over-stimulation. These gestures or behaviors can help a child regulate back into their own safe state, thus allowing them to relax and obtain a neuroception of safety; and (4) activities such as clicker training, agility training, or trick training with an animal, which can also aid in providing regulation as well as self-esteem and confidence building. In addition to the interventions used in AAPT, the metaphors that develop through the child's play are just as crucial in AAPT as in traditional play therapy (VanFleet & Faa-Thompson, 2019; VanFleet et al., 2019).

While dogs and horses tend to be the most common animals involved in AAPT work, other practitioners involve animals such as cats, goats, rabbits, and guinea pigs. Sessions can be conducted across the nondirective to directive play therapy spectrum, but this is more often dictated by the individual strengths, interests, and needs of the animal involved rather than the practitioner's theoretical orientation. Because AAPT involves specific training, knowledge, and skills, this chapter does not prepare readers to incorporate this approach into their practice. Instead, it presents a connection between AAPT and the Polyvagal theory. Additionally, it should be noted that not all animals (even our own beloved pets) are appropriate for involvement in AAPT, just as this model is not appropriate for all clients (VanFleet & Faa-Thompson, 2017b; VanFleet & Faa-Thompson, 2015a; VanFleet & Faa-Thompson, 2015b).

AAPT has many benefits but requires multiple specialized skill sets, including knowledge of child-specific play interventions and animal-assisted therapy, animal-specific training, species-specific knowledge, and behavioral principles. This model combines several well-researched and valuable fields (animal-assisted therapy, play therapy, ethology, anthrozoology, and animal sciences, among others), which creates more effective treatment options for individual clients. With multiple relationships (client/therapist, client/ animal, and therapist/animal) present to focus on, there are more opportunities to observe and understand behavior within a single session and over time. The playfulness an animal can bring to the session can help children who struggle to play because their challenges are so significant. AAPT also improves social skills, provides modeling opportunities, and can help with emotional and behavioral regulation.

AAPT can be conducted from various play therapy theories, frameworks, and approaches. Polyvagal theory is one such theory that blends well with AAPT. Polyvagal-informed approaches to AAPT can help children and their caregivers achieve more profound levels of safety and connection, which is crucial to the success of therapy. The primary polyvagal concepts at work in AAPT are the neuroception of safety and co-regulation. Both neuroception of safety and co-regulation are dependent on relationships. The therapeutic relationship has repeatedly been shown to be incredibly important within the therapeutic process. The therapeutic relationship also includes the animal involved, providing additional opportunities through neuroception and co-regulation. Particularly for clients who have experienced significant trauma or abuse, the relationship with the animal may initially feel safer than the relationship with the play therapist.

Neuroception of Safety in AAPT

Neuroception is a subconscious system that allows us to determine whether situations or people are safe or dangerous (Porges, 2011). Polyvagal theory suggests that a natural order of response is evident in all human experiences (Porges, 2011). We come into the world ready to connect and to feel safe in our bodies, environments, and relationships. The primary principle of AAPT is that there must be reciprocal and mutually beneficial relationships (VanFleet & Faa-Thompson, 2017a). AAPT is not about controlling the animal to do what the therapist desires but about recognizing the animal's innate nature, accepting it, and building a relationship around it.

According to Porges (2011), the ventral vagal pathway responds to safety cues and supports feeling engaged and socially connected. In contrast, the dorsal vagal pathway responds to signals of extreme danger. It takes us out of connection and awareness and into a protective state of numbness. In AAPT, the animal can serve both as a model and as a physically grounding presence, particularly in terms of touch. Like humans, animals also experience the same sympathetic nervous system responses and demonstrate their own signals related to calmness and stress. The animal can serve directly or indirectly as a metaphor for the client with the therapist helping the client learn, recognize, and respond to calming signals the animal is displaying, indicating their arousal state and need to counteract those feelings of arousal.

Physical touch between the client and animal may also provide a sense of grounding when a client is having sympathetic nervous system responses, but the presence of an animal in and of itself can create a calming effect in the body. Studies with dogs, specifically, have shown that people relax in the presence of a dog, displaying loosened muscles and easing pain (Sakson, 2007). Interactions between dogs and humans have also been shown to increase levels of oxytocin (commonly regarded as the "love hormone") in both the dog and the human (Beetz et al., 2012). Parish-Plass (2008) suggests that an animal's presence in a setting contributes to the perception of a safe environment. There is also a direct and reciprocal connection between the animal's neuroception of safety and ours. The human nervous system picks up on the animal's neuroceptive expressions, affecting the human's neuroception of safety and vice versa. This perception of safety is the core of AAPT and serves as one of the guiding principles as outlined by VanFleet and Faa-Thompson (2017a).

Even being in the presence of a play therapy animal can directly affect our nervous system by providing nonverbal cues of safety and connection. Dogs, for example, have reciprocal engagement systems just like humans. Dogs are great companions and listeners, make no judgments, are very accepting, and usually enjoy the company of humans. VanFleet (2018) reframes the common characterization of dogs as being unconditional in their interactions with humans to being accepting and tolerant of many things while still having individual limits and boundaries. Dogs can give nurturance and love to us as well. Children often indicate they feel safer when dogs are around (Thompson, 2009).

Co-Regulation in AAPT

Self-regulation (managing one's feelings) is developed only through the experience of co-regulation (managing feelings with help)—most mammals co-regulate. Regulating emotions can be difficult when stuck in the dorsal or sympathetic states. Therapy animals can be a part of emotional regulation strategies to help people move from a state of heightened arousal to a more regulated state of ventral vagal. While dogs and cats are the most studied examples, other animals, such as horses, are known to co-regulate as well.

Studies have supported the physiological effects of interacting with an animal. Many people do not accurately label canine body language and communication, missing essential cues and signals. A wagging tail itself is not always a sign of enjoyment. Dogs also wag their tails when nervous, stressed, or cautious, but it is the speed, tension, and height of the tail wag that communicates what the dog is truly experiencing. Typically, when a dog is in a state of safety, they get closer to you. They become more playful, have increased eye contact, and their tails, ears, and eyes express their safety. Across species, animals communicate their sense of safety through their body language, including posture, facial or body tension, ear placement, etc. Human nervous systems can pick up on their security cues, causing a neuroception of safety within us.

One common effect of trauma, abuse, and neglect is difficulties in both self-regulation and co-regulating. These difficulties can manifest in problems with establishing and maintaining healthy relationships. Until such clients can develop their abilities around self-regulation, co-regulation and a sense of safety in the presence of another appropriate mammal (human or animal) is a key component of promoting the clients' optimal wellbeing (Hrdy, 2008).

Our mammalian companion animals, like dogs, become a part of our families, a process which has also been supported by work on the human-animal bond (see Barba, 1995; Triebenbacher, 2000; Selby & Rhoades, 1981). Connections with animals during early childhood have been linked to the development of nurturing and caring behavior in children (Mueller et al., 2019; Triebenbacher, 1998). The presence of and interactions with a pet have been shown to activate the release of serotonin and dopamine (the neurochemicals associated with feelings of happiness and relaxation) (Charnetski et al., 2004), as well as oxytocin (Beetz et al., 2012). These same benefits of having an animal within a household can be mimicked in the interactions provided through AAPT.

According to Porges (2011), other animals, such as reptiles, do not have the same social engagement system as mammals. This system promotes social interactions such as play, co-regulation, and intimacy (Porges & Dana, 2018). These species do not need to co-regulate with one other. There is no social engagement system or facial affect, as they are basically in a constant state of mobilization or immobilization. Reptiles and other non-social species of animals are not involved in AAPT work for these exact reasons.

There are a variety of different co-regulation strategies commonly seen in AAPT. The sensory stimulation of touching or stroking animals can provide a comforting tether for clients. In AAPT, engaging clients in attending to and nurturing the animals through grooming, providing food and water, and other caretaking activities can reduce hyper-arousal symptoms. Animals can often be a "social lubricant," reducing client experiences of isolation and disconnection. The mere presence of an animal often attracts attention and engagement, even with strangers. The connection between the client and animal in AAPT often happens naturally but also intentionally, as animals should be selected for involvement with consideration for their interest in and enjoyment in interacting with people. All interventions are conducted with the safety and welfare of the animal and the human participants always at the forefront.

The animal's mere presence can help facilitate a trust-building bond between the therapist and the client. In AAPT, play and playfulness are integral to the process. Play occurs naturally in animals, and many naturally goofy animal behaviors can be harnessed while ensuring that the activities are enjoyable and meaningful for all involved. In play therapy, the client's play is considered their "work." This holds true in AAPT, but the playful interactions with the animal provide additional psychological distance for the client by shifting the focus from the client's difficulties to the animal. Through these non-threatening interactions, animals can help clients focus on complex issues such as processing complicated feelings, engaging in a meaningful and nonjudgmental relationship, and learning and practicing new skills. The animal and their emotions, behaviors, wants, and needs often become the metaphor for the child, providing psychological safety to take therapeutic risks towards healing and growth. The animal offers nurturance through a presentation of acceptance throughout the therapeutic process.

Therapeutic Powers of Play

Schaefer and Drewes (2014) identify 20 specific therapeutic powers of play. These serve as the foundation of play therapy and help explain how and why play therapy works. While many of the therapeutic powers of play identified by Schaefer and Drewes are applicable to integrating AAPT with Polyvagal theory, we will highlight a few that are most relevant to the connections made in this chapter. Primarily, these most applicable therapeutic powers of play come from two categories: "Enhances Social Relationships" and "Increases Personal Strengths" and align directly with the goal areas of AAPT identified by VanFleet and Faa-Thompson (2017a): self-efficacy, attachment and relationship, empathy, self-regulation, and problem-solving.

All four therapeutic powers of play from the "Enhances Social Relationships" category apply to AAPT: therapeutic relationship, attachment, social competence, and empathy. Relationship is a guiding principle of AAPT. First and foremost, the relationship between the therapist and the animal must be mutually respectful, empathic (attuned), and securely attached (VanFleet & Faa-Thompson, 2017a). In this way, the relationship between the therapist and the animal serves both as a model of a healthy social relationship and the foundation from which the client can then build their own reciprocal relationship with the animal based on care and trust.

Clients, especially child clients, tend to gravitate naturally to animals (Melson, 2001), and the animals involved in AAPT are no different. We find that children demonstrate attachment to our animals in a variety of ways in both direct interactions with the animal (e.g., talking to the animal, choosing an activity/treat that the animal enjoys, etc.) and in indirect interactions with/or about the animal (e.g., sharing about their session with a caregiver, verbalizing joy at the animal remembering the client between sessions, etc.).

AAPT has a strict requirement of nonaversive methods being used on or towards the animal (VanFleet & Faa-Thompson, 2017a). Animals have agency and choice in whether to participate in an activity. These practices are intentional in the implicit message they send to clients about the respect that should be shown to their bodies, their choices, and others, encouraging respect and empathy.

The client can develop and practice social competence in interactions with the animal and the therapist through AAPT interventions. The therapist might prompt or encourage the client to notice, recognize, and respond to the animal's reactions to verbal or nonverbal cues, movement, etc., during play. This allows the client to practice attuning to the animal and offers them the opportunity to make choices within the relationship in response to the animal's reactions. The client learns how to engage reciprocally with the animal, improving their social competence. This reciprocity can later be bridged outside of the playroom into interactions with others.

Under the category of "Increases Personal Strengths," the therapeutic powers of play of resiliency, self-regulation, and self-esteem are most significant. Many AAPT practitioners incorporate positive, relationship-based animal training practices into their sessions with clients. Scaffolding clients in an AAPT intervention where the client is trying to teach the animal a new behavior provides an underlying lesson in resilience. The same is true when the client asks the animal to engage in an activity that the animal has not done before, such as negotiating an obstacle course. In these instances, we often see clients attempt to help the animal so that they can be successful at the new activity, especially when the animal becomes discouraged or confused. In a game where the client has hidden bits of food for a dog to find, the client can encourage the dog towards where the food is hidden or move it from a more hidden spot out into the open. As the client helps the animal persist or succeed, the client also reinforces their own sense of resiliency.

Self-regulation is increased through the relationship with the animal in safe but playful interactions. By encouraging a client to recognize and respond to the animal's emotional state and wellbeing, the therapist helps the client practice recognizing and regulating their own emotional responses. Clients can engage with the animal, practicing new behaviors in real time based on the animal's reactions without fear of shame or embarrassment.

AAPT offers multiple opportunities for the client to experience an increased sense of self-esteem. Clients often display a sense of mastery through this work. While this can take different forms, it can include accomplishments such as developing animal training skills, an increased knowledge of a species or a particular animal, successfully negotiating an obstacle course with the animal, or more personal intrinsic gains (e.g., increased problem-solving skills, increased perseverance, decreased anxiety, etc.). The relationships in AAPT also feed a client's self-esteem through genuine acceptance and support.

Effectiveness of AAPT and Polyvagal Theory

Polyvagal theory provides a neurophysiological framework for working with animals in play therapy. All people need to be in the right autonomic state to use their social capacity. Through AAPT, we can intentionally assist clients in identifying emotions and support our social engagement system through touch, movement, connectedness, and play with a therapy animal. Research supports the effectiveness of animal connections in regulating our autonomic nervous system. Parish-Plass (2008) claimed that the presence of the therapy dog in play therapy provides a less threatening atmosphere and enhances feelings of safety for a child. A study by Martin and Farnum (2002) showed that children exhibited a more playful mood, were more focused, and were more aware of their social environments when in the presence of a therapy dog. Thompson (2009) found that AAPT is beneficial in establishing rapport, decreasing aggression, and improving self-esteem in children diagnosed with anxiety disorders. Purewal and colleagues (2017) found that interacting with a dog is generally beneficial for children across multiple domains (cognitive, social, emotional, behavioral, and educational). Overall, there is a significant amount of support for the connection between AAPT work through a Polyvagal lens in promoting attachment, creating a sense of safety, building self-esteem and confidence, and increasing empathy.

Caregiver Involvement

There are numerous options for engaging caregivers in AAPT, providing those caregivers with the same benefits of neuroception and co-regulation as the client. As previously mentioned, AAPT can be conducted as part of family sessions, allowing opportunities for the caregiver to be involved throughout the process and to be directly engaged in the interventions along with the client. As noted previously in this chapter, the individual animal and their strengths, interests, and needs will guide whether the interventions are conducted from a nondirective or a more directive play therapy orientation. The level of structure is then aligned with the client's goals.

When AAPT is used to work with a client individually, often there are opportunities to bring the caregiver into the session to highlight the client's progress, including demonstrations with the animals that show the client's skills and relationship. The practitioner may also structure the caregiver's involvement, where the client gets the opportunity to teach the caregiver some of the things they have learned. Such interactions give the client an opportunity to show-off and receive positive attention for their work. Involving the caregiver also provides the opportunity to help bridge the client's relationship with the animal into relationships outside of the playroom. New relationship dynamics are added to the mix (caregiver/client and caregiver/animal), with the client helping create the neuroceptive link.

Finally, the AAPT practitioner may engage in caregiver consultation as part of or in addition to client sessions. During consultation, the practitioner works with the caregiver to further support the client by gathering additional information, answering questions, making suggestions, providing resources, teaching skills, etc. The therapist can involve the animal directly (the animal is present and involved in the consultation), indirectly (the animal is discussed but not involved), and even metaphorically (the animal serves as a metaphor for the child) as part of consultation to both showcase client progress and to describe the client's continued needs.

Case Example: Polyvagal Theory and AAPT in Action

Stevie was an eight-year-old child who presented with his mother for play therapy with one of the authors (Mary) due to parental divorce. Stevie was a highly anxious and depressed child who exhibited some social, emotional, and academic delays. However, from the initial session, it was clear that Stevie was depressed and hurt by his father's absence following the divorce.

The play therapy process was explained at his first session with a therapy dog named Jenga. At the time, Jenga was a five-year-old Sheltie who had been trained to be involved in the AAPT partnership with her owner, Mary. Jenga showed a strong interest in play, as evidenced by frequent play bows, tracking children as they play, and engaging with them when requested. She was best suited for nondirective play sessions, as even with a relatively high energy level, she could settle and relax quickly when needed. This skill set is very beneficial when working with children needing co-regulation skills.

Most of the sessions consisted of Stevie petting Jenga while telling her about losing his father's attention. This was an excellent example of how AAPT can assist clients in identifying emotions and support the social engagement system through touch, connectedness, and play with a therapy animal. For Stevie, this connectedness was crucial and seen at every session. It should be noted that although Stevie engaged in verbally sharing his feelings with Jenga frequently in sessions, the goal is not to get the child to process their feelings verbally. It is the play activities and metaphors that develop as part of the play that is the primary area used to address the client's difficulties.

Typically, Stevie came into sessions and started by telling Jenga something new going on in his life, and then they ended the session with an agreed-upon play activity. Sometimes Stevie and Jenga played fetch, a game of Feelings Jenga (in honor of his favorite pup), tug, or tag. Other times Stevie and Jenga worked as an agility team or played hide and seek, learning the value of problem-solving, teamwork, and regulation. The two even created new interventions together. These play activities were essential to Stevie's ability to co-regulate, especially following emotionally charged conversations about his father.

After several sessions, Stevie's mother called the therapist requesting an emergency session after Stevie's father abruptly told him he was terminating his parental rights. As soon as Stevie entered the playroom, he went straight to the spot where he and Jenga would sit together, curled up on the pillow with Jenga, and while crying, told her about his phone call with his dad. As Stevie told his story to Jenga, she licked his hand and his tears as they fell while his therapist provided reflective statements, validated his feelings, and supported and encouraged him to share his emotions. Together Jenga and the therapist were able to support Stevie where he was, allowing him to remain in a regulated and safe state. This neuroception of safety gave Stevie the signal that he was safe to continue to process this traumatic experience. It helped his autonomic nervous system to climb up the polyvagal ladder. After the session, Stevie's mom reported that Stevie was feeling much better.

After that pivotal moment, the bond between Jenga and Stevie grew. In each of Stevie's sessions, Jenga played a critical part in his feeling safe enough to process his trauma. The interactions they shared through touch, movement, and play supported Stevie's social engagement system, as the Polyvagal theory proposes. AAPT helped Stevie access safe ways of regulating and restoring his nervous system to a balanced state of calm, resilience, and growth. It lightened his mood and promoted a feeling of safety and acceptance, which allowed him to remain in the ventral vagal pathway, facilitating his ability to deal with his trauma successfully.

Conclusion

Animal-assisted play therapy is one modality of play therapy that is highly compatible with the Polyvagal theory concepts of neuroception of safety and co-regulation. Opportunities to develop both experiences are built out of the various combinations of relationships and interactions between the animal-assisted play therapist, the animal involved, and the client. The flexibility of animal-assisted play therapy offers practitioners a wide range of options to develop a client's individual neuroception of safety and co-regulation skills based on practitioner theoretical orientation and the type, personality, and strengths of the animal involved.

 Treatment Takeaways

- AAPT is a specific treatment modality requiring specialized training, knowledge, and skills.
- The Polyvagal theoretical concepts of neuroception and self-regulation can be used to help understand some of the therapeutic dynamics occurring during AAPT.
- The various relationships within AAPT provide multiple avenues to establish and maintain a sense of neuroception.
- AAPT offers unique opportunities for developing a client's ability to co-regulate as well as to learn self-regulation through relationship and intentional AAPT interventions.

References

Barba, B. E. (1995). A critical review on the human/companion animal relationship. *Antrhozoös*, 8, 9–15.

Beetz, A., Uvnas-Moberg, K., Julius, H., & Kotrschal, K. (2012). Psychosocial and psychophysiological effects of human-animal interactions: The possible role of oxytocin. *Frontiers in Psychology*, 3, 234–234.

Charnetski, C. J., Riggers, S., & Brennan, F. (2004). Effect of petting a dog on immune system function. *Psychological Reports*, 95, 1087–1091.

Hrdy, S. B. (2008). *Mothers and others: The evolutionary origins of mutual understanding*. Belknap Press.

Jalongo, M. R., Astorino, T., & Bomboy, N. (2004). Canine visitors: The influence of therapy dogs on young children's learning and well-being in classrooms and hospitals. *Early Childhood Education Journal*, 32(1).

Martin, F., & Farnum, J. (2002). Animal-assisted therapy for children with pervasive developmental disorders. *Western Journal of Nursing Research*, 24(6), 657–670.

Melson, G. F. (2001). *Why the wild things are: Animals in the lives of children*. Harvard University Press.

Mueller, M. K., Fine, A. H., & O'Haire, M. E. (2019). Understanding the role of human–animal interaction in the family context. In A. H. Fine (Ed.), *Handbook on animal-assisted therapy* (5th ed., pp. 351–362). Academic Press.

Parish-Plass, N. (2008). Animal-assisted therapy with children suffering from insecure attachment due to abuse and neglect: A method to lower the risk of intergenerational transmission of abuse? *Clinical Child Psychology & Psychiatry*, 13(1), 7–30.

Porges, S. W. (2011). *The Polyvagal theory: Neurophysiological foundations of emotions, attachment, communication and self-regulation*. Norton.

Porges, S. W., & Dana, D. (2018). *Clinical applications of the Polyvagal theory: The emergence of polyvagal-informed therapies*. Norton.

Purewal, R., Christley, R., Kordas, K., Joinson, C., Meints, K., Gee, N., & Westgarth, C. (2017). Companion animals and child/adolescent development: A systematic review of the evidence. *International Journal of Environmental Research and Public Health*, 14(3), 234.

Sakson, S. (2007). *Paws & effect: The healing power of dogs*. Alyson Books.

Schaefer, C. E., & Drewes, A. A. (Eds.). (2014). *The therapeutic powers of play: 20 core agents of change* (2nd ed.). Wiley.

Selby, L. A., & Rhoades, J. D. (1981). Attitudes of the public towards dogs and cats as companion animals. *The Journal of Small Animal Practice, 22*(3), 129–137.

Thompson, M. J. (2009). Animal-assisted play therapy: Canines as co-therapists. In G. R. Walz, J. C. Bleuer, & R. K. Yep (Eds.), *Vistas: Compelling counseling interventions 2009* (pp. 199–209). American Counseling Association.

Triebenbacher, S. L. (1998). Pets as transitional objects: Their role in children's emotional development. *Psychological Reports, 82*(1), 191–200.

Triebenbacher, S. L. (2000). The companion animal within the family system: The manner in which animals enhance life within the home. In A. Fine (Ed.), *Animal-assisted therapy: Theoretical foundations and guidelines for practice* (pp. 337–375). Academic Press.

VanFleet, R. (2018). Ameliorating children's stress and trauma: Roles for dogs in counseling, therapy, and disaster relief. In M. R. Jalongo (Ed.), *Children, dogs and education—caring for, learning alongside, and gaining support from canine companions* (pp. 211–227). Springer.

VanFleet, R., & Faa-Thompson, T. (2015a). Animal assisted play therapy to empower vulnerable children. In E. J. Green & A. C. Myrick (Eds.), *Play therapy with vulnerable populations: No child forgotten* (pp. 85–103). Rowman & Littlefield.

VanFleet, R., & Faa-Thompson, T. (2015b). Short-term animal assisted play therapy for children. In H. G. Kaduson & C. E. Schaefer (Eds.), *Short-term play therapy for children* (3rd ed., pp. 175–197). Guilford.

VanFleet, R., & Faa-Thompson, T. (2017a). *Animal-assisted play therapy.* Professional Resource Press.

VanFleet, R., & Faa-Thompson, T. (2017b). Animal assisted play therapy with reticent children: With a little help from friends. In C. A. Malchiodi & D. A. Crenshaw (Eds.), *What to do when children clam up in psychotherapy: Interventions to facilitate communication* (pp. 217–237). Guilford.

VanFleet, R., & Faa-Thompson, T. (2019). *Manual of animal assisted play therapy techniques.* Play Therapy Press.

VanFleet, R., Fine, A. H., & Faa-Thompson, T. (2019). Application of animal-assisted interventions in professional mental health settings: An overview of practice considerations. In A. H. Fine (Ed.), *Handbook on animal-assisted therapy* (Vol. 5, pp. 225–248). Elsevier/Academic Press.

18
Digital Play Therapy™

Harnessing the Felt Sense of Safety in the Digital Space

Jessica Stone and Rachel Altvater

Overview

The use of digital play in therapy has been discussed for decades. Gardner (1991) pondered the use of Nintendo games in psychotherapy in 1991. Clarke and Schoech discussed the use of computer-assisted games with adolescents in 1994, as have many others over time, such as Favelle, 1995; Mineo et al., 2009; Ceranoglu, 2010; Stone, 2019. A complete list would be quite lengthy. These early rumblings remained predominately underground until the 2019 COVID-19 pandemic impacted the world. Suddenly the power of connection through digital means was discovered and explored further by so many who had either been previously quiet about the use of such tools in therapy or those who had dismissed the inherent value without exploration. Today we celebrate new horizons in many directions.

This chapter bridges the relationship between Polyvagal theory, Digital Play Therapy™, and the ability to foster, recognize, and experience the felt sense of safety in digital spaces. The therapeutic value of digital tools within the therapeutic relationship for the autonomic nervous system is highlighted through the descriptions of Digital Play Therapy, Polyvagal theory, and the therapeutic powers of play. Recognition of the powerful states of the dorsal and ventral systems during digital play, and consequently the impacts the attuned, attentive, and informed therapist can have for the client, is critical for the digital native client.

DOI: 10.4324/9781003352976-18

Digital Play Therapy™

Digital Play Therapy (DPT) is a play therapy modality which is grounded in the therapeutic powers of play (Schaefer & Drewes, 2014), prescriptive play therapy (Kaduson et al., 2019), and the DPT 5 Cs: competence, comfort, culture, congruency, and capability (Stone, 2019, 2022). Defined as "a modality that utilizes highly motivating, immersive activities to incorporate areas of client culture and interest into the play therapy process to deepen relationships, gather information, implement interventions, and advance the treatment plan forward," DPT provides a structure and foundation for the use of digital tools in therapy (Stone, 2022, p. 16).

Consisting of three levels of use, DPT allows the client and therapist to engage in ways that are congruent, comfortable, and safe for many clients. Level 1 includes the discussion of anything to do with digital hardware or software. This could be a device, game, or experience *that the client deems important.* The openness of the therapist to listen and/or discuss (verbally or non-verbally) is imperative, as it allows the client to understand that their whole-self is accepted within the space. Acknowledging and incorporating the client's culture, including their interest in digital hardware and software, allows the client to feel accepted, seen, heard, understood, and valued by the play therapist.

Level 2 includes the incorporation of a digital tool to look up, watch, witness, share, etc. any content that the client or therapist would like to bring into the session. This can include watching YouTube® or looking up the lyrics to a song, etc. In this level, a device is displaying information which both the client and therapist are attending to. Level three includes co-play. The therapist and client are engaging in play together within a particular software using compatible or common hardware. Each level of DPT has merit and value, with the therapist displaying interest and openness to the whole client in an effort to connect, engage, and understand the client and their needs (Stone, 2022).

Through the combination of a strong theory foundation and knowledge of the client, along with knowledge of a variety of digital hardware and software, and activated components within the interactions, the play therapist can foster an environment and experience which provide a neuroception of safety. This allows the treatment plan to move forward. With millions of programs available, the therapeutic interactions can be customized to the client's needs, particularly those which impact the emotional, physical, cognitive, and neurological systems. Ultimately, digital items are just another tool in the playroom, and they can be very powerful when used properly.

Applying Polyvagal Theory to Digital Play Therapy

Polyvagal theory, which Dana (2018) refers to as the "science of safety," combines physiological and psychological constructs to comprehend our internal processes. The nervous system is of primary importance when working with clients, as it shapes and informs perspective, ongoing experiences, and connection with self and others. When humans have a felt sense of safety, the environment affords an opportunity for more secure attachments and deeper reparative healing experiences. Conversely, if the nervous system perceives threat or uncertainty, it is wired for protection and is likely to behave in a manner that is rooted in survival.

Psychotherapy is intended to be a cathartic holding space, meaning the client is able to safely express, process, and work toward resolution of challenging internal and external experiences. A felt sense of safety is imperative within this holding space, as a perceived lack of trust and protection inhibits connection and therapeutic processing. In play therapy treatment specifically, this felt sense of safety is facilitated through a client being seen, heard, understood, and valued. Foundational play therapy tenets are to meet clients, namely children, where they are and to speak their language of play to encourage this process (Axline, 2011; Landreth, 2012). As explored in the previous section, the digital realm is often a space of comfort, expertise, and interest for many digital native children. This digital play space of easement and familiarity aids healthy autonomic nervous system responses and co-regulation within the therapeutic process.

Neuroception

Neuroception, a concept defined by Porges (2004), "describe(s) how neural circuits distinguish whether situations or people are safe, dangerous, or life threatening" (p. 19). He explains that neuroception occurs in the primitive parts of the brain, thus transpiring outside conscious awareness. So the body often responds prior to the individual cognitively recognizing a perceived threat. Oftentimes, there is a response or feeling that results from these neuroception experiences; however, pinpointing triggers or contributors are not always as clear and potentially further complicate connections and an ability to regulate experiences. A lack of awareness of the reason for a somatic response or other feeling often keeps individuals on high alert for self-preservation purposes. Therapy aims to uncover and clarify possible reasons behind behaviors, which improves insight, a sense of power and control, and ultimately a felt sense of safety.

Entering into a new environment or meeting a stranger can activate a threat response within the nervous system. In the introductory stage of play therapy, it is common for clients to experience anxiety and uncertainty of the space and play therapist. Regularly, the first several sessions are focused on building rapport, establishing a strong therapeutic alliance, offering opportunities for exploration, and working toward establishment of a felt sense of safety. Perceived safety cues within the environment, such as toys, child-friendly decor, a warm, welcoming environment, and a general sense of comfort and familiarity, aid in a neuroception response that promotes positive physiological experiences.

The digital realm, in particular, offers various well-known safety cues from the start of services as children are typically well-acquainted with, and are masters within, this space. Environments which are familiar, safe, and nourishing "invite connection and inspire an enlivening of ventral energy. When we inhabit spaces that are filled with signs of safety, spaces that invite us to enter and stay awhile, we move toward well-being" (Dana, 2022, A Ventral Space card, para 1). Comfortable, familiar, and safe digital environments can reduce the need to protect oneself within the therapeutic dynamic.

When children are immediately encouraged to enter into an expert role and guide the play therapist through the digital ecosystem in manners that are relevant and therapeutic for them, they transition from a space of apprehension and defensiveness to social engagement and alleviation. Of note, some digital spaces are unsafe and uncomfortable, especially when associated with trauma, age or developmentally inappropriate experiences, or predatory interactions. Digital play therapists remain aware of and set parameters for safe digital play when necessary to protect clients and support beneficial neuroception experiences.

Autonomic Nervous System

The autonomic nervous system consists of the sympathetic and parasympathetic branches. The sympathetic nervous system is activated when confronted with cues of danger and triggers the fight-or-flight or freeze-or-fawn response; we can become disorganized and flooded (Dana, 2022; Frothing-ham, 2021; Cannon, 1925). This sympathetic system works as an adaptive survival mechanism to keep the person safe. Such cues and triggers are important human responses, and the ability to understand, respond, and reg-ulate is a critical component of human development.

The parasympathetic nervous system has two pathways in Polyvagal theory—dorsal and ventral vagal. The dorsal vagal pathway is activated when cues of extreme danger are present. The result is a freeze response, which is dis-connection, at times dissociation, and a "protective state of collapse" (Dana, 2018, p. 9). When this happens, we are removed from connection and aware-ness, which are both critical for moving out of the dorsal state (Dana, 2022). The importance of digital play within a therapeutic environment, connected with an attuned therapist, is highlighted here: the pathway from a dorsal state to a ventral state includes a titration of energy to avoid flooding—too much too quickly can return the system to a dorsal state. A connected and observant therapist can guide and moderate the play, as appropriate, to avoid flooding and assist in the process toward regulation. The ventral vagal pathway responds to cues of safety, which fosters comfort, connection, and co-regulation, along with the ability to connect with something greater than oneself, and each can be activated within the digital play.

Opportunities to transition between the various autonomic nervous system responses in an attempt to safely experience and overcome troubling encoun-ters becomes possible within the safety of the client-play therapist dyad. In particular, this relationship appears within digital play and allows for the safe exploration and practice of a number of resources and reactions. Dana states: "It is important to have a range of resources available to you so that you can reach for a resource that matches your energy level in the moment" (2022, Meeting the Moment card, para 1). This safe exploration and ability for safe repetition allows the client to add to their dorsal-to-vagal response repertoire.

Play therapy provides a working-through experience for children to pro-cess psychological distress from a *safe enough distance*. Clients externalize or project onto therapeutic toys, which in digital play might be represented as avatars/characters or objects within the play space. As an example, if a client is engaging in a fear-based video game, they might guide their char-acter through various obstacles and try out alternate solutions to overcome those obstacles. Scary music, ominous backdrops, or antagonistic characters are likely to activate the sympathetic or dorsal vagal nervous system. When there is a felt sense of safety within the therapeutic relationship and a deeper sense of comfort and self-trust within a familiar digital space, clients are bet-ter able to confront and overcome these frightening encounters. This results in activation of the ventral vagal pathway and reduction of ongoing psychological distress within anxiety-provoking situations. Additionally, engaging in digital play which activates this process can allow the client to discern between historical patterns of protection and other available options. The ability to explore, and ultimately choose, an intentional response rather than a habitual one allows for generalizable change.

Co-Regulation

Polyvagal theory "identifies co-regulation as a biological imperative: a need that must be met to sustain life" (Dana, 2018, p. 4). Regulatory experiences are strongly encouraged to tame undesirable nervous system activation. Of note, some sympathetic and dorsal vagal responses can be adaptive for ongoing survival and safety; however, heightened and prolonged activation are quite detrimental to the mind and body. Compassionate, connecting, co-regulating experiences ease heightened nervous system responses and aid in positive neuroception and ventral vagal experiences.

A primary benefit of Digital Play Therapy is co-play, which is collaboratively or competitively playing a game together, through taking turns, or via parallel play (Stone, 2022). Co-play fosters relationships, is likely to enhance connection and understanding, and can be a positive experience for all involved, even if the game itself activates frustration, conflict, or negative feelings. Encounters within co-play provide opportunities for communication, validation and nurturance of emotion, safe exploration with support and potential for additional resources, and so much more. Children often express passion, enjoyment, and fulfillment with playful digital realms, and the attention, interest, and connection of a supportive person in this space makes more of an impact than one might realize. When adults are disconnected from children in this space and games or other digital interactions are dismissed or belittled, children often feel that what matters to them lacks value, importance, or relevance to others. These messages are likely to result in dysregulating experiences and further misalignment and disengagement from others and intensification of psychological distress.

Amplified Integration of Polyvagal Theory and the Therapeutic Powers of Digital Play Therapy

Polyvagal theory amplifies the therapeutic powers (Schaefer & Drewes, 2014) of Digital Play Therapy (Stone, 2022). As described by Dana (2018), "adding a Polyvagal perspective to clinical practice draws the autonomic nervous system directly into the work of therapy, helping clients re-pattern their nervous systems, build capacity for regulation, and create autonomic pathways of safety and connection" (Book Summary section). Digital play presents an ideal platform and experience for this to occur, as it facilitates communication, fosters emotional wellness, increases personal strengths, and enhances social relationships for the digital native client (Schaefer & Drewes, 2014).

Clients who communicate through words and/or actions in digital play have the chance to therapeutically release and regulate, returning the sympathetic nervous system to a ventral state. Sometimes children lack the developmental ability to articulate their psychological distress, which often leads to increased frustration and dysregulation. Technology, a present facilitator of language, offers a desirable medium to express oneself and begin to conceptualize what is occurring, even if only metaphorically. The greater awareness a child gains into their distress, the better equipped they can become at managing it. Play-based communication serves as the gateway for the play therapist's, and subsequently the child's, understanding.

Digital play also fosters emotional wellness through a felt sense of safety through the screen. Children are able to enter into play-based spaces riddled with danger cues from a safe enough distance and work on alternate methods of calming the nervous system responses. During emotionally intense play, such as an aggressive and competitive battle royale game, the pathways of the nervous system are activated, and clients navigate situations and regulate the nervous system in the presence of a deeply attuned play therapist. Some digital games, particularly in virtual reality, also foster movement, which can also assist in the release of physical and emotional energy. Skills which foster emotional wellness can then be generalized to triggering or aggravating scenarios in their off-screen day-to-day interactions.

Clients have many opportunities within digital gaming to increase personal strengths, which greatly assists with ventral vagal experiences. Children want to encounter situations where they can advance their skillset, feel a sense of empowerment, and enhance their self-esteem. Many digital games implement recurrent reinforcers as a method to draw children back into the game or continue leveling up. Therapeutically, this is beneficial because it aids a child in improving their self-perception as capable, and they are likely to continue trying and working toward reaching their goals and aspirations.

Aforementioned, co-play is a primary benefit of Digital Play Therapy, as it allows for enhancement of social relationships. When children connect with another person on the digital platform, there is a sense of camaraderie. New situations that typically might make clients feel lost, alone, and vulnerable and that would be avoided are more likely to be approached with a play therapist in the space. This presence and co-play experience mitigates neuroception threat responses. As humans, we feel safer when we are able to enter into unfamiliar terrain with a safe person.

Caregiver Connection and Regulation Through Co-Play

Oftentimes, when caregivers bring their child to therapy, they are grappling with their own internal dysregulation. Whether it be because they are experiencing anxiety about their child's psychological challenges or they are navigating their own mental and emotional struggles, distress is a common occurrence. Guiding caregivers in regulating their nervous system supports the process of providing external regulation for their child. Imparting psychoeducation to caregivers about Polyvagal theory and Digital Play Therapy at the start of treatment is recommended to encourage support and to enhance awareness about therapy. A lack of knowledge about the process further fuels the already-heightened emotionality.

Caregivers are also strongly encouraged to spend time engaging in co-play with their child between sessions. A regularly scheduled digital playtime is advantageous for consistent connection and regulation. Benefits of family game nights include developing strong character, promoting problem-solving skills, stress reduction, fostering togetherness toward a shared goal, prosocial skills, enhancing communication, and promoting family bonding (Atkins, 2017; Stone, 2022).

By leaning into the child's world and understanding their perspective, caregivers begin to develop clearer cognizance of their child's inner and outer worlds. Humans desire to be seen, heard, and understood. When caregivers connect to their child's interests on the digital platform, and even share some of their own, they enhance familial relationships. These deepened connections further support ongoing nervous system regulatory experiences.

Case Example

Robert was an eleven-year-old 6th grade student who presented with interpersonal relationship difficulties. His parents reported that he had difficulties at home with siblings, with neighborhood peers, and at school. He was able to make friends easily; however, he was not able to maintain the friendships. Robert attended play therapy sessions both face-to-face and via a telemental-health platform.

One of Robert's favorite games to play was a Roblox® game called SCP Roleplay (Roblox Wiki, n.d.). This game is categorized as a horror game and "takes place on a fictional containment site, where dangerous anomalies of SCPs <sic> are contained from the public" (para 1). SCPs are creatures with different features and are identified by numbers, such as 457, 096, 049, 966, and 008. The player initially chooses a default role such as Security Department (SD) who act as guards, Scientific Department (ScD) who research and perform experiments, or Class-D (CD) who were previous jail inmates relocated to be used as test subjects with the SCPs. This basic information will assist with understanding the dynamics within the play. It is important to note that Robert's parents were aware of him playing this game and consented to the play within the therapy session. More discussion of communicating with caregivers can be found in Stone (2022).

Roblox is a "largely misunderstood phenomena in the therapeutic realm" (Stone, 2022, p. 239). Although it is often discussed as a platform specifically for children, billions of people of all ages play on the user-created-content platform. In fact, 30.6 billion hours of Roblox content was played between 2008 and December 31, 2020 (Roblox, 2021). There is great value to be found in many of the games within Roblox, and it is very important that the therapist understand the different types of games available, as they are played by all age groups.

Robert enjoyed the thrill of each SCP space. The therapist was new to the game, to the concept, and to the gameplay, so Robert was automatically the expert. He initially thrived within this dynamic. He felt a sense of safety and control outside of the locked SCP rooms, but also the thrill of going into the rooms, being killed, and then respawning within his solo play, and even more so when the therapist joined in Level 3 DPT play. His dorsal and ventral vagal systems were constantly activated and reactivated within this play.

The process of leading the therapist into the spaces was exciting for Robert. He really enjoyed his level of knowledge of the game play—knowing what the SCP was, what it looked like, what it would do to the therapist, and knowing the therapist was not aware what was in that locked room. He giggled as he led the therapist into the room, stating firmly that all would be OK and working to regulate the therapist, who was exhibiting fear of the unknown. The therapist was initially soothed by this and felt safe with the client who stated, "We are going to go look at something in this room together." The therapist quickly learned that going into the room led to being attacked and killed by the enclosed SCP.

The next time the client attempted to soothe, to say it would be OK "*this time*," the therapist would be killed again and again by the creature. Each creature was different in name, appearance, and features and led to new unknowns to the therapist. The client repeated this pattern for a number of consecutive sessions, each time attempting to soothe the therapist into believing that the experience would be safe, only to have the therapist die quickly. Additionally, the client escaped the room in time and left the therapist to be attacked and respawn alone. This meant the client and therapist were now in different areas of the game, as the spawn point was not close to where the client was exploring.

After a number of sessions where a perception of the neuroception of safety was provided by the client to the therapist, along with attempts at co-regulation, only for the therapist to be led and deceived, the pattern needed to change. The therapist allowed the client to display the pattern over time, and when the therapist indicated verbally and non-verbally that this was no longer a positive experience, the client did not appear to know how to change the pattern. This indicated a need for change initiated by the therapist. Therefore, the therapist declared verbally that she would no longer enter the SCP rooms. The client attempted to soothe the therapist and convince her to continue to participate in his ploy; however, the therapist would not. She would look in the window to the SCP room but would not enter. His cajoling went unheeded. The therapist verbalized her internal process; she wanted to feel safe and cared for, wanted to trust the lead of the client, his words, and the experience; however, they only led her to be deceived and into danger. These experiences led to feelings of distrust and not wanting to play together—she pondered aloud what that might be like for other kids if they had this happen during play (it was a known dynamic within this client's social difficulties).

After two more sessions where the client attempted to convince the therapist to join in the room, and the therapist describing the emotional reaction from both her perspective and those of others who might have experienced this dynamic, the client once again attempted to ensure the therapist's safety. Interestingly, something had changed in the interaction, and the client appeared more sincere: no longer giggling, his speech more purposeful and with an inflection and tone of seriousness. He was also making intentional eye contact. The therapist verbalized these noticings and the impact they had on her, one being neuroception of safety. She verbalized her thought process to model and highlight what she perceived as different and what might alter someone's decision to engage with him in other situations. She also verbalized a strong hope that this was a truthful situation and not a deception, as it would be really hard to trust him in the future if this was not sincere.

With trepidation, the therapist accompanied the client into a SCP room. The room was foggy, and the SCP was not visible. The therapist continued to verbalize her hopes, fears, and decision-making process along the way. The SCP in that room was cute and cuddly and did not attack either of them. Subsequent play did not repeat the previous patterns in this game or future games. The pattern had been broken, and Robert appeared to have integrated the experience into his interpersonal response patterns.

Conclusion

The use of the Roblox game and the process of autonomic nervous system activation within Digital Play Therapy allowed the therapist to understand and experience a common dynamic for this client within a variety of his social interactions. Once the dynamic was understood further by the therapist, it could be paired with the knowledge of the client's interactions outside of the play therapy room. The verbalization of the sympathetic and parasympathetic processes, along with the verbalization and non-verbal cues of the internal experiences of the therapist, allowed the client to further understand the impact of his behaviors on his play partner. The new approach of joining and providing an interaction of safety and trust for the therapist appeared to provide a new experience of pride and protection for the client.

📝 Treatment Takeaways

- Digital Play Therapy is rich with experiences and opportunities to express, create, explore, practice, and communicate.
- The Polyvagal system is activated within Digital Play Therapy, and the client-therapist dyad can work through facets of regulation through the play.
- Utilizing such tools within therapy allows the therapist to enter the client's world and honor their culture. Technology is a subculture. In order for us to exercise cultural humility, it is imperative to work toward understanding our digital native clients on this platform.

- Learn about and lean into perspectives and experiences that diverge from your own.
- Engage in digital co-play during sessions and encourage families to do the same outside of sessions.
- There are a plethora of benefits that accompany this playful, therapeutic engagement.

References

Atkins, M. (2017). *Benefits of family game night.* Mommy University. https://mommyuniversitynj.com/2017/02/01/benefits-of-family-game-night/

Axline, V. (2011). *Play therapy: The inner dynamics of childhood.* Hesperides.

Cannon, W. B. (1925). *Bodily changes in pain, hunger, fear and rage.* D. Appleton and Company.

Ceranoglu, T. A. (2010). Video games in psychotherapy. *Review of General Psychology, APA, 14*(2), 141–146.

Clarke, B., & Schoech, D. (1994). A computer-assisted game for adolescents: Initial development and comments. *Computers in Human Services, 11*, 121–140.

Dana, D. (2018). *The Polyvagal theory in therapy.* Norton.

Dana, D. (2022). *Polyvagal card deck.* Norton

Favelle, G. K. (1995). Therapeutic applications of commercially available software. *Computers in Human Services, 11*, 151–158.

Frothingham, M. B. (2021, October 6). Fight, flight, freeze, or fawn: What this response means. In *Simply Psychology.* www.simplypsychology.org/fight-flight-freeze-fawn.html

Gardner, J. E. (1991). Can the Mario Bros. help? Nintendo games as an adjunct in psychotherapy with children. *Psychotherapy: Theory, Research, Practice, Training, 28*, 667–670.

Kaduson, H. G., Cangelosi, D., Cangelosi, D. M., & Schaefer, C. E. (Eds.). (2019). *Prescriptive play therapy: Tailoring interventions for specific childhood problems.* Guilford.

Landreth, G. (2012). *Play therapy: The art of the relationship* (3rd ed.). Routledge.

Mineo, B. A., Ziegler, W., Gill, S., & Salkin, D. (2009). Engagement with electronic screen media among students with autism spectrum disorders. *Journal of Autism and Developmental Disorders, 39*, 172–187.

Porges, S. W. (2004, May). Neuroception: A subconscious system for detecting threats and safety. *Zero to Three, 24*(5), 19–24.

Roblox. (2021). *Powering imagination.* https://corp.roblox.com/

Roblox Wiki. (n.d.). *SCP roleplay.* https://roblox.fandom.com/wiki/SCP_Roleplay_Community/SCP:_Roleplay

Schaefer, C. E., & Drewes, A. A. (Eds.). (2014). *The therapeutic powers of play: 20 core agents of change* (2nd ed.). Wiley.

Stone, J. (2019). *Digital play therapy: A clinician's guide to comfort and competence* (1st ed.). Routledge.

Stone, J. (2022). *Digital play therapy: A clinician's guide to comfort and competence* (2nd ed.). Routledge.

Index

Made in the USA
Monee, IL
09 April 2024

56661656R00155